A Nation of Singing Birds

Born in Skewen and educated at Neath Grammar School, Ronald Rees taught historical geography at the University of Saskatchewan and, as adjunct professor, at Mount Allison University, New Brunswick. He has written books on the Canadian prairies, the Maritime provinces of Canada, garden history, and on science and industry in south Wales. He lives in St Andrews, an historic resort on the Bay of Fundy in New Brunswick.

A NATION OF SINGING BIRDS

SERMON AND SONG IN WALES AND AMONG THE WELSH IN AMERICA

RONALD REES

To Erin Rees, musician and chorister

First impression: 2021

© Copyright Ronald Rees and Y Lolfa Cyf., 2021

The publishers wish to acknowledge the support of
the Books Council of Wales

Cover photograph: © David Hurn / Magnum Photos
(The Last Chapel Walk, Six Bells, Abertillery)
Cover design: Y Lolfa

ISBN: 978 1 912631 29 2

Published and printed in Wales
on paper from well-maintained forests by
Y Lolfa Cyf., Talybont, Ceredigion SY24 5HE
website www.ylolfa.com
e-mail ylolfa@ylolfa.com
tel 01970 832 304
fax 832 782

Contents

Foreword

THIS BOOK IS about the Welsh proclivity for song. Many years ago, after hearing a group of exuberant Welshmen sing a popular hymn, an English friend turned to me and said appreciatively: 'You know, it isn't so much that the Welsh can sing; it's that they *do* sing.' The observation may not have originated with him, but it was original to me and it has coloured the way in which I've listened to Welsh choral and congregational singing ever since. Why we sing as fervently as we do and why in general we behave, as the journalist René Cutforth remarked, like 'Italians in the rain', is a mystery. Today we sing less frequently, and in far fewer numbers than formerly, but to declare Welsh nationality almost anywhere in the Western world is to risk being asked if one has a voice. Choral and congregational singing, which is the kind the Welsh are renowned for, came into their own with the singing of hymns, and even though the chapels have emptied and the choirs have greyed and thinned, hymns remain our tribal songs. At international rugby games in Wales the crowd sings 'Cwm Rhondda' with almost as much fervour as the national anthem itself, and at pivotal moments when the warriors need heartening, the refrain very often is Max Boyce's 'Hymns and Arias' – not a hymn of course, but sung in an appropriately solemn key. It is a reminder that we still revere song, even though we may have no particular gift for singing.

Although hymn singing is the overarching subject of this book, music and religion do not figure prominently in it.

This may seem paradoxical, but my objective (I am neither a musician nor a historian of music) was to explore how hymns, and the religious movements and Revivals of which they were part, fired the Welsh imagination. Other nations were drawn to the siren-like power of hymns, but perhaps no other has sung them with such fervour. In the nineteenth century, that fervour gave rise to a unique institution, the *cymanfa ganu*, a hymn-singing festival attended not by trained choirs but by the folk, the *werin*. Choirs followed, but it was from the chapel congregations that they drew their recruits. By the middle of that century Wales, thanks to a repertoire of appealing hymns and an easily-learned form of musical notation, was the fabled sea of song. In Welsh settlements overseas, and in America in particular where the Welsh settled in numbers, they continued to sing. It was a group of Welsh migrants to Utah, led by John Parry, who formed the nucleus of the famed Mormon Tabernacle Choir.

Musicality, however, was not confined to the singing of hymns. The American classicist Harry Caplan defined preaching as a 'sacred art', suggesting that sermons were performances, vocal exercises as well as pedagogical ones. To engage their audiences, Welsh preachers at home and in America often delivered their sermons with a discernible cadence or rhythm in which sound could be as important as meaning. By combining the persuasive power of the word with the emotive power of music, assemblies could be brought to states ranging from spiritual readiness to hysteria. In our own times there are echoes of the mesmerizing, cadenced style in the recorded speeches of Dr Martin Luther King and the poetry readings of Dylan Thomas. Thomas's great-uncle, Gwilym Marles Thomas, was a Welsh Congregationalist minister.

Two particular incidents led to the writing of this book. The most recent was my reading of Barbara Ehrenreich's *Dancing in the Streets*. Her book is about the need, manifested throughout human history, for communal expressions of feeling – in dance, parade and song. In Wales the Methodists and other Nonconformists, the progenitors of the great hymnwriters, were extremely successful, paradoxically, in suppressing native song and dance. But the need for what the anthropologist Victor Turner called *communitas* is not easily eliminated, and what the folk, the werin, were denied in popular song and dance they sometimes made up for in ecstatic religious ritual. Fervent hymn singing during the religious revivals and at the hymn-singing festivals, the cymanfaoedd canu, was a manifestation of his thesis. It allowed for the shedding of the self, the *id*, and the corollary of this, the relief and deep pleasure of merging the self with the whole.

The earlier incident was a combined concert and cymanfa ganu held at St David's Hall, Cardiff, about forty years ago. The concert performers were members of Rhondda's peerless Pendyrus Choir led by their charismatic conductor, the late Glynne Jones. The organizers of the event had advertised widely, attracting chapel congregations from Cardiff and from the valleys above the city. The latter arrived by the busload and packed the upper tiers of the hall. Between renditions by the choir, the audience, led by Glynne Jones, sang well-known Welsh hymns. The singing, much of it in four-part harmony, was hair-raising. Had the writer and broadcaster Wyn Griffith been there, he might have repeated an observation he had made much earlier: 'Singing so intense in its emotional powers as to be almost compelling, suborning thought and speaking directly to something older. No one who has not heard a body of Welsh men and women singing in this state can form any idea of the effect of the repetition, in harmony, of a couplet or a verse of a hymn; it can bring about what can only be called an incandescence of the spirit.'[1] As the final, repeated chorus in St David's Hall died, a deeply moved Glynne Jones let the hall grow silent and said quietly and reverently: 'This is who we are.'

1

Breaking the Silence

THE HYMN, AS a song of praise sung in the vernacular by the congregation, dates from the Reformation. At the time of Martin Luther's ordination (1507), song and chant in the Catholic Church were the preserve of the clergy and the choir; the congregation, in the body of the church, was silent; its only involvement, known as 'the blessed mutter of the mass', was to put money in the collection plate. Biblical psalms set to slow metres, and sung and chanted in Latin, were the musical fare, and even if the congregation had wanted to sing it would have found the music too difficult and the language too unfamiliar. To involve the congregation, and enliven church services, Luther advocated radical reforms. They began with language. He thought the psalms, and the Bible itself, should be translated into the vernacular, the language of the people, and that the congregation should join in the singing. To complement the psalms, which were verse translations of the Hebrew originals, he proposed – in what proved to be an inspired intuition – that there ought to be uplifting new works written in German. His own compositions – Luther played the flute and had a light tenor voice – were poems on religious subjects whose verses could be sung to the same tune. Like a traditional folk song, a hymn consisted of easily understood verses, each with the same number of lines and the same structure of stresses and syllables. Taking his cue from folk and popular songs, Luther set his hymns to simple, pleasing tunes that could be sung, according to the compiler of one hymn book, by 'the peasant at his plough, the servants at their labour, the children in the street'.

Until the congregation at his parish church in Wittenberg was ready to sing, its members simply read the printed hymns sung by the choir, but once won over (a process that took four to five years) they sang enthusiastically. Other reformers followed Luther's lead. John Calvin heard the spirited Lutheran hymn singing in 1538 while exiled in Strasbourg and, although not a musician, he could see its energizing effects. He directed that in the Reformed churches the entire congregation should sing and that it should do so unaccompanied by choirs and soloists. Like Luther, he thought the words should be in the language of the people and that the singing should express 'the deep feeling of the heart'. But, unlike Luther, he had reservations about original verse, contending that the language of the Biblical psalms needed no embellishment. With help from well-known poet Clément Marot, distinguished scholar Théodore de Beze, and several musicians, he produced a hymnal consisting almost exclusively of Old Testament psalms.

The German hymns and psalms were a revelation. A Protestant refugee in Geneva, who had fled England in 1553 on the accession of Mary Tudor (the Catholic 'Bloody Mary'), noted their appeal:

> A most interesting sight is offered in the city on weekdays, when the hour for service approaches. As soon as the first sound of the bell is heard all shops are closed, conversation ceases, business is put on one side, and from all parts the people hasten to the nearest church. Arrived there, each one draws from his pocket a small book which contains some psalms with notes, and thus the congregation sings before and after the sermon, while everyone testifies how great consolation is derived from this custom.

Huguenots (sixteenth- and seventeenth-century French Calvinistic Protestants) were so captivated by hymns that the Catholic authorities declared them siren-like and heretical and threatened to cut out the tongues of the singers. The threat produced the smallest hymn book ever: the two-inch-long gantier, so-called because Huguenot women used to conceal it in their gloves.

The return to England of the Protestant refugees, and the accession of Elizabeth I following the death of Bloody Mary, led to a small but significant lifting of the clergy and the choir's monopoly on song. In an injunction to the former, Elizabeth decreed that the congregation be allowed to join in the singing of a hymn or 'such-like song' at the end of Common Prayer. Keen to follow Luther's example, early Anglican reformers wanted English hymns brought into the body of their services, but they had no writers to compose them and no tunes for any that might have been written. In Wales, the translation of the Book of Common Prayer into Welsh in 1567, and of the Bible in 1588, led to suggestions that translation be extended to the psalms. The first attempt, by William Middleton – an Elizabethan sea captain who commanded one of Admiral Howard's vessels in the West Indies – foundered. He completed the translations in 1595, but his metres were so eccentric that no tunes would fit them and no mouth could sing them. His book, according to Howell Elvet Lewis, was a 'pious failure'[1]. Middleton's translations were followed by the more conventional translations of Edmwnd Prys, Archdeacon of Merioneth. In 1621 he published a book of psalms, *Llyfr y Salmau*, in popular metres that might be sung and memorized by whole congregations. It was the first metrical psalter to be published in Welsh and the first book in Welsh printed with music. There were twelve psalms, some set to tunes of Welsh origin. No other collection of psalm tunes would appear for at least a century. Prys's intention had been to prepare a fresh psalm for each Sunday, but illiteracy and the scarcity of printed material seems to have prevented their wholesale adoption despite their popularity. Between 1672 and 1727 they were republished fifteen times.[2]

In churches where only a handful of the congregation could read, or which had few hymn or psalm books, the minister or a delegate would usually read the psalm or hymn through to convey the meaning and then repeat each line before it was sung. The practice, known as 'lining out' or 'deaconing', eventually graduated from one line to two and because the Scots, in particular, took to it, the practice became known as the Scots manner. In Wales, however, official resistance to the participation of the congregation persisted. Few Anglican ministers wished to change the structure or the tempo of their services, and Dissenters, who in theory ought to have been more sympathetic to the idea of the involvement of the congregation, seem to have placed little importance on singing. They allowed strictly biblical metrical psalms in their meeting houses but, until the Toleration Act of 1689, the singing was subdued, in part from fear of being heard. In the days of the Stuart persecutions their meetings were furtive, often held in houses and even barns. Tom Lewis described a conventicle meeting at Cwmglo, near Merthyr, in 1620:

> Cwmglo was inconspicuous. A dingle of sylvan beauty, it was screened by a profusion of dense copses and tall, overhanging trees where tradition states the nightingale often sang. But even in the delicious seclusion of Cwmglo the Dissenters were not free from molestation. Though their minds were fixed on the things of the spirit, their ears were always alert for the footsteps of the informer. A shaking bough, or a quivering bush, or the snap of a twig in the undergrowth, made their hearts beat faster, their blood run cold. The soothing influence of hymn and sacred song was denied them. Hostile ears might be listening in the thickets.[3]

In Pembrokeshire and western Carmarthenshire, in a practice dating to at least Tudor times, congregations engaged in a form of high-pitched chanting of biblical texts, *canu pwnc*, sometimes making striking harmonies. The purpose was to extend knowledge of the Bible at a time when many people might not have been able to read. The chanting, which at times was prolonged, might be regarded as a precursor to congregational singing.

In the established churches, itinerant and volunteer singing teachers tried to improve standards of singing, but most were untrained and ineffective. Often, the teachers were the *clochydd*, the officer who rang the church bell and dug the graves. In services, few hymns were sung and only a half-dozen of the old psalm tunes seem to have been in general use, and these were not sung correctly. Musical instruments to lead and support the singing might have helped but there was no support for these. Even William Williams, Welsh Methodism's greatest hymnwriter, opposed musical accompaniment of any kind. He wrote in 1762: 'When the blessed gift of the Holy Spirit came upon the people the "spirit within" was of itself sufficient to the whole man, body and soul, to praise the Lord without any musical instruments other than the media of graces ordained by the Lord, namely, preaching, praying and singing.'[4] In England, Anglican Communion services closed with a hymn but resistance to the singing of psalms and hymns during the service persisted.

To ring with song, like the churches in Germany and central Europe, churches in England and Wales had to free themselves of Anglican restraint or 'formalism', the suppression of any expression of strong emotion. Advocates for change within the Established Church, disturbed by what they perceived as general lassitude in matters of faith, pressed for more dynamic church services. Their targets were the inattentive inside the church as well as the Sabbath-breakers outside. Ellis Wynne, the cleric and satirist, complained in 1703 of sparse attendance, whispering and laughter during services, and of attention drifting from the liturgy to the dress of neighbours, in the case of women, and, in the case of young men, to the more alluring girls and young ladies, and in the case of young women and girls, to the more attractive boys.[5] For the indifferent or the irreligious outside the church, Sunday – the only work-free day for most – was a day for pastimes and sport: football, wrestling, bowls, skittles, cock-fighting, ferreting and dancing to the tunes of pipes, fiddlers, harpists and minstrels. If people were to be roused from their indifference and folly, restrained prayer and measured sermons in English, if the incumbent was not Welsh, would not be enough. The engines of change would be dramatic, highly charged sermons accompanied by fervent congregational singing.

The aim of the reformers, or Methodists as they described themselves, was to revitalize the Established Church, not undermine it. In spite of bishops who knew no Welsh, and clergy who were often English and sometimes absent, the Church itself was held in affection and loyally supported by a great majority of Welsh people.[6] The most influential of the early reformers was Griffith Jones, a curate at Laugharne and, after 1716, rector of Llanddowror, a parish five or six miles west with which his name is now associated. He is known best for his remarkable system of more than 3,000 circulating schools where children during the day and adults at night learned to read the Bible. In due course, they were also able to read hymn books. Although asthmatic and melancholic, Griffith Jones was a preacher of such magnetism that the churches in Laugharne and Llanddowror could not hold the numbers who came to listen to him. On Sundays he attracted gatherings of 500 to 600, 'crowding the churches to capacity [and] transforming graveyards into churches', according to William Williams. For preaching outside his own parish without the permission of the incumbent, Griffith Jones fell foul of his bishop and in order to remain within the Church, and protect his schools, he avoided any public alignment with the Methodists. As a pioneer evangelist he was an early exponent of the open-air or field sermon, possibly the most effective weapon in the Methodist armoury. With no church threshold to cross, and no Christian symbols to intimidate them, people who attended churches or meeting houses irregularly, or not at all, flocked to listen to him. There was also, of course, no limit to the numbers who might attend.

Griffith Jones's successors were two younger associates, Howell Harris and Daniel Rowland, the chief instruments in Wales of The Great Awakening, a label coined in New England and adopted by Welsh writers. In his account of Welsh charity schools, John Evans remarked that Harris and Rowland came from the same stable: '[Both were products of] Mr Jones' shop with their heads turned exactly the same way'.[7] Harris was a schoolteacher from Trefeca-fach in Breconshire, and Rowland an Anglican Church curate in the parishes of Llangeitho and Nantcwnlle in mid-Cardiganshire. Rowland had been converted by a Griffith Jones sermon in 1737 and, encouraged by Jones, he pursued ordination. Harris was never ordained. Like Griffith Jones, both acolytes were spellbinding preachers with, like their mentor, a taste for open-air gatherings. Harris visited Griffith Jones regularly during the first fifteen years of his career and, like both Jones and Rowland, he had remarkable rhetorical gifts. Because he was not ordained, he described himself as a *cynghorwr*, an exhortationist, rather than a preacher. His English Methodist counterparts went by the milder term 'lay preacher'. In 1763, after more than two decades of practice, he could blandly record that he addressed 'a vast crowd' at Llangammarch 'without any subject for three hours'.[8] Equally matter-of-fact was his observation that he sometimes took his text from whichever page 'the Book opened [to]'. Like Chaucer's Pardoner (For I kan al by rote that I telle), he could preach without preparation on any topic. At other times Rowland took no particular text, his subject 'all given unto me in an extraordinary manner without the least premeditation'.

Rowland, too, was a marathon orator who on one occasion is said to have preached for six hours without intermission, to a spellbound multitude.[9]

Harris measured the success of his sermons by the force or 'power' he was able to generate, and when the current was in full flow he admitted that he 'could hardly contain [himself]'. Power, or fervour, was the antidote to the measured sermons of the Anglicans and the restrained intellectualism of the 'dry' Dissenters. In Welsh, the word for the power or concentrated energy that Harris referred to is *hwyl*; it is also the word for a sail. A ship was said to be in full hwyl when leaving port with full and spread sails under a favourable breeze. The Welsh for breeze is *awel*. If there is a connection between sailing and preaching, it is that the preacher and the sail concentrate energy, both expanding in the process. From a quiet and contained, but expectant beginning, the preacher or speaker ascended a scale of intensity that frequently culminated in a rapt congregation. In its unadulterated form, hwyl, as seen by Methodists and Methodist historians, was simply a case of the divine or the holy spirit inhabiting and energizing the body of the preacher. William Williams, poet and hymnwriter, in an elegy to a lay preacher, draws the parallel between wind and power:

> Feeling was his life and essence,
> Heaven's breeze his only aid;
> With no breath of God attending
> Fixed his vessel would have stayed;
> Sturdy oars not his to row with,
> But the gale from heaven above
> All the saints would bring with triumph
> To the paradise of love[10]

In Wales, hwyl, or power, was an expected, or at least hoped for, feature of Methodist sermons, and preachers were graded on their mastery of it. In 1749 Harris complained of the 'lukewarmness' of the Dissenters and earlier, at St Paul's, London, in 1742, he had dismissed a sermon on the grounds that 'there was no power with it'.[11] The origins of hwyl, to convey intensity and fervour, are unclear, and it seems to have come into common usage only in the eighteenth and nineteenth centuries when applied to the delivery of revivalist preachers. What is certain is that the sermon, when delivered by Methodist exhorters, was a vocal exercise aimed directly at the emotions. Harris himself was unequivocal about the target of his sermons: 'we preach chiefly to the heart and the spirit … faith in the heart rather than enlightenment in the head.' Charles Wesley described Harris as 'a son of thunder and consolation', while his brother John, who acknowledged that Harris was a 'powerful orator both by nature and grace', noted that his sermons 'owe[d] nothing to art or education'.[12] For Harris's more cerebral listeners, who might have welcomed some of both, his message, as the Welsh historian John Davies has pointed out, was terrifyingly simple and compelling: convert or suffer eternal torment. E.P. Thompson, the English social historian, characterized the practice as 'religious terrorism', the effect of which on the working class was to suppress revolt by enjoining obedience.[13] Philosopher and historian Élie Halévy's argument in *The Birth of Methodism* is similar: the discipline imposed on the workers by the Methodists helped to avert in England and Wales upheavals of the kind that occurred on the Continent.

Daniel Rowland's early career paralleled Harris's. Like Harris, he began as a missionary preacher, travelling throughout Wales on foot and on horseback, but as an ordained priest he did so on sufferance. When the Bishop of St Davids suspended his license in 1763 due to maverick behaviour, he confined himself to Llangeitho, a village near the headwaters of the River Aeron in the remote interior of Cardiganshire. Thereafter, as A.H. Dodd remarked, he was generally content to let the mountain come to Mohammed. In Llangeitho he leased a plot of land and built a spacious chapel or meeting house. He entered the pulpit through a door directly behind, allowing for a sudden and, if desired, dramatic entry. In a voice, according to one report, that was 'sonorous and marvellously effective' he would announce a psalm or hymn. The opening sentences of the address that followed 'soon led up to a striking, perhaps thrilling, remark – "like the opening of a box of precious ointment", and the fragrant incense seemed to fill the place and graciously affect the whole audience. Henceforth they were in his hands.'[14]

After 1750 the Methodist movement spread widely in south and south-west Wales, and Rowland quickly began attracting crowds. On Sundays, when they overflowed the chapel, he preached in the open air, holding additional indoor services during the week. The tracks were deplorable but people still came; some, on his monthly Communion Sundays, even sailing from north Wales and disembarking in harbours on the Cardiganshire coast. Howell Harris had taken the Revival to north Wales but until late in the eighteenth century the north drew on the inspiration and energy of the south. These northern pilgrims, as Professor E.G. Bowen contended, followed the same amphibious routes as those used by prehistoric traders and the Celtic saints. To avoid the dangerous currents at the tip of the Lleyn peninsula, the traders and the saints left their boats on one side and portaged by cart and wagon across to the other side where they picked up fresh boats, repeating the exercise on the return journey. Professor Bowen suggested that the early Methodists used the same routes, gathering at harbours in Anglesey and on the north coast and sailing down to the Lleyn peninsula to convenient crossing points. After the land crossing they boarded vessels that would take them across Cardigan Bay and land them at harbours such as Aberystwyth, Llan-non and Aberaeron.[15]

At the larger gatherings in Llangeitho, the crowds were so great that hundreds of temporary sheepfolds had to be raised to contain and protect the frightened animals, and a way had to be found to feed them.[16] Many of the walkers met at a mountain spring about two miles from Llangeitho, where they rested and refreshed themselves before the final leg of their journey. They arrived singing hymns, and upon hearing them as he walked and mused before his sermon, Rowland was heard to remark: 'Well, here they come, bringing heaven along with them.'[17]

Rowland could summon even more power than Harris and the effect usually was electrifying. For Communion services, held on the last Sunday of each month, people descended on Llangeitho by foot, horseback and wagon, and in villages for miles around services were cancelled. At the eleven o'clock service, Rowland would preach to crowds of 2,000 in winter and 3,000 in summer; later in the day 1,200 to 1,500 would take Communion at a service conducted by Rowland and two or three assistants. Houses and farms on what, in effect, were pilgrimage routes provided food and shelter, and when no beds were available people slept in the open or on straw in barns. On Mondays the pilgrims went home, as they had arrived, singing and praying.

Rowland's thunder and its effects inspired, on his death, this elegaic verse by fellow evangelist William Williams:

His name was Boanerges,
Son of thunder, flaming, true;
Shaking heaven and earth together
With a voice both strong and new;
'Come! Awake!' his voice in echo
Calls to all, 'our town's ablaze.
Flee this moment without turning;
God to ashes all will raze.'
…
Five Welsh counties heard the thunder,
And with awesome, fearful dread,
Fell with slaughter and with terror
On the ground, in heaps as dead.[18]

To stumble upon a Rowland sermon without forewarning of its power, as happened to one English visitor to Wales, could be unsettling: 'I came accidentally to a place in Wales where Rowland was preaching to an immense congregation in the open air. Indeed, I never witnessed such a scene before. Oh! The striking appearance of the preacher: his zeal, animation and fervour were beyond description, and such effects as descended on the congregation under him as never came within the sphere of observation before.'[19]

For clergyman David Griffiths, who would have known of Rowland's power, only the rising swell of a tempestuous sea was a sufficient analogy:

> This great preacher in his public ministrations resembles the gradual swelling and bursting of the waves of the ocean, when the wind agitates the bosom of the deep. The overwhelming power of the mighty influences of the Spirit in his ministry came on gradually, in manner like a wave of the sea, increasing more and more. He commences his address calmly, but as he advanced, both his matter and his manner increased in interest ... At length his eloquence attained its climax, and then his preaching, under divine influence would most nobly break forth like the rising swell of the sea, and would overwhelm the great concourse of people in an astonishing manner.[20]

To fall under the spell of a Rowland sermon it was not even necessary to understand it. An Englishman, who had no Welsh, listened to him preach in Llangeitho and was enthralled: 'I heard much of him, but it never could have entered into my heart to conceive of the mighty energy and power that accompanied his preaching. His words did fly like darts.' Rowland himself, of course, was fully aware of what his power could do. In February 1743 he wrote to George Whitefield, the most passionate of the English Methodists: 'And thus I was obliged to leave my whole congregation, being many hundreds, in a flame, the one catching it from the other. It would have set your heart in a flame to see them, and to feel the flame that runs through; and this is our condition generally every Sabbath!'[21]

For a Rowland, as for a Harris sermon, people would travel many miles. On his way to Llanddewibrefi, Cardiganshire, one Sunday in November 1741, Howell Harris tells of 'seeing some running to hear the Word' at five in the morning! In July 1741 three 'dear sisters travelled the 40 miles or so from Llanidloes to Ystrad-ffin to hear Rowland preaching, crossing some of the wildest and roughest terrain in Wales to do so'. Even in old age Rowland could attract huge crowds: 'Saturday morning by 12 noon to Llangeitho to hear Saturday's noon sermon from old Mr Rowland. There were that day about 4,000 souls, but on Sunday, when the father and the son preached, they were obliged to have a pulpit erected in a field, where by a moderate computation of those who were pretty good judges, there were at least 14,000 people.' Such preaching wrought, according to William Williams, a magical change in behaviour: 'Now the tone of whole districts was changed; instead of playing games on the Sabbath, dancing, swearing, blaspheming the name of God, singing unworthy songs, empty talk, gossiping … instead of all this … the shepherds would sing hymns in the valleys, the ploughmen and the driver of his oxen often sing psalms and spiritual songs together in the fields.'[22]

In England, Methodism's standard bearers were the brothers John and Charles Wesley, and George Whitefield. In December 1738 Whitefield, then the undisputed leader of English Methodism, wrote to Howell Harris, and the following year (March 1739) the two men, both just twenty-four years old, met in Cardiff where Harris impressed upon Whitefield the effectiveness of field or open-air preaching and his methods of oratory. Outside church walls the preacher could speak dramatically and with far greater freedom. Whitefield thought field preaching a 'mad Trick' but he took to it soon after his return to London. His first attempt was at Kingswood, near Bristol, where he addressed a gathering of coal miners. John

Wesley recorded the occasion in his journal: 'In the evening I reached Bristol, and met Mr Whitefield there. I could scarce reconcile myself at first to this strange way of preaching in the fields of which he set me an example on Sunday; having been all my life (till very lately) so tenacious of every point of decency and order, that I should have thought of the saving of souls almost a sin, if it had not been done in a church.'[23]

Wesley relented to become one of the great open-air preachers, but his associate Rowland Hill took to the practice immediately. He regarded field preaching as the salvation of Methodism: 'I know the Lord puts honour upon it, and am sure that as soon as ever that custom dies, methodism will die with it.'[24] More than a century later Edward A. Ross, a social psychologist, endorsed Hill's supposition. He pointed to a fact then known to every experienced orator: that the response of a standing crowd in the open is very different from one seated indoors, and the orator changes his style accordingly. He cited the example of the French theatre of the old regime where the standing portion of the audience (the pit) was always more emotional and violent in its demonstrations than the sitting portion (parquet), and that the provision of seats for the pit audience quieted their demeanour. Although Hill enjoyed his 'field campaigns', he noted, when travelling and preaching in Wales in 1774, that he 'liked the fire, but he did not like the smoke', that is, the warmth and informality of the meetings but not the hysteria they sometimes generated.

As ordained Anglican priests, Whitefield and the Wesleys could not, as a matter of practice rather than doctrine, preach in the churches of dioceses for which they held no licence. Like Welsh revivalists under similar restraints, they confined their gatherings outside their own parishes to the hours before or after church services, informing the resident clergy of their intentions whenever possible. The churches, in any case, could not have accommodated the crowds and they would not, like the Rev. William Grimshaw, have welcomed some of the responses. In 1742, Grimshaw, a friend of John Wesley and a leading evangelist, attended a Revival meeting at his church in Haworth, Yorkshire. As the time for the meeting approached the church filled: 'My church began to be crowded, insomuch that many were obliged to stand out of doors. Here, as in other places, it was amazing to see weeping, roaring, and agonies many people were siezed with at the apprehension of their sinful state, and the wrath of God.'[25]

*

The Wesleys' unique gift to evangelism was to recognize that it could be driven by hymns and congregational singing, not just invigorated by them. In England, Isaac Watts, a young man from a family of persecuted Hampshire Nonconformists, had pointed the way forward earlier in the century. Watts's father was a deacon in the Independent Church of Southampton and his mother the child of a Huguenot refugee. The son complained of the flatness of the psalms and the quality of the singing in his father's church, and, after his own ordination, his family challenged him to write something with more appeal. He responded with an original verse that was in effect a statement of intent:

> Behold the glories of the Lamb
> Amidst his Father's throne;
> Prepare new honours for his name
> And songs before unknown

Eschewing slavish scriptural paraphrase, Watts wrote some 600 songs or hymns, composed of original or 'unknown' verse, the first collection of which he published in 1705. They were models of simplicity. His metres and rhymes, now known as hymn metre, were quatrains of four lines of alternating rhyme based on English folk poems and ballads. Set to familiar psalm tunes, and couched in language within reach of an unlearned reader, Watts's hymns could be sung on first hearing. Watts used rhyme as a mnemonic, and usually he took care that each line made sense on its own, even though it might have been part of a longer sentence.[26] Benjamin Franklin reissued the hymns in America where they were adopted in the 1730s and 1740s by the leaders of The Great Awakening. In his account of the 1734–5 Revival in Northampton, Massachusetts, Jonathan Edwards specified the singing of Watts's hymns as a key element. More than a century later, Emily Dickinson, who as a child heard them in a church in Amherst, Massachusetts, adopted hymn metre (in preference to the customary iambic pentameter) for her striking, laconic verse.

As the architect of the modern English hymn, Watts had raised a platform on which the Wesleys were able to build. Of the seventy hymns in John Wesley's first hymn book, published in America in 1737, more than a third were by Isaac Watts. But a more immediate influence on Wesley than the hymns of Watts was an encounter with a group of twenty-six Moravians aboard the *Simmonds*, the vessel that carried Wesley and his brother Charles to America in 1736. According to David Stowe, it was nothing less than 'the most momentous encounter in the long history of [Anglo-American] sacred music'.[27] They and their two companions, all members of Oxford University's Holy Club, were going to proselytize among American Indians. On each evening of the two-month voyage, the Moravians gathered on deck for their *Singstunde* (singing hour) at which they sang hymns from memory. The singing, as the Moravians liked to describe it, was from the heart and Wesley was deeply moved. He was also in awe of their calm demeanour at the onset of an Atlantic storm, continuing their singing hour even as the mainsail began to shred. 'In the midst of the psalm wherewith their service began ... the sea broke over, split the mainsail in pieces, covered the ship, and poured in between the decks, as if the great deep had already swallowed us up. A terrible screaming began among the English. The Germans looked up, and without intermission calmly sang on. This,' Wesley wrote in his diary, 25 January 1736, 'was the most glorious day I have hitherto seen.'

On their return to England in 1738, John and Charles travelled to Herrnhut, the chief Moravian settlement, located in what is now the Saxony region of Germany. John Wesley's second exposure to Moravian singing convinced him that people should sing their way to salvation, on waves of melody and rhyme. He advised fellow Methodists that if they wanted to hear fine psalmody they had better go to Herrnhut, or Fulneck in West Yorkshire. Charles Wesley, the more gifted writer of the two brothers, continued to compose hymns. He published his first collection in 1739–40, under the title *Hymns and Sacred Poems* and followed this with a tune book. He would eventually write 6,000 hymns. Fourteen of the tunes in his first collection were of German origin. Frustrated (like Watts) by the dearth of available tunes, he adopted popular ones. When preaching in Cornwall he was interrupted by a group of drunken sailors who sang a bawdy parody of 'Nancy Dawson', a ballad in praise of a popular dancer. Charles registered the tune and the measure and, to forestall interruption at the next meeting, he distributed the words for a hymn set to the sailors' tune.[28]

As well as encouraging the singing of hymns, John Wesley also prescribed the ways in which they should be sung. He found the singing of psalms at his father's church, in Epworth, Lincolnshire, to be slow-paced and lifeless, and in his *Directions for Singing* he advised speed: 'Take care that you sing not too slow. This drawling way naturally steals on all who are lazy.' He repeated the instruction in *Sacred Harmony* (*c*.1789): 'Sing lustily, and with good courage. Beware of singing as if you were half dead, or half asleep; but lift up your voice with strength. Be no more afraid of your voice now, nor more ashamed of its being heard, than when you sung the songs of Satan.' At the same time he cautioned against undisciplined, unrestrained singing: 'Sing modestly. Do not bawl, so as to be heard above or distinct from the rest of the congregation, that you may not destroy the harmony; but strive to make your voices together, so as to make one clear melodious sound.'

As for the music itself, he insisted on simplicity. In *Thoughts on the Power of Music* (1779), he wrote that choral music was most affecting when 'the sound had been echo to the sense', and when the composer had attended to melody, not harmony. He attributed the popularity of Scotch and Irish airs to their simplicity 'in the highest degree'. He thoroughly disliked counterpoint and complicated music and he had no tolerance for music unaccompanied by song: 'Music without words is sounds without sense.' It was an article of faith with him that congregational music, because it was for the congregation not the choir, ought to be, in Carlton Young's phrase, 'simple, singable, moving, memorable and teachable'.[29] A good hymn, like a good folk song, ought to be easy to learn and hard to forget, the melody brief, the chorus repeating, and the rhymes leading from line to line. Anthems, with their complicated harmonies, were Wesley's bête noire: 'a psalm which no one knew, in a tune fit for an opera, wherein three, four, or five persons sang different words at the same time!' A notable transgressor was a church choir in Neath:

> [Neath, Thursday, 9 August 1768] I began reading prayers at six, but was greatly disgusted at the manner of singing: (1) twelve or fourteen persons kept it to themselves, and quite shut out the congregation; (2) these repeated the same words, contrary to all sense and reason, six or eight or ten times over; (3) according to the shocking custom of modern music, different persons sung different words at one and the same moment; an intolerable insult on common sense, and utterly incompatible with any devotion.

Wesley reiterated the sentiment at Pebworth, Worcestershire, ten years later (March 1778): 'In the evening, I preached at Pebworth church; but I seemed out of my element. A long anthem was sung; but I suppose none beside the singers could understand one word of it. Is not that "praying in an unknown tongue"? I could no more hear it in a church of mine than Latin prayers.'[30]

His insistence on melody and simple language was a winning formula. Methodists everywhere became known for their singing, and Methodist ministers would as soon have been without their Bibles as their hymn books. In Cornwall, Methodists were known as the Canorum, from a Cornish word *canor*, meaning a singer. Thomas Vivian, the curate of Redruth, noted in 1747 that in public prayer the Methodists frequently shed tears, especially when singing their hymns. After hearing Methodists sing in London, in 1759, Johan Henrik Lidén, a professor at the University of Uppsala, commented in his journal: 'The song of the Methodists is the most beautiful I ever heard. Their fine psalms have exceedingly beautiful melodies composed by great masters. They sing in a proper way, with devotion, serene mind and charm.'[31]

One captive of Methodist hymn singing was a young Welshman, Thomas Olivers, a shoemaker from Tregynon, near Newtown, who as a young man had lived dissolutely. After listening to a Whitefield sermon in the west of England, he began attending Methodist meetings, leaving when public preaching ended – society meetings were for members only – but to listen to the singing that followed he went into a field at the back of the preaching house. Olivers became a successful evangelist and an accomplished composer of hymns, the best known of which, 'Helmsley', was a particular favourite of Queen Victoria's.[32]

In places where Methodists gathered, their hymn singing immediately attracted attention. An unnamed American Congregationalist, quoted by Leland Howard Scott, urged his colleagues to follow the lead of the Methodists: 'We sacrifice too much to taste. The secret of the Methodists lies in the admirable adaptation of their music and hymns to produce effect; they strike at once at the heart and the moment we hear their animated, thrilling choruses, we are electrified.' After a large Methodist gathering in Philadelphia, in 1739, at which George Whitefield had preached and hymns had been sung, Benjamin Franklin noted how 'one could not walk through [the city] in the evening without hearing psalms sung in different families of every street'.[33]

After one Whitefield sermon, Franklin, one of the Founding Fathers, noted: 'every accent, every emphasis, every modulation was so perfectly well turned and well placed, that, without being interested in the subject, one could not help being pleased with the discourse; a pleasure of much the same kind with that received from an excellent piece of musick.'[34] Ebenezer Pemberton, the only minister to offer Whitefield a pulpit on his arrival in America in 1739, spoke of his 'clear and musical voice' and how its 'heavenly cadence' used to entrance his audiences.[35] The English actor David Garrick once said that Whitefield could bring an audience to tears merely by intoning the word 'Mesopotamia', and that he would give a hundred guineas if he could say 'Oh' like Mr Whitefield.

Wedded to metrical versions of the psalms, most of the established churches resisted the introduction of Methodist hymns, and saw their support drain away. In a letter to Jane Austen, the playwright and novelist Fanny Burney noted that 'Mr Cooke, our vicar … complains that the Methodists run away with the regular congregations, from their superiority in vocal devotion, & he wishes to remedy this evil by a little laudable emulation'. In general, however, the Anglican Church attempted little in the way of laudable emulation. In Sheffield matters came to a head in 1819 when Thomas Cotterill, in an attempt to stem the outflow from his church, introduced Methodist-style hymns against the wishes of his conservative congregation. The dispute reached the Diocesan Consistory Court which, in a careful compromise, declared that because the metrical psalms themselves had no legal standing in the Anglican liturgy, despite their wide use, the Court was in no position to outlaw hymns. By the middle of the century, however, the more intransigent Anglicans had relented. The perennially popular *Hymns Ancient and Modern* appeared in 1861 and, by 1906, although outnumbered by the Nonconformist denominations, Anglicans were the largest single religious community in Wales.[36]

*

Any debts owed by English Methodists to the Welsh in the matter of field preaching were repaid with interest by reciprocal lessons in the benefits of hymn singing. By 1740, translations of Whitefield's booklets on the Revivals in New England and the history of the Moravians were already in circulation. Howell Harris had also read Jonathan Edwards's account of the Northampton Revival and discussed the mechanics of it with Daniel Rowland.[37] Early Welsh attempts at hymn writing had not been encouraging. There were few Welsh hymns and even fewer hymn tunes to which they could be adapted. In 1725 Thomas Baddy, an Independent minister, published a small collection of hymns in Welsh, but he had chosen to write in the language of the scriptures, not in a contemporary idiom, and they did not engage. In the late 1730s, Howell Harris and John Games (a travelling teacher of psalm-singing from Talgarth) brought singing to the *seiadau*, small support groups or societies of Methodists. Harris recorded how, soaked to the skin, he sang psalms on the road between Ystrad-ffin and Llanwrtyd, and how at Llanwrtyd in 1740 he was transported by the singing of a hymn given out by a young minister. William Williams, the celebrated Methodist hymnwriter, was in Llanwrtyd in September 1740 and it is tempting to think that he was the young minister who gave out the hymn.[38] Harris also wrote hymns but only one may be found in modern hymn books. But in spite of the faltering start and a limited repertoire, by 1740

29

hymns were part of the Methodist agenda. Hymn singing was taught at the seiadau, and at the first meeting of the Association of Welsh Methodists, the *Sasiwn*, in 1742, the delegates agreed that a hymn should be sung at the beginning of each society meeting.

Daniel Rowland also tried his hand at hymn writing. A collection of 69 hymns, *Hymnau Duwiol* (Godly Hymns), published in 1744, bore the inscription 'mainly by Daniel Rowland'. That same year Rowland published a sequel, *Rhai Hymnau Duwiol* (Some Godly Hymns), in which he introduced a number of new metres, influenced, it is assumed, by the hymns of the Wesleys and Isaac Watts. Although Rowland's verses were rudimentary, exhorters and leaders of the seiadau copied them. In his letters and diaries, Harris referred to a progression from psalm to hymn singing, proof that hymn singing at the seiadau was no mere formality. It is also evident from the content of an *anterliwt* (interlude), a popular and often satirical form of verse play performed at fairs and markets that was sometimes commissioned by Nonconformist opponents of the more extreme Methodist ways. The anterliwt players for the most part were itinerants who performed in the open on wagon floors and improvised stages. In one anterliwt, sub-titled the 'Scourge of the Methodists', published in 1745, Howell Harris instructed Dafydd Siencyn Morgan (a former Anglican and itinerant singer teacher) on how to be a successful Methodist:

> In the first place you must sing and shout
> Hymns by the score if you would be devout,
> Then you must frighten to death with your roar
> The people asleep in the house next door.

Unaffected by the banter and the Established Church's distrust of hymns, Welsh Methodism produced its own great hymnwriter in the middle of the eighteenth century. William Williams's conversion to Anglicanism, and then Methodism, is now legendary. Born near Llandovery to Congregationalist parents in 1717, he was known either as Williams Pantycelyn, or simply Pantycelyn, the name of his mother's family farm. As well as identifying the owner, a farm name conferred status. Summoned by the sound of bells one Sunday morning when passing through the village of Talgarth, in 1737 or 1738, he entered the parish church. After a desultory service, the congregation, instead of hurrying home, gathered in the churchyard, waiting. A small, thin, unsmiling man eventually appeared and, standing on one of the gravestones, began to preach. It was Howell Harris. Williams was transfixed. He was about to embark on a career in medicine but, persuaded by Harris, he sought ordination in the Established Church to which Harris still belonged and within which it was the intention of the founders of the Methodist movement to remain.

After his ordination as a deacon in 1740, he was licensed as a curate of two small and unprofitable churches under the vicar Theophilus Evans, the future author of *The History of Modern Enthusiasm* (1752), an anti-Methodist rant. Williams's career in the Established Church was over before it had properly begun. His Methodist sympathies, his habit – following the practice of Harris and Rowland – of preaching outside the parish, and Theophilus Evans's scrutiny, scotched any hope of advancement. His bishop refused to ordain him priest and in 1744 he left his curacies to devote himself to Methodism.

As a preacher, Williams may not have had the power of Harris and Rowland, but like them he aimed for the heart rather than the head: *nid crefydd y talcen, ond crefydd y galon*. He would also preach anywhere and from any stage: a pulpit, a horse-block or horse-stand, a table, in a field, a house or a barn, anywhere; in short, wherever a crowd could gather and be addressed. By his own reckoning, he travelled 150,000 miles within Wales (3,000 miles a year), preaching, inspecting Methodist societies, and selling copies of his many publications. He characterised his ministry in a letter to Lady Huntingdon in 1769: 'roveing, and rangeing, over the rude mountains, and wild precipices of Wales, in search of poor illiterate souls chain'd in the dens of darkness and Infidelity.'[39] A couplet he wrote in praise of the reach of Daniel Rowland's ministry could have applied equally to his own: '*O Dyddewi i Lanandras, O Gaergybi i Gaerdydd*' (from St Davids to Presteigne, from Holyhead to Cardiff). Inasmuch as he saw Wales as a geographical unity, his couplet is reminiscent of Woody Guthrie's 'This land is your land', a part of his hymn chorus to the geography of America.

The circumstance that raised Williams to the throne of Methodist hymn writing is fabled, but sadly, so it is now thought, apocryphal. At a meeting of Calvinistic Methodists at Llanddeusant, Carmarthenshire, in 1740, attended by Harris, Rowland, Williams and two or three other exhorters, it was agreed that before the next meeting each should compose a few lines of verse to see who had the hymn writing gift. Williams won hands down, Howell Harris pronouncing '*Williams piau y canu*', Williams owns the singing.

To compose his hymns, Williams drew on the traditions of Welsh folk song and poetry, rejecting the restrained language and stiff metres of many of the psalms and hymns in favour of a mixture of literary language and dialect: the idioms and phraseology of his own locality. It was a combination that, as literary critic Glyn Tegai Hughes has pointed out, had some chance of being understood by the unlearned. As an approach, it had been initiated by John Wesley. In the preface to his 1779 hymn book Wesley wrote: 'Here are, allow me to say, both the purity, the strength, and elegance of the English language; and at the same time, the utmost simplicity and plainess, suited to every capacity.' By combining in new ways literary Welsh and village Welsh, Williams produced a body of literature that could be understood by the common man. His other strength was his appeal, against which the Welsh have little resistance, to the sentiment known as *hiraeth* – the nostalgic longing for home and the things connected with it.

William Williams published his first collection of hymns, *Aleliwia*, in 1744, and he and Daniel Rowland began the practice of singing a hymn at the conclusion of each service. His most definitive work, however, *Caniadau y rhai sydd ar y môr o wydr* (Songs of those upon a sea of glass), published in 1762, proved so popular that 1,200 copies sold within a few months. Further editions followed until his death in 1791. Much of his imagery came from the fields around Pantycelyn and from the Black Mountains beyond. He wrote in free verse and he is now widely regarded as Wales's first romantic poet. Confronted, like the earlier hymnwriters, by a dearth of tunes and measures to which to set his verse, he turned to folk and popular songs, some of them of English origin. One entitled 'Lovely Peggy', he qualified with 'Moraliz'd', an unmistakeable Calvinist suffix. He demonstrated his musical catholicity by his, and his wife Mary's, response to a baiting crowd at the Bridgend Tavern in Llangefni, Anglesey, where the Williamses were staying. Mary Francis (Williams) had a full and melodious voice. The crowd pushed its way into the public parlour and a fiddler among them asked the Willamses if they would 'have a tune'. Falling in with the banter, Pantycelyn replied 'anything you like'. The fiddler began playing a jig and Mary, after a word with Pantycelyn, began to sing one of his hymns (*Gwaed dy Groes sy'n codi i fyny*) in the same metre, following the fiddler note for note. At the close, the crowd left quietly. Charles Wesley on the south coast had done no better.[40]

Pantycelyn's success encouraged several contemporaries, among them Dafydd Jones of Caeo and Morgan Rhys of Efail Fach. Jones translated the hymns and psalms of Isaac Watts, as well as composing his own, and Morgan Rhys, whose hymns in his day may have been as popular as Pantycelyn's, for a while taught at Griffith Jones's circulating schools. Dafydd Jones was a cattle drover and buyer who learned English while delivering cattle to English markets. A popular pub singer, he had been converted by a hymn sung at the Independent chapel in Troedrhiwdalar, Breconshire, that he entered on one of his returns to Wales. He subsequently joined the Independent chapel at Crugybar, Carmarthenshire, and remained a prominent member for the rest of his life. The publication in 1753 of a collection of his jubilant hymns and psalms is seen as one of the first concessions to the Methodist spirit by the traditionally austere Nonconformists.[41]

Nourished by the hymns of Pantycelyn, Morgan Rhys and Dafydd Jones, evangelism took flight, the hymn books, like seeds in receptive ground, sprouting mini Revivals wherever they landed. Few parts of Wales escaped the downpour. Congregational singing, an adjunct to the 1742 Revival, had become the engine of the second, traditionally dated from the publication of Pantycelyn's *Caniadau* in 1762. In March 1763 Howell Harris recorded in his diary: 'Met Wm Wms & many of my former friends that I have not seen since the Separation … my spirit crying to catch their fire & life, the Lord having awakened many in these parts by a spirit of singing and blessing the Lord who continue whole nights in that exercise.'[42] That same year he wrote of 'the spirit of singing that is fallen on various parts, and of several hundreds awakened in Cardigan, Carmarthen, and other shires, and the vast flock coming to hear'. People in small communities, as author, musician and choir director R.D. Griffith pointed out, are reported to have walked miles to fellowship meetings, singing jubilantly all the way. Among them was the legendary Nancy Jones, 'Miriam of the Revivals', who led singers from from Caeo and Crugybar to Llanwrtyd.[43]

By the end of the eighteenth century, hymns were regarded as critical to the success of any Revival gathering. A clergyman writing at the end of that century noted that for every person 'turned away by doctrine, ten have been induced by music'.[44] Even Wesley complained of 'dead audiences' whom even his charisma and loquacity could not rouse. Early in his ministry he learned that the surest way to attract an audience was to sing first. Standing at the end of a street in Newcastle-upon-Tyne with his associate John Taylor, he began to sing the hundredth psalm: 'Three or four people came out, who soon increased to four or five hundred. I suppose there might be twelve to fifteen hundred before I had finished preaching.'[45]

Wesley and all experienced evangelists understood that before a group would respond to preaching, prayer, and suggestion, it had to take on the character of – as psychologists would later define it – a 'psychological crowd', that is one in which a mere physical aggregate had been changed into a like-minded collectivity. For this to happen, the inhibitions or barriers between individuals had to be dissolved. In this process of transformation the hymn, psychologist and moral philosopher James Bisssett Pratt argued, was central.

> The hymn has two great advantages. In the first place all can take part in it; the emotions which have been swelling up in the hearts of individuals can thus be given vent ... Thus it comes that the hymn is especially valuable for suggestion and auto-suggestion. By singing out ... the sentiments and ideas which the revivalist desires to instill into him, each member of the audience suggests them to himself ... And he also at the same time passes on the suggestion to his neighbor. The whole audience thus acts upon each individual ... and so acts and reacts upon itself, thus spreading the desired suggestion by geometrical progression.

Pratt concluded that the most effective hymns are the kind that run on in the head and sing themselves: simple melodies, simple language and rhymes allowing everyone to take part with ease.[46] Writing a few years later, fellow psychologist Sidney G. Dimond introduced a qualifier: that hymns sung in the minor key were the most effective of all. They might have virile and jubilant qualities, but they were 'peculiarly calculated to kindle emotions of awe and wonder, and an attitude of repentance and hope'.[47]

*

Assessments of the reactions to impassioned preaching and singing at Methodist gatherings divided observers then, and divide historians still. What is not in dispute is the intent of the sermons: they were dramatic, often orchestrated performances designed to induce maximum states of expectation and tension. After comparing Daniel Rowland's rhetorical technique to a rising storm at sea, the clergyman David Griffiths turned to its effects upon his audience:

> [At the height of the storm] the intenseness of their feelings found relief ... in a simultaneous burst of hallelujahs and ascriptions of praise to the most high God. The preacher would then pause for a short interval, until the people had enjoyed the feast ... He would then commence another paragraph of his sermon ... his voice, his countenance, and his discourse gradually altering, and that in a wonderful manner as he was advancing; and when his evangelical and extraordinary eloquence arrives at its climax, it was most glorious, it went forth like the bursting of another wave. And the great mass of people was again overpowered by their feeling, and again burst into loud Hosannahs to the Son of David.

Even Howell Harris trembled before Rowland's power. In a letter to George Whitefield, he described a gathering at Llangeitho in the winter of 1743:

> I was last Sunday at the Ordinance with Brother Rowland where I saw, felt and heard such things as I can't send on Paper any Idea of. The power that continues with him is uncommon. Such Crying out and Heart Breaking Groans, Silent Weeping and Holy Joy, and shouts of Rejoicing I never saw. Their Amens and Cryings Glory in the Highest &c would enflame your Soul was you there. Tis very common when he preaches for Scores to fall down by the Power of the Word, pierced and wounded and so overcom'd by the Love of God and Sights of the Beauty and Excellency of Jesus, and lie on the Ground. Nature being overcomed by the Sights and Enjoyments given to their Heaven born Souls that it can't bear.[48]

Anglican observers, however, were less convinced of a Godly or heavenly connection. Pandemonium, not heaven, is the guiding image for a description of a meeting at Llangeitho in 1746. The observer was a relative of Daniel Rowland's.

> Mr Rowland made a long extempore prayer before his sermon which … worked so upon most of his audience that some cry'd out in one corner 'Rhowch Glod' [Give Praise], others in different parts of ye church bawled out as loud as they possibly could, 'Bendigedig, rhowch foliant' [Splendid, Give Praise], and so on, that there was such a noise and confusion through the whole church that I had much ado … to make any sense of anything he said. His preaching … flung almost the whole society into the greatest agitation and confusion possible, some cry'd, others laughed, ye women pulled on another by ye caps, embraced each other, caper'd like, where there was any room, but the perfectionists continued as before their huzzas. By this time poor me began to be uneasy too (I am sorry to say it) so much madness, so much irreverence in the house of God … I am sorry I had no time to speak to Mr Rowland upon this subject.[49]

A reaction peculiar to Wales, and to outsiders more perplexing even than the shouting and ecstatic swaying and swooning that they might have experienced at evangelical gatherings elsewhere, was prolonged and rhythmic jumping. Two letters, both written from Carmarthen to a London newspaper, described the phenomenon: 'They have a sort of rustic dance in their public worship, which they call religious dancing, in imitation of David's dancing before the Ark. Some of them strip off their clothes, crying out "Hosannah!" etc. in imitation of those that attend our Saviour when He rode into Jerusalem.' The other, written a year later: 'The worship of the day being over, they have kept together in the place whole nights, singing, capering, bawling, fainting, thumping, and a variety of other exercises. The whole country for many miles round have crowded to see such strange sights.'[50] One of the most damning witnesses was the poet Iolo Morganwg (Edward

Williams) who, in his irreverent 'Jumpers' Hymn' comments on the effects of the preaching of Rowland Hill. Hill himself, however, considered the jumpers distasteful: 'the caricaturists of religion' and their jumping 'mummery and nonsense'.

> Come, all ye true believers
> Of Calvin's ranting sect;
> Tho' deemed by some, deceivers,
> We are sure the Lord's elect
> And a-jumping we will go.
> …
>
> With mad fanatic jumping,
> With folly bawled aloud,
> With rant and pulpit thumping,
> We charm the silly crowd,
> When a-jumping we do go.[51]

Jumping appears to have been nationwide, and to some extent denominational, following the tracks of the evangelists. An observer, who understood no Welsh, left this impression of a Methodist meeting at Caernarfon. 'After the raving of the preacher, interspersed by noises from the congregation, a psalm was sung, during which … part of the assembly were seen jumping in small parties of three or four together, and lifting up their hands, beating their breasts, and making the most horrid gesticulations.' Jumpers moved en masse to and from meetings, rather as mediæval flagellants moved from town to town, beating themselves. So extreme were some of the reactions that critics accused Wesley and others of giving the jumpers halicababum, a dried herb, to induce frenzy. John Wesley suggested, one senses without much conviction, that the frenzied cries indicated that 'Satan was tearing [people] apart so that they might come to Christ'. Thereafter, he appears to have turned a blind eye to bodily contortions.[52] George Whitefield, a more intense character than Wesley, was more comfortable with extreme emotion. In *The History of Modern Enthusiasm* (1752), Theophilus Evans noted that while 'WHITEFIELD is most luxuriant in Enthusiastical Rants ... Mr Wesley ... generally more upon his Guard'.

Yet another feature of Welsh meetings that disturbed Wesley were long sessions of trance-like praying and singing. An account of a Revival meeting at Carmarthen, on 27 August 1763, gave him pause. 'It is common in congregations attended by Mr W.W. [William Williams] and one or two other clegymen, after preaching is over for anyone that has a mind, to give out the verse of a hymn. This they sing over and over with all their might, perhaps over thirty, yes, forty times. Meanwhile the bodies of two or three, sometimes ten or twelve, are violently agitated, and they leap up and down in all manner of postures, frequently for hours together.' Wesley's response was unconvincing: 'I think there needs no great penetration to understand this. They are honest, upright men who really feel the love of God in their hearts. But they have little experience, either of the ways of God or the devices of Satan. So he serves himself of their simplicity in order to wear them out, and to bring discredit on the work of God.'[53]

Although strong, frenzied reactions were associated with large crowds and open-air meetings, they were not restricted to them. When preaching at his father-in-law's house at Llanfynydd, in 1772, John Thomas reported that some of his listeners had to leave the house because their cries drowned the sermon: 'the fiery ones went out singing praises and leaping along the yard towards the barn ... silence having been restored inside the house, I began speaking, and others broke out in like fashion, then the ones who were outside came in, it was like the joining together of two fires, so that I was obliged to be silent and let them sing, praise, pray and otherwise give utterance for hours on end before they finally left.'

Methodist questioning of the emotional, and apparently hysterical, nature of some of their meetings was understandably muted. Anglican critics, however, had no reason for restraint.

As members of a hierarchical church, in which authority flowed from the top down, they regarded as presumptuous the notion that one could approach the deity directly through feeling, dispensing with the mediation of a priest. Belief might ultimately require a leap of faith, but for Anglicans the safe approaches to it passed through the cool regions of the head, not the fiery chambers of the heart. In Wales, the strongest attack on the Methodists came from Theophilus Evans, Pantycelyn's immediate superior at Llanwrtyd. The epigraph on the title page of the *The History of Modern Enthusiasm* is a stark warning: 'Beware what Spirit rages in your Breast;/ For Ten inspir'd, Ten Thousand are possess'd.' The text is a blazing attack on the exhorters: 'The natural Tendency of their Behaviour, in Voice and Gesture and horrid Expressions, to make People mad, which very frequently has been the case with a great many of their Followers.' The evangelists' claim, that their extempore preaching issued directly from the Holy Ghost, he dismissed as nothing more mysterious than an artful combining of scriptural phrases – of which the exhorters had a ready stock – with a voluble tongue, presence of mind, and a convenient boldness.

Even though the Nonconformist denominations were to embrace the Revival and adopt the 'Methodist way', or the Methodist spirit, their conservative members deplored the leaping and dancing and the preaching with 'strange fire'. The most vitriolic attack on the new ways came from the Baptist Nathaniel Williams: 'There are some, when they ascend to the pulpit, you may see them changing their appearance and hear them assuming a strange tone of voice, – their body mannerisms are unseemly as they bend forward and backward ... beating the pulpit with their feet and hands, making as much noise as someone beating a drum.' As for their preaching, 'they clear their throats and drag out the words with a long drawn out note ... like an ass braying ... drawing in the breath with such a rush that the windpipe roars while the man fumes, sweats and gnashes his teeth like a madman.'[54] Just as damning of the histrionics was William Williams, also a Baptist, of Cardigan, who blamed in particular the itinerant preachers. He also disliked the beginning and finishing of a service with a hymn, singing without knowing the words, and above all, the repetition.[55]

Historians were no less severe. W.E.H. Lecky referred to 'religious terrorism' and 'religious madness': 'A more appalling system of religious terrorism, one more fitted to unhinge a tottering intellect and to darken and embitter a sensitive nature, has seldom existed.'[56] More recently, J.H. Plumb, in his history of eighteenth-century England, saw it as a reaction to the 'Age of Reason': 'There was nothing intellectual about Methodism; the rational attitude, the most fashionable attitude of the day, was absolutely absent, and Wesley's superstitions were those of his uneducated audiences.'

When defending enthusiasm, Howell Harris advised caution against hasty and irascible judgements. He thought it perfectly understandable that God's people should rejoice, and that they could not help crying out 'when so penetrated by the word'. Their singing together on the way to and from meetings he regarded as an innocent exercise that required no explanation: '[it] has much simplicity in it. The heart being thus kept heavenward, trifling thoughts as well as idle talking are prevented. When my heart is warmed by love, I cannot help singing even if I am hoarse.' William Williams concurred: singing, shouting for joy, laughing, leaping and dancing were all manifestations of a 'fervent love within', and thus all pleasing to heaven.[57] But not everyone was convinced of the innocence of the practice. In some of the open-air meetings the frenzied removal of clothes and abandoned dancing and jumping were regarded by some as invitations to sexual congress. The Calvinist doctrine that declared faith, not behaviour, to be the passport to heaven, gave licence, as an amused Alfred Russel Wallace noted during his days as a railway surveyor in the Neath valley, to what he perceived to be the natural hedonism of the Welsh. Half a century later, at Revival meetings in the American Midwest, John Steinbeck's Jim Casy would discover that the more fervent the sermon the greater the animal excitement generated. In a letter to Lady Huntingdon, Anglican evangelical revivalist John Berridge spelled out the dangers besetting the field preacher. 'No trap so mischievous to a field-preacher as wedlock and it is laid for him at every hedge corner.'[58]

English attacks on the jumpers were simply dismissed by the Welsh. One nation's hysteria was another's elation: 'You English blame us, the Welsh, and speak against us and say, "Jumpers, jumpers". But we, the Welsh, have something to allege against you, and we most justly say of you, "Sleepers, sleepers".' The rejoinder was Daniel Rowland's. In his biography of Rowland, Eifion Evans attributed jumping to feelings of transcendence. Commenting on a young convert's justification for her behaviour during the 1762 Revival, Evans wrote: 'That is what "jumping" was about: the unmixed, fresh, irresistible joy of salvation. Energy, emotion, understanding, memory, natural senses, spiritual desires, all – and more besides – were transposed to hitherto unimaginable heights of reality in the enjoyment of God.'[59] To a charge that trance-like singing, jumping, swooning and swaying were symptoms of mass hysteria, fellow historian, Derec Llwyd Morgan, also issued a categorical rejection: 'It does not survive a moment's reflection. The gathering is not that of a mass but of a number of individuals each of whom is moved by both an aspiration and a need.'[60]

History, to some degree, is on their side. Citing biblical scholars, Barbara Ehrenreich noted that singing, probably with musical accompaniment, dancing and swooning were old Christian practices. Early Church services, she suggested, were not just festive, but probably noisy and charismatic as well. She quoted the French sociologist Émile Durkheim who regarded ritually induced passion or ecstasy (which he defined as 'collective effervescence') as the cement that not only binds societies but that ultimately is the basis of all religion.[61] Anthropologist Victor Turner's term for the feelings of fellowship inspired by ecstatic ritual, that he regarded as a universal human need, was *communitas*.[62]

Europeans customarily have associated ecstatic ritual with primitive societies, but the behaviour, at least in its more muted forms, was not confined to 'savages' and non-Europeans. In Europe, ritual dancing and singing were never completely suppressed, despite the Church's censure. On St Eluned's Day in Breconshire in the twelfth century, Giraldus Cambrensis recorded: 'You can see young men and maidens, some in the church itself, some in the churchyard and others in the dance which wends its way round the graves. They sing traditional songs, all of a sudden they collapse on the ground, and then those who, until now, have followed their leader peacefully as if in a trance, leap up in the air as if siezed by frenzy.'

Barbara Ehrenreich points out that the 1730s Paris 'convulsionary' cult offered scenes as wild as anything that could be found among 'savages'. 'While the assembled company redoubled their prayers and collectively reached extreme heights of religious enthusiasm, at least one of their number would suddenly lapse into uncontrolled motor activity ... They thrashed about on the floor in a state of frenzy, screaming, roaring, trembling and twitching.' The excitement, which could go on for hours, was horrifying to the upper classes who associated emotionalism and extreme or abandoned behaviour with savages and the lower classes. They reacted, in Ehrenreich's phrase, by walling themselves up in 'a fortress of ego and rationality against the seductive wildness of the world'. But the tactic didn't always work. When witnessing a black Christian service in New Orleans, Frederick Law Olmstead, the nineteenth-century American landscape architect, was swept up by the 'shouts and groans, terrific shrieks, and indescribable expressions of ecstasy – of pleasure or agony' to the point where he found his own face 'glowing' and feet stamping, as if he had been 'infected unconsciously'. Clinton Furness, a traveller to South Carolina in the 1920s, was similarly affected while watching an African-American ring-shout, or danced form of religious worship whose movements were not unlike those of Welsh jumpers: 'I was gripped with the feeling of mass-intelligence, a self-conscious entity, gradually informing the crowd and taking possession of every mind there, including my own ... I felt as if some conscious plan or purpose were carrying us along, call it mob-mind, communal composition, or what you will.'[63]

In *Ecstatic Religion*, anthropologist Ioan M. Lewis noted that new faiths usually announce their advent with a flourish of ecstatic revelations, but once established they have little tolerance for enthusiasm. By circumventing the mediation of the priesthood, the religious enthusiast threatened the established order. As the early Christian community became the institution of the Church, all forms of enthusiasm – in the sense of being filled with or possessed by the deity – came under attack. When the believers could no longer access the deity on their own through ecstatic forms of worship, they were reduced to a state of dependence on central ecclesiastical authorities. Prophesying became the business of the priest and singing, as Barbara Ehrenreich has pointed out, the prerogative of a specialized choir.[64]

The fewer occasions for expressing collective joy in both the community (through carnival) and the Church coincided with what several historians of European culture consider to have been a fundamental psychological change, nothing less than a mutation in human nature. They contend that until the late sixteenth or early seventeenth century people had no strong sense of themselves as autonomous beings with distinct identities. While there must always have been a sense of selfhood, only with the rise of subjectivity and the discovery of the inner self were people made to confront the world as an autonomous 'I' separate from 'them', the group. The price for this new sense of separation and autonomy according to Yi-Fu Tuan, the distinguished cultural geographer, was 'isolation, loneliness, a sense of disengagement, a loss of vitality and of innocent pleasure in the givenness of the world'.[65] Émile Durkheim's name for the condition is *anomie*.

One antidote for anomie, posited by Richard Browne in *Medicina Musica* (1729), was song: 'Thus we may see what a vast influence Singing has over the Mind of M, and with Pleasure reflect on its joyful Consequences, and at the same time be amaz'd that it should be a Diversion or Exercise so little practis'd, since the Advantages that may be reap'd from it are so very numerous.' Browne also recommended regular doses of dancing 'in a due and regular time', preferably 'an Hour or more at a convenient time after every Meal'. Sixteenth- and seventeenth-century doctors also asserted that singing brought physiological benefits; the pressure of the air in the lungs clarified the blood and dissolved humoral deposits. But they also warned that care should be taken to avoid 'melancholy and languishing tunes' which would drive spirits further into depression.[66] Barbara Ehrenreich argues that rituals involving song and dance break down the sufferer's sense of isolation and reconnect him or her with the human community. They encourage the experience of 'self-loss', of release from the prison of the self, or, in Nietzsche's extreme phrase, '[from] the horror of individual existence'. The 'immense tragedy' for northern Protestantism, Ehrenreich concludes, is that the same social forces that disposed people to depression also swept away a traditional cure – the mind-preserving, lifesaving techniques of ecstasy.

In the epilogue to the *Devils of Loudun*, Aldous Huxley addressed the 'deep-seated' human need to transcend or escape the self. 'Always and everywhere human beings have felt the radical inadequacy of their personal existence, the misery of being their insulated selves' and, the corollary of this, the need (he quoted Wordsworth) for something 'far more deeply interfused'. The easiest way of escaping insulated selfhood (and inducing what others have called boundary loss) is to yield to 'downward self-transcendence' induced by rhythmic movement and rhythmic sound. Upward transcendence, the spiritual way, is difficult and fatiguing and therefore, Huxley asserted, we have invented short cuts that lead to a rejection of the self, dragging it downward to what seems like liberation but is, in actuality, enslavement.

When long-drawn and repetetive, rhythmic movement and sound can be hypnotic, resulting in uncontrolled jigging, swaying and head-wagging. In public worship, the repetition of particular words or phrases is almost always associated with rhythmic sound either chanted or intoned. The same word or phrase, constantly repeated, may induce states of light or even profound trance. Huxley dared any man, however civilized, to listen for very long to African drumming and Indian chanting and retain intact his critical self-conscious personality. A biting satirist, Huxley famously added Welsh hymn singing. While at Oxford his rooms were opposite Balliol Chapel, and he wrote that on Sundays he was 'made unhappy by the noise of people singing hymns'.[67] Not only did he dislike hymn singing, but when fervent and repetitive he distrusted it. Prolonged exposure to any form of unrestrained rhythmic chanting or singing, he argued, posed the danger of downward transcendence, herd intoxication, and hysteria. Citing Christ's 'Where two or three are gathered in my name, there am I in the midst of them', he warned that if the number is increased to 200 or 300, the divine presence becomes more problematical, and when the numbers run into thousands the likelihood of God being there, in the consciousness of each individual, declines almost to vanishing point. Priests and politicians, Huxley contended, who could not be unaware of the manipulative possibilities presented by downward self-transcendence, seldom proclaimed its immorality. He concluded that people, when in a light hypnotic trance, will act upon any command or exhortation.

'To men and women under the influence of herd poison, whatever I say three times is true, whatever I say three hundred times is Revelation.'[68] On Solidarity Service Days at the Fordson Community Singery, in Huxley's *Brave New World*, the communicants drink from their soma-laced, ice cream filled cups and sing solidarity hymns. After the third hymn the excitement becomes intense, a voice chants 'Ford, Ford', again and again, and the communicants feel as though they are melting and about to be visited by the Greater Being. They form a circle and chant to a feverish drumbeat, all sense of individuality lost. The circle eventually breaks and they fall down exhausted.

2

Controlling the Voices

In Capel Hebron the choirs are singing
And Martha and Jane and Hywel and Emrys
Are lost in the rapture of anthem and chorus
And the walls of the chapel are shaking with song

Idris Davies

DRIVEN BY THE successes of Nonconformity, enthusiasm for the hymn and congregational singing continued in Wales, achieving by the last quarter of the nineteenth century a popularity perhaps unsurpassed at any other time or in any other place. The formal divorce of the Calvinistic Methodists from the Anglicans, in 1811, swelled the official ranks of the Nonconformists and prompted a massive increase in chapel building to house the newly independent Methodists. Nonconformist congregations, which numbered just over 100 in 1742, increased to almost 3,000 by 1861, encompassing roughly three-quarters of the Welsh population. Unrestrained by Anglican formalism, the chapel-going Welsh embraced the sermon and the hymn. In a society without theatres, concert halls and even popular fiction, these inevitably became a diversion as well as a source of religious instruction. The most charismatic preachers, heirs to Howell Harris and Daniel Rowland, coursed the length and breadth of the country on foot, horseback, carriage, and (after 1840) rail, enthralling the thousands who turned out for open-air meetings, or who on cold, wet days crowded into chapels and barns. Unlike the established churches, chapels were not sacred spaces so they could, without fear of sanction, be used for dramatic sermons and unscripted fervent song.

Under the Nonconformist onslaught and the associated temperance movement, popular and traditional entertainments wilted. Thomas Charles of Bala, who orchestrated the Methodist break with the Anglican Church, led the charge, declaring Wales to be sunk in superstition and vice. Backing him was an army of preachers and lay readers who disparaged, as carnal entertainments, dancing, drinking, and cock-fighting. Even outdoor sports and recreation, with their inevitable emphasis on the body, were seen as a threat to public morality. In her study of Welsh emigration to Ohio, the geographer Anne Kelly Knowles recorded how farm labourers in Cardiganshire were in the habit of going to Aberaeron on Sundays to bathe and play on the beach. In the wake of a Methodist Revival, lay readers in the town decided, in 1818, that their admonitions against what they regarded as a shameless desecration of the Sabbath needed the force of economic sanction. Backed by the local gentry, who would have been Anglican, they instituted a penalty of five shillings for unruly behaviour, the equivalent of a week's wage. The measure worked – Aberaeron's beaches were silent on Sundays. Games at Llan-non, a popular Sunday venue for men's football, public dancing, and a game for girls known as 'First to the Gap', suffered a similar fate.[1]

Folk tunes, songs and dances also suffered. In 1806, Iolo Morganwg, the antiquary and poet, complained that the singing of popular hymns in taverns threatened to supplant traditional music and song. For *penillion* singers, *crwth* players, fiddlers and harpists, all on the margins of respectability at best, taverns were refuges, and without alternative stages their numbers could only decline. Denunciations of fiddlers and harpists began in the early eighteenth century when Ellis

Wynne, the scourge of the inattentive during church services, in *Gweledigaethau y Bardd Cwsc* (Visions of the sleeping bard) condemned four fiddlers to eternal torment for enticing would-be church-goers into taverns on a Sunday. As the hymn and choral and congregational singing appropriated the cultural stage, the harp, the traditional accompaniment to song, gave way to the harmonium and the piano. Dancing stopped and the best fiddlers and harpists went to London. Some repented, however. At Llannerch-y-medd fair, Hugh Morgan offered his crwth to Howell Harris, and Richard Jones from Anglesey his fiddle to a Methodist preacher from the south. But most fled or were so discouraged that they simply stopped playing. Whole genres of folk culture that remained largely intact in Catholic Ireland, Brittany and the Hebrides, disappeared from Wales.[2]

Seasonal festivals also fell before the Nonconformist fire. The *gŵyl mabsant*, or *mabsant*, a wake or holiday held originally to celebrate the local parish saint, by the early nineteenth century had become a secular three-day fair associated with the late summer and autumn harvests when food was plentiful and money in circulation. Wales was one of the few countries in Protestant Europe where saints' days were still celebrated, however tangentially. The mabsant had suffered Puritan censure since the first half of the seventeenth century, but with the rise of the Methodists the attack on the annual revels intensified. The chief entertainments, which took place in and around the parish church and churchyard, were dancing, singing, the performing of interludes, and a variety of races, games and contests, some of which, such as wrestling and bando – a kind of rough field hockey – were physical and sometimes bloody. All were fuelled by natural high spirits reinforced by large quantities of cider and beer. The dances – an essential feature of all wakes – were traditional jigs and reels accompanied by harpers and fiddlers. A wake without music was unthinkable.[3]

The Established Church tolerated the wakes because of

their religious associations and because, however roughly in some cases, they perpetuated folk custom and practice. Clergy and the local gentry attended them, presenting the prizes and often calling the dances. For the Nonconformists, however, the drinking, gambling and rowdiness endemic to the wakes were intolerable and they attacked them relentlessly. Knowing that he would be unlikely to meet the revellers in a church or at a field meeting, Howell Harris confronted them on their own ground. Before a crowd of 2,000 at a mabsant in 1739, he rebuked an attending parson and two magistrates for countenancing 'pride, swearing and drunkenness'. The revellers, as we have seen, returned the fire in their interludes. Taking heart from Howell Harris, English Methodists also bearded the lion. Before intervening at a fair in Basingstoke, George Whitefield wrote that he had 'resolved to follow the example of Hywel Harris in Wales'. At a wake in Glamorgan, in 1741, Charles Wesley preached against revels, some of which he noted disapprovingly, were 'honoured with the presence of gentry and Clergy, far and near'.

Following the lead of the charismatic field-preachers, Nonconformist exhorters throughout Wales campaigned against the revellers. At Methodist Association meetings in Aberystwyth and Bala, in 1823, chapel members were advised under the rules of discipline not to attend gŵyl mabsantau and other 'gatherings for foolish pleasure'. A single, powerful sermon from John Elias, the Methodist leader who was known as the Methodist Pope, in the 1820s is said to have ended all Sunday fairs in Flintshire. Methodists also used lay officers to punish the revellers. In Montgomery a high constable, who was also a Methodist preacher, prosecuted at the Courts of Quarter Sessions the actors in an 'indecent' interlude performed at a wake. By the 1830s and 1840s the organizers of most of the mabsantau had yielded to Nonconformist pressure, the chapels having appropriated the day of the mabsant for special meetings of their own. In Cardiganshire, in 1833, a scriptural competition between neighbouring Sunday schools supplanted *y bêl ddu* (the black ball), a riotous football match. But the symptoms were evident much earlier, with Edward Jones, an accomplished harpist and an embittered Anglican, lamenting in 1802:

> The sudden decline of the national Minstrelsy and Customs of Wales, is in great degree to be attributed to the fanatick impostors, or illiterate plebeian preachers who have too often been suffered to over-run the country ... dissuading [the common people] from their innocent amusements, such as Singing, Dancing, and other rural Sports and Games, which heretofore they had been accustomed to delight in, from the earliest time. In the course of my excursions through the Principality, I have met with several Harpers and Songsters, who actually had been prevailed upon by those erratic strollers to relinquish their profession, from the idea that it was sinful. The consequence is that Wales, which was formerly one of the merriest, and happiest countries in the World, is now become one of the dullest.[4]

*

As the second, supporting wave of evangelists, nineteenth-century preachers might not have had quite the impact of Howell Harris and Daniel Rowland – the shock troops of the Methodist Revival – but the more prominent of them (the Methodist John Elias, the Baptist Christmas Evans, the Independent Williams of Wern, and David Davies of Swansea), the 'big guns' of the denominations and 'the rock stars' of their generation, as Professor Sioned Davies has characterised them, were household names in Wales. Blessed, like Harris and Rowland, with great powers of invention and recall they could preach extemporaneously and were as comfortable in the field as in the chapel. Preaching tours, and their corollary 'sermon tasting', were in great vogue and wherever the more celebrated preachers went they attracted huge audiences. For large meetings, sometimes referred to as 'religious fairs', shops closed and business, except for innkeeping, was laid aside. If a meeting was indoors, windows were opened or removed so that the people gathered outside could hear. For the listeners, denominational affiliations were irrelevant. Nine out of ten of the followers of the itinerant preachers, noted an Anglesey vicar in 1914, were indifferent to which sect the preachers belonged.

In an essay on the Welsh pulpit for the *Titan*, the Scottish poet and novelist James Hogg stressed the importance of the Welsh preacher's ability to address the folk in a language they could readily understand.[5] He contended that this characteristic, more than any other, distinguished the Welsh from the English pulpit. The gulf between the language of the educated and the uneducated, which he regarded as unbridgeable in England, did not exist in Wales. He attributed the shared language to the greater cohesion of Welsh society. In Wales there was no large commercial class and no landowning class that was qualitatively different from their workers, tenants and labourers. The result was less political agitation than in England, and the absence of unbridgeable social gulfs allowed ideas – religious and others – to permeate the entire nation. Welsh preachers, Hogg continued, had the gift of wrapping abstruse principles in the homeliest language. He cited Williams of Wern who put 'the thoughts of a philosopher in the language of a child'. Kenneth Morgan, the modern historian, has endorsed Hogg's view, characterising the nineteenth-century preachers as essentially populist, *gwerinol*, in way of life and rhetoric, enjoying a natural, spontaneous relationship with their congregations.[6]

Contemporary, nineteenth-century accounts suggest that the sermons of the more celebrated preachers were vocal as well as pedagogic exercises. All were adept at readying the congregation (*porthi'r gynulleidfa*) by repeating or reiterating key words or phrases and modulating the tone and rhythm of their delivery. They could also address crowds of thousands without seeming to raise their voices and without dramatic gestures. Bodily movement, as in the performance of a singer at a classical concert, seems to have been deliberately restrained to allow both the speaker and the congregation to concentrate on the voice. David Davies's gift for enunciation and projection was so remarkable that he announced his own hymns in quiet, natural tones that reached without apparent effort to the edges of the crowd. Davies's voice also enchanted: so like 'a silver bell', according to one witness, that 'the strongest men could scarcely endure his ministry without being melted by it'.[7]

For economy of movement and gesture, John Jones, the rector of Nevern and an eminent Welsh bard, regarded John Elias as a latter-day Demosthenes: 'For one to throw his arms about is not action, to make this or that gesture is not action. Action is seen in the eye, in the curling of the lip, in the frowning of the nose – in every muscle of the speaker ... every movement that he made was not only graceful, but it spoke.' Action, when used, was telling. To claim the attention of a congregation made restless by the previous minister at a *cymanfa bregethu* (preaching festival) in Amlwch, Elias approached the edge of the stage, slowly removed his hat and placed it on the reading platform. He then took off his gloves, just as slowly, and placed them in his hat, touched his hat again and moved it slowly away from him. With all eyes now on him he began to speak. He could do so with fiery intensity, one Anglican clergyman remarking that he was like 'a flaming seraph in the pulpit'; and another, that he preached as if 'taking fire down from heaven'. But Elias also understood, from listening to sermons as a child, that in the quieter passages sound and rhythm could be as important as meaning: 'For a long time I listened without understanding much of what the preacher was saying. Yet I would derive pleasure from the sound of the sermons.'[8]

In a study of folk preaching in present-day America, Bruce A. Rosenberg notes that in sermons where the subject of the narrative is a matter of accepted faith, and the lessons to be drawn from it unassailable, then the preacher is free to experiment with the structure, pace and rhythm of his address. Rhythm, he asserts, is the essssence of the preacher's 'musical art', and to be truly effective it must be sustained and properly paced throughout the sermon. Like the young John Elias, Rosenberg found, when listening to folk preachers in or from the American South, that sound could, without diminishing the impact of the sermon, sometimes supersede meaning: 'Much of what he [Rubin Lacy] was saying was unintelligible. What was intelligible was his driving rhythm, his musical chanting and the great passion he exuded through emphasis, expression and gesture.' Fellow American James Weldon Johnson, in *God's Trombones*, goes further. As a youth he attended services where the congregation was 'moved to ecstasy by the rhythmic intoning of sheer inconsistencies'.[9]

The celebrated Welsh preachers may never have been incoherent but equipped, as Abel Evans and James Floy noted, with 'the mystic power of an unknown tongue' they could, like musicians, evoke sympathies 'scarcely dependent upon words'.[10] The English as well as the Welsh fell under their spell. Paxton Hood, a Congregationalist minister and well-known writer, described their sermons as 'a sort of song, full of imagination'. In his biography of Christmas Evans, Hood noted how, at open-air meetings, Evans, as 'a master of the instrument of speech', drew bystanders inward, siren-like, from the hedges and the byways.[11] Abel Evans and Floy could not decide where Christmas Evans's greater strength lay: in the magic peals which made his hearers tremble or in his marvellous allegorical and dramatic power. Williams of Wern had comparable gifts. He was a singularly quiet preacher but when 'in full sail', noted a contributor to the *Biographical Magazine*, his voice was 'never surpassed in compass and elasticity'. He handled it, the writer continued, 'as doth a songster', adding that 'in no country in modern times is the voice modulated in public speaking as it is in Wales ... Entirely without art – simply from an instinctive choice of key and variety of note to strike and please. The ear, while congruous to the subject and to its variety of treatment, the skillful preacher pours forth thought and passion, poetry and melody, intertwined in such a flood of subduing power and sweetness that the congregation is often literally bathed in tears.'[12]

David Davies of Swansea, a poet and hymnwriter as well as a preacher, had a voice, according to Paxton Hood, of such 'overwhelming compass and sweetness' that he was known as the 'Silver Trumpet of Wales'. In his appraisal of Davies, Dr Thomas Rees of Swansea was more prosaic, but just as admiring: 'What the old people tell you about him is wonderful. It was in his voice – he could not help himself; without any effort, five minutes after he began to speak, the whole congregation would be bathed in tears.' Unable to leave, people remained for a long time, singing, weeping and praising. Many regarded David Davies as the heir to Daniel Rowland, and the highest praise that could be bestowed on Swansea and, by extension, on Davies, was to say that it was 'another Llangeitho'. He was, Hood concluded, 'a singer, a prophet of song, and the swell and cadences of his voice were like many voices which blend to make up one complete concert. He was not only a master of the deep bass notes, but he had a rich soprano kind of power, too.' When Davies raised his voice to a higher pitch than ordinary, it increased in melody and power, and its effects were 'thrilling in the extreme; there were no jarring notes – all was the music of elegance throughout.' He was, Hood concluded, 'an organ in a human frame'.[13]

To encapsulate the vocal talents of the four, Paxton Hood treated them as a singing group: 'Thus, if we were to speak of these four men as constituting a quartette in the harmony of the great Welsh pulpit, we should give to John Elias the place of the deep bass; to Davies the rich and melting soprano; to Christmas Evans the tenor; reserving, for Williams of Wern, the place of the alto.'[14] As songsters, the Welsh preachers had the advantage of a language whose strong stresses and lilting quality were, to some ears, already halfway to music. In his late eighteenth-century *Journey through Part of Wales*, Lord Lyttleton noted that when he first passed some of the Welsh hills and heard the harp and the melodious voices of the Welsh women, he could not help indulging the idea that he had descended the Alps, and was enjoying the harmonious pleasures of the 'Italian Paradise'.[15] Even preachers renowned for their symphonic performances outdoors could, when indoors, play softly as upon a single instrument. Thus Lady Llanover could say of Edward Matthews (Matthews Ewenni) that he would preach at her home in a voice more enchanting than the harp on St David's Day.[16] Of John Jenkins, a gentle Baptist preacher, it was said that his words descended like the dew, leaving the faces of his hearers washed with tears.[17]

During the Revivals, and at gatherings to mark significant events in the Nonconformist calendar, the preaching sessions, cymanfaoedd pregethu, could last all day and they were attended by very large crowds. To create an amphitheatre-like effect, the organizers often set the stage in a hollow, or at the bottom of a slope, the audience sitting or standing on the sloping ground. And, as in any rock concert, the star attractions were kept to the end.[18] At these gatherings ordinary preaching, Christmas Evans insisted, would not serve: 'Common preaching will not rouse sluggish districts from heavy slumbers ... Indeed, formal prayers and lifeless sermons are like bulwarks raised against these in England; and this evil genius has also entered the principality under the pretence of order. Five or six stanzas will be sung as dry as Gilboa, instead of one or two new verses, like a new song, full of God, of Christ and the Spirit of grace, until the heart is attuned for worship.'[19]

For a Methodist quarterly meeting at Bangor, during the 1859 Revival, more than 50,000 people are said to have gathered. Sermons, from a succession of preachers, began at 6a.m. and went on into the night. A year later at Caernarvon between 15,000 and 20,000 assembled for a similar Methodist meeting. Tyssul Evans caught the flavour of a cymanfa bregethu held at Penygroes:

> In the field adjoining the churchyard ... a rude stage or platform was erected roofed over with canvas and fitted with seats ... The public meetings began on the field at two o'clock; three sermons were preached in the afternoon and three in the evening ... Wednesday was the chief day of the feast. The first meeting was at seven o'clock in the morning, at which there were two sermons, but the great meeting of the gathering was held at ten o'clock. To this people came in thousands from all parts of the country ...

At the great field-sessions, sermons, prayers and hymns followed each other in sequence:

> The rough stage is filled with ministers and religious leaders, the field is dotted over with people, a few sitting on the raised planks, but the majority sitting in an expectant mood. The minister gives out a hymn, the plaintive melody is taken up by the vast congregation and rises and falls like the waves of the sea. After a reading of the Scriptures another hymn is sung and an earnest prayer is directed to heaven ... the people become more and more animated ... sway to and fro under the power of his mighty eloquence ... and when the speaker comes to an end the tension is relieved by the singing of a hymn ... Another sermon follows and after the singing of a hymn still another. The tide of feeling runs high and the refrain of the last hymn is repeated again and again by the assembled thousands.[20]

*

By the middle of the nineteenth century, the musical, cadenced quality of the sermons of the popular preachers became more pronounced and, in some quarters, it dominated. Hwyl, which had been used to describe fervent impassioned preaching, became 'the hwyl', a quasi-musical preaching technique.

58

Erasmus Jones described it in an *Atlantic Monthly* essay, 'The Welsh in America'.

> The effect often produced by the popular Welsh preacher is wonderful. There is one peculiarity connected with their preaching which differs entirely from anything that I ever observed in English pulpits; it is usually marked by a great variety of intonations. I do not know the origin of this chanting style of preaching prevalent among the Welsh, though it probably was introduced by the founders of Calvinistic-Methodism. The judicious use of it is confined to the more passionate or pathetic parts of a sermon. It differs entirely from that monotonous tone that is heard in English churches, or the chromatic chanting of the mass before Papal altars; it is melody of the purest nature. It is not an easy matter to import ... a clear idea of the genuine Welsh hwyl, or that musical style in which the minister pours forth his pathetic passages when under 'full canvas'. A clergyman who has not an ear for music can never charm his hearers with this melodic hwyl, and it would be exceedingly unfortunate for him to attempt it, for it embraces the tones and semitones of the scale ... The best description I can give of this peculiarity is this: it is the application of sentences in a chanting style to portions of the minor scale. The minister is never at a loss how to apply the words to the melody; they appear to run together as by mutual attraction. The sentence is started, for instance, on E minor. The minister has his own peculiar melody. It ranges here and there from the first to the fifth, often reaching the octave, and then descending and ending in sweet cadence on the key-note. I am sure that in the genuine hwyl the intonations are always in the minor mode. The introduction and the deliberative parts are in the major voice, and the voice continues until the emotional point is reached, then it glides triumphantly into a thrilling minor, which generally continues to the close.[21]

It was the phonic, musical character of Welsh preaching at its most dramatic that also preoccupied Paxton Hood in his 1883 biography of Christmas Evans:

> The Welsh preacher seeks to play upon [words] as keys ... hence, as he rises in feeling he rises in variety of intonation, and his words

sway to and fro, up and down, – base, minor, and soprano all play their part, a series of intonings. In English, this very frequently sounds monotonous ... even affected; in Welsh the soul of man is said to have caught the hwyl, – that is, he is in full sail, he has the feeling and fire: the people catch it too ... Great Welsh preaching is very often a kind of wild, irregular chant, a jubilant refrain, recurring again and again. The people catch the power of it; shouts rise – prayers! Bendigedig ... Amen! Diolch byth! and other expressions rise and roll over the multitude; they, too, have caught the hwyl.[22]

In his history of Congregationalism in Wales, R. Tudur Jones pinpoints the origins of hwyl in its theatrical late nineteenth-century guise. His source is David Williams of Troedrhiwdalar, born in 1779, who remembered a time when the practice was unknown. As the first exponent of the method of chanting the emotional parts of the sermon, Tudur Jones names David Davies (1775–1838), a Methodist preacher of Sardis, Myddfai, in Carmarthenshire. Endowed with a melodious voice and an engaging personality, Davies was encouraged to preach by his namesake, David Davies of Swansea. So great was his appeal that he quickly found imitators. The best known of them was Daniel Davies of Neath, a preacher with a voice, so it was said, of 'incomparable sweetness'.[23]

Two more recent scholars, Sioned Davies and Sally Harper, have sought a longer pedigree for hwyl, examining possible links with the chant or declamatory tones used by medieval poets, harpists and storytellers (*cyfarwydd*). As performers, Davies suggests, Welsh preachers would often use the same techniques as their medieval counterparts, creating drama through a compelling combination of sound and meaning.[24] Harper quotes a definition of hwyl by Owen Thomas, the biographer of John Jones of Talysarn (1796–1857): 'a kind of recitative, half-chant and half-speech (though closer to speech).'[25] For those too young to have heard the dying strains of the hwyl in the 1940s and 1950s, its cadences, as author and literary critic John Ackerman has indicated, may still be heard in the recorded poetry readings of Dylan Thomas.[26]

For Howell Elvet Lewis, a poet, hymnwriter and Independent minister, hwyl was the end to which all true oratory tends: 'All true oratory is instinctively, unconsciously set to music; the tune can be discerned by a listener with a good ear, set down and copied in notes and rhythm. But this is especially noticeable in Welsh preaching, more so, perhaps, than in any other tongue. There is a manufactured form of it; there are extravagant varieties of it; but when it comes naturally, with the rising warmth of emotion, and ... with the aid of a well-modulated voice ... it sways a congregation almost at will.'[27] In its unrestrained form, however, the hwyl was merely histrionic, sound without meaning. 'The hwyl was the culminating point of any sermon, and if the preacher was endowed with a sweet voice, modulated to advantage; the hwyl, if it is well done, covered all poverty of thought in the introduction and exposition ... The hwyl could not possibly explain nor argue, more than a piece of music explains or argues.'[28] The Nonconformist pulpit, having banished the fair, the interlude, the fiddlers and the crwth players had, at its most theatrical, become what it disdained – a stage, an entertainment.

*

While the voices and rhetorical skills of Welsh preachers drew widespread praise, informed evaluations of congregational singing were less enthusiastic. Critics complained that its quality had not improved since the 1762 Revival, some contending that it may even have lost ground.[29] The complaints ranged from shouting and the seemingly endless repetition of verses to a sluggish tempo and drawling. Other irritations were the hypnotic swaying of body and head, and the clapping of a hand to the ear so that the singer could hear his or her own voice more distinctly. In what was called 'praise singing', the congregation would repeat the chorus of a favourite tune, singing in an elongated drawl, with hand on ear, head trembling.[30] The most popular Welsh hymns were sung at a slow pace in a minor key, a practice that could lead to drawling or 'dragging'. Sydney Smith, the eighteenth-century cleric and wit, objected to minor key singing because it had a depressing effect on his nerves. On one occasion he complained to the organist of St Paul's: 'Mr Goss, no more minor music, if you please, while I am in residence.'[31] Others were more forgiving. The musicologist James Lightwood maintained that when minor melodies were sung at a moderate pace, people in general revelled in them, and when sung by the Welsh the effect could be 'wonderful'. The Scots, he noted, sang scarcely anything but minor melodies for centuries.

Yet however moving or exhilarating Welsh congregational singing might have been at its best, by formal musical standards it was crude. Professor T.J. Morgan of Swansea likened it to a great river flowing unharnessed toward the sea, great in volume and energy but lacking control and finesse.[32] The singers needed guidance. Although slow to adopt singing in their services, some of the earliest directions came from the Baptists. In 1797 John Williams, a minister and teacher of singing, produced a pocket-sized choral primer, *Y Gamut*, in which he offered the rudiments of scale, clef, tonality and metre. It was used by travelling singing teachers and often published with a collection of hymns. Another Baptist, Joseph Harris of Swansea, who thought the entire congregation should sing, offered this caveat: 'Let everyone who sings try to make it as harmonious and melodious as he can while avoiding extremes of virtuosity which hamper congregational singing.' From 1821, hymn tunes appeared regularly in *Seren Gomer*, the Baptist periodical. Instruction, and printed hymns, improved the quality of Baptist singing but the new, restrained style did not please everyone. Christmas Evans lamented the loss of the old practice of treasuring hymns in the memory, and the exuberance of singing from the heart, *canu o'r galon*. The new style, he argued, encouraged showmanship. When a member of the congregation at his chapel in Caernarfon drew a collection of printed hymns from his pocket, Evans remarked, 'You won't have those in heaven, put it back in your pocket.'[33]

But the mood was for change. To instruct the Welsh in 'the old craft of singing', Owen Williams, a church musician from Anglesey, in 1817 and 1818 brought out two volumes on the principles of singing. In one of them a set of eight pictures showed how the mouth was to be shaped for effective voice production.[34] In 1839, John Roberts of Henllan published a collection of Revival hymns, *Caniadau y Cysegr* (Songs of the sanctuary), harmonized by the author. His aim was to improve the quality of 'praise singing' by separating the low and high voices and by making the tunes more dance-like and buoyant. Mindful of the musical limitations of most congregations, he did not, in his introduction to *Caniadau y Cysegr*, suggest singing in parts.

The manuals and instructional books were mainly for choir leaders and conductors; the singers needed direction. One of the first to offer it was Robert Williams, a young man with strong interests in singing and pedagogy. He arrived in Bethesda in 1819 having memorized Williams's *Gamut*. He came to work on a farm but, fatally as it turned out, he soon found work at the Penrhyn slate quarry. On Saturday afternoons, and occasionally on weekday evenings, he organized classes for children and young people to whom he taught both reading and hymn singing. The hymns were sung in the Sunday service to such effect that the members of Carneddi Chapel came to be known as 'the singing congregation'. John Elias urged people to go to Carneddi where they could 'not expect to hear better singing this side of heaven'.[35] Robert Williams died after an accident at the quarry, in 1828, at the age of thirty-seven. Friends and supporters organized a singing society (The Society of the Religious Singers of the Cairn) that over the next decade spawned similar societies in many places in north and mid Wales. The societies were non-sectarian; singing in Wales, as the American Congregationalist Lincoln Hartford pointed out, was a neighbourhood affair.[36]

These early efforts to raise the level of congregational singing, however, were outshone by the achievements of the gifted Mills brothers, John and Richard, the grandsons of Henry Mills whom Thomas Charles had asked to improve singing in Methodist Sunday schools in and around Bala. John Mills (1812–73), who was a Calvinistic Methodist minister and leader of a singing society in Llanidloes, wrote essays on music for Welsh periodicals under the pen-name Ieuan Glan Alarch, and lectured on music in south and west Wales. In 1838 he published a musical grammar, *Gramadeg Cerddoriaeth*, an attempt to explain musical composition to Welsh readers, that ran to six editions. After he moved to London in 1846 to work in a Jewish mission, he and his brother Richard published, in 1847, *Y Cerddor Eglwysig* (Church musician) in which, to accommodate the usual assortment of high and low voices in any congregation, they advocated part-singing after the tune had been learned:

> Teach the tune to the body of the congregation ... put the number of men with the strongest voices to sing the bass; young men whose voices are breaking sing the middle part ... and boys whose voices have not started breaking take the top part ... We think this is the most natural arrangement, and the only one that gets the whole congregation singing.[37]

So popular and effective were the brothers that in an address to the United Singers of Bala in 1845, the Reverend Lewis Edwards appealed for the use of Welsh tunes exclusively, arguing that the work of John and Richard Mills had dispensed with the need to continue the singing of 'the poor tunes born from England'.[38] Richard's most significant work was *Caniadau Seion* (1842). Like John Roberts of Henllan, he refrained, in his introduction, from laying down any rules of singing: 'some have the men only to sing the accompaniment (air) and the women to sing the tune; and others vice versa. This perhaps is the most correct way in choral singing although I would not think this was the best with congregational singing; thus I leave the choice to the leaders of voice and to their best judgements.' Earlier, W.E. Hickson in *The Singing Master* (1836) had issued similar advice. He thought that instruction in singing, as in the teaching of language, should start with rhythms, sounds and (in the case of singing) melodies, and once these had been mastered only then proceed to the grammar – the technicalities.

To raise the levels of congregational singing in the eastern valleys in the 1830s, Moses Davies, a Merthyr plasterer and self-taught musician, held three singing classes a week at different chapels. He considered singing at full power to be the height of vulgarity: 'I used to lay much stress on the necessity of making it a rule to sing in rather a subdued manner, so as to produce music and not noise.'[39] Davies's refrain was taken up by Rosser Beynon. Born in Glyn-nedd in 1811, he came to Merthyr with his parents in 1815. He began work in a coal mine at age eight and, according to his brother John, he was self-taught '[depriving] himself of hundreds of hours of sleep to master some musical problem'.[40] At eighteen he conducted singing practices at Soar Chapel and, like Moses Davies, he held evening singing classes. He was so well regarded as a teacher that he gave weekly lessons in Cardiff and occasional lessons to congregations throughout south Wales. He also wrote hymns and compiled and edited a hymn-tune book, but his strength lay in teaching.

The great breakthrough in teaching choral singing to congregations, as distinct from choirs or 'singing groups', was the circumvention of conventional staff notation, the immoveable obstacle for the musically illiterate. A few years before the arrival in the Tawe valley of choir director and tinplate manufacturer Ivander Griffiths, John Henry Vivian,

Swansea's leading copper manufacturer and its enlightened Liberal MP, invited to Swansea the author of a system of sight-reading or sight-singing that was then being taught in English schools and colleges. John Hullah's services at the time (June 1842) were in great demand in London and it is a measure of Vivian's standing that he was able to persuade him to spend a few months in Swansea. Hymn-singing leaders and ministers from valley communities and the town came as many as three nights every week to receive lessons at the rate of a shilling an hour. Hullah, who had studied at the Royal Academy of Music, was a protegee of Dr James Phillips Kay-Shuttleworth, founder of the Battersea Normal College training school for teachers and secretary to the education committee of the Privy Council. Kay-Shuttleworth, a physician who had worked in the slums of Manchester during the 1832–4 cholera epidemic, was a passionate advocate of shorter hours and better education for workers. In 1839 he appointed Hullah to Battersea as part of a programme of studies that encompassed the methods of Pestalozzi in arithmetic, Mühlhäuser in handwriting, and Lautier in reading. Hullah, the lecturer in music, offered singing classes to trainee teachers based on a scheme devised by L.M. Wilhelm, a music teacher in Paris.[41]

The classes were popular and in 1841 Kay-Shuttleworth, with the Privy Council's blessing, organized a series of classes for practicing teachers at Exeter Hall in London, a more public arena. In less than a year, the classes were thrown open to all-comers. National recognition followed. Kay-Shuttleworth's and the Council's objectives, as spelled out in Hullah's 1842 manual, were undisguisedly social and political: 'Amusements which wean the people from vicious indulgences are in themselves a great advantage: they contribute indirectly to the increase of domestic comfort, and promote the contentment of the artisan … The songs of any people may be regarded as an important means of forming an industrious, brave, loyal and religious working class.' Lord Wharncliffe, president of the Council of Education in the Peel administration, was more direct. He hoped that the programme would keep people out of the taverns. To mark their appreciation of Hullah's efforts, in 1842 the first workingmen's singing class presented him with a music stand (made entirely by members of the group) in the shape of an angel, gilded and bearing a palm branch.

Hullah's system had a mixed reception from musicians and the press. The method, commonly called the 'fixed Doh' (based on the key of C), was a novel form of music notation related to the tonic sol-fa, a later refinement. The teaching, involving complicated hand and arm movements, was difficult. As each pupil repeated notes in the ascending scale, he or she raised his or her right arm and opened and closed his or her fingers at stated intervals. The five fingers represented the five lines in the staff notation. The pupils kept their left hands open at waist level while the right had moved swiftly in four predetermined directions before finishing with a clap in their left palms. The *Illustrated London News* found the exercise, accompanied by the alarming cry of 'crotch, crotch, crotch' (short for crotchet) 'not a little grotesque'. The independent and radical press, after an initial burst of enthusiasm, was not pleased. Not only was the system difficult to teach but there was a suspicion that it might have been technically unsound. More threatening perhaps was the charge that by tying students to their manuals the system obstructed efforts at 'musical culture' made by other means. In other words, by making the reading of music available to all it threatened the authority of staff notation.

Hullah's fixed Doh system improved the quality of singing, but by restricting singers to a single key it meant that some voices were strained while others were under-used. That every voice might have something it could manage required a system that would allow singing in different keys. The solution was the tonic sol-fa. Sarah Ann Glover, the daughter of a Congregationalist minister who ran a Dame school in Black-Boy Yard, Norwich, began experimenting with her own notation in 1812. Using the initials of the old scale names, she devised a ladder-like chart that demonstrated how a change of key affected the sound of the notes. Freed from standard musical symbols, her pupils learned quickly to sing from sight. At her father's church she assembled a remarkably proficient children's choir and, in 1828, she broadcast her success in a book: *A Scheme for Rendering Psalmody Congregational*. The book ran to many editions but it was the communicator John Curwen who, as we might say, took her scheme and ran with it. Curwen was a young Congregationalist minister with no musical training who had been unable to teach members of his own Sunday school to sing anything but the melody. But he was a gifted teacher, and delegates to a Nonconformist Sunday School Union conference in 1841 considered him the ideal candidate to recommend a reliable method for teaching singing at Sunday schools. Unable to master staff notation without the help of a teacher, and frustrated by Hullah's fixed Doh system, Curwen fell upon Glover's book. He found that he could read a psalm tune from her notation and, even more convincing, that he could teach a child at his lodgings to sing.[42]

In 1842 Curwen, then twenty-five, published a series of articles, entitled 'Lessons on Singing', in the *Independent Magazine*, a Congregationalist journal that he edited. He changed Glover's sol-fa names to the now-familiar doh, ray, me, fah, soh, la, te, and to emphasize the scheme's key-centred nature, he named it tonic sol-fa. The system was easily learned and, invaluable to a singer, it conveyed a sense of accurate time and accurate relative pitch. Armed with sol-fa, a singer could tackle any music, not just set pieces that could be learned parrot fashion and, no small advantage in working-class Britain, sol-fa was much cheaper to print than staff notation. Curwen devised methods of mass producing tonic sol-fa versions of music as complex as oratorios, masses and even operas at prices chapel congregations could afford. He had struck gold. He resigned his ministry in 1856, established his own printing press in 1862, and in 1869 he founded the Tonic Sol-fa College in London. Long before his death in 1880, sol-fa was the recognized method of teaching music in chapels, churches and schools not only in Britain and Europe but throughout the English-speaking world and wherever English speakers were found. By 1907 a scheme that the inspector of Normal (teachers') Colleges in Belgium lauded as 'the admiration of Europe' was being taught to schoolchildren in Japan and Sioux Indians in America.

By the mid-1860s Curwen's sol-fa had replaced Hullah's system in England's elementary schools and teachers' colleges. Curwen's stated intention, like Sarah Glover's, had been to regard it as a ladder to staff notation and music's broad uplands, but instead of leading to a larger world it proved, in most cases, to be a cul de sac. When tonic sol-fa could be applied to any hymn tune or chorus, who but a music enthusiast would tackle staff notation? Sarah Glover, who may have been dismayed by what her invention had wrought, refused for more than twenty years to endorse Curwen's modifications.

*

For a people disposed to sing, but with only instinct to guide them, tonic sol-fa was heaven-sent. Its emissaries in Wales were two Welsh Sunday school superintendents from Liverpool, Eleazar Roberts and John Edwards, who, in 1859, attended in Liverpool an exposition of tonic sol-fa by Curwen himself. They were immediate converts, and with Curwen's permission translated his handbook into Welsh. Curwen was delighted, exclaiming: 'Hurrah for the first Tonic Sol-fa book in the Cymric tongue.' Sol-fa classes were organized in Sunday schools throughout the country and by 1866 there was hardly a school without one. Sidelined, staff notation became known as *hen nodiant*, old or, more accurately, old-fashioned notation. After 1872 the choristers could sing from song sheets printed at Isaac Jones's Treherbert print shop, one of the first in Wales to publish choral music in the new notation.[43] Among the learners were ministers and hymn-singing leaders. The effect was to transform, in Lincoln Hartford's phrase, 'the babble of Wales ... into the ravishing beauty of chapel singing'.[44]

After the opening of the Sol-fa College in 1869, Welsh ministers and hymn-singing leaders descended on London in such numbers that Welsh speakers had to be appointed to the examining panel. In most years, Welsh candidates took the lion's share of the advanced certificates and some of these were able to evade the cul de sac. In 1892 the name of David Evans appeared five times in the honour rolls. David Evans was a coal miner from Resolven who went on to a doctorate of music at Oxford and a professorship of music at Cardiff.[45] He was one of three doctors of music produced by Resolven, a mining village of a few hundred people in the Neath valley. The others, both former boy coal miners, were Thomas Hopkin Evans and William Rhys Herbert. The son of musical parents, Hopkin Evans left Resolven for London at seventeen, where he 'rubbed shoulders' with musicians of all sorts. He returned to Resolven and founded a choral society that won prizes at the National Eisteddfod in 1905, '06 and '07.[46] That led to the directorship, for fourteen years, of the Neath Choral Society and further honours. William Rhys Herbert graduated from tonic sol-fa to staff notation thanks, in part, to the enterprise of his fellow villagers who held a concert at Jerusalem Chapel to raise funds to pay for lessons with T.J. Davies, a Bachelor of Music in Swansea. Herbert also bought a harmonium, the first in the village, that was delivered by train and, followed by a crowd of children, hauled by cart through the village. When only twenty-two Herbert followed his tutor to America and became an organist and conductor at a large church in Minneapolis.

Most students of tonic sol-fa, however, were content to remain within its orbit and many became accomplished teachers and conductors. By 1910, of the 500 licentiates of the Tonic Sol-fa College, 300 were Welsh. For workingmen with no access to colleges and universities, certificates from the Sol-fa College were prized and they were framed and hung with pride on living-room walls. Constant exposure to the letter notes at school, Sunday school, and chapel, made possible sight-singing competitions for individuals and choral groups in local eisteddfodau and during intervals at concerts. The notes were so familiar that they could be applied, with the assurance that they would be understood, to the cadences of speech. Each cadence in the sermons of John Jones of Talysarn, for example, is said to have ended in ray soh, with the doh on C.[47]

Curwen's tonic sol-fa would always have had an audience in Wales, but that it should have arrived when people once again were taking up their hymn books was providential. In 1859–60, Wales was in the throes of a religious Revival. Through emigrant letters and church and denominational bulletins, news of an American Revival reached Wales – and an expectant population well-versed in Charles Finney's immensely popular *Lectures on Revivals of Religion* – in 1858. The Revival's vehicle in Wales was twenty-seven-year-old Humphrey Jones of Tre'r ddôl, a returnee from America. Jones's parents had left Tre'r ddôl, in north Cardiganshire, for Wisconsin in 1847, leaving their son to be brought up by an aunt. The younger Jones, who started preaching at fifteen, had ambitions for the Methodist ministry but when his candidacy failed he followed his parents to Wisconsin. He arrived in 1855 when Wisconsin, like the rest of America, felt the first tremors of a Revival, and as an itinerant he preached in Wisconsin, Illinois and New York State. Inspired by his success in America, he returned to Tre'r ddôl in 1858 determined, as he told one minister, 'to set Wales ablaze'. He began preaching daily, starting at 5a.m., even during the harvest, and continuing for five straight weeks. His approach worked: 'Only with the greatest difficulty was it possible to drive the carriage past the chapel, such was the crowd. The chapel was crammed full, and the road in either direction past it for about half a mile was packed with people, young and old, some worshipping, some praying and others praising ... the sound of song and praise could be heard in the houses and in the fields throughout the locality.'[48] Prayer meetings were held nightly throughout the district, most of them spontaneous and all apparently unstructured. People prayed and sang as the spirit moved them, and often through the night so that by morning arms and legs were stiff and their owners, in some cases, stupefied. From Tre'r ddôl the Revival mood spread and settled over much of Wales.

A curious feature of both the Welsh and American Revivals of 1857–8 was a phenomenon known as singing in the air. Witnesses at Revival meetings reported the sound of heavenly angelic voices, sweetly and softly joined in harmony, that rendered the listeners incapable of movement. It was as if, according to one account, they were nailed to the spot. In Wales there were reports of earlier occurrences at Beddgelert, in 1817, and Staylittle, Montgomeryshire, in 1851. At Staylittle, David Vaughan, a minister's son dismayed by what he perceived to be spiritual torpor, urged his father to conduct a week of prayer meetings. The meetings failed to trigger the hoped for Revival, but on their way home on the last evening the walkers heard the sound of sweet and melodious singing from an invisible choir in the sky. When they related the incident the following day, others in the district claimed to have heard the same sounds.[49] In his book on Welsh chapels, Anthony Jones cited an incident (no date) during an evening prayer meeting at a chapel in Blaenpennal, near Aberystwyth. In spite of stormy, tempestuous weather, the chapel was crowded. During the singing of the hymn 'He who Speeds the Lightning's Flash' there was, so it was reported, 'wild confusion. The chapel was overcome by Heavenly discords [and the] rejoicing and shouting was chaotic.'[50]

*

Hindsight suggests that what was gathering in Wales during the 1850s were the ingredients for an explosion of song: a people predisposed to sing, a religious Revival to generate emotional intensity, and a system of music notation that, within limits, was easily learned. To combine the ingredients and release the energies within them, what was needed was a sound repertoire of hymns and a disciplined framework in which to sing them. John Roberts, known by his bardic name Ieuan Gwyllt, was in many ways an unlikely saviour of congregational singing in Wales. Gwyllt was born near Aberystwyth, in 1822, to parents who were prominent singers at their chapel. His mother had a fine voice and his father was the precentor, the lead singer. Gwyllt's early life lacked direction. He worked first, from 1842, as a clerk in an Aberystwyth pharmacy, but after two years gave that up to teach at a local school. After a few months he left for London to train as a teacher, but on failing to get a certificate, probably because of ill health, he returned to Aberystwyth in 1845 where he was still able to open a Nonconformist 'British School', supported by government grants tied to attendance and results. The school closed after nine months, and for the next seven years Gwyllt worked as a solicitor's clerk; in his spare time he edited a short-lived monthly music magazine, involved himself in the music of his chapel, and attended classes conducted by John and Richard Mills.

In 1852 there was another shift in direction; he left for Liverpool to be the assistant editor of *Yr Amserau* (The Times), and quickly became its editor. Journalism suited him but he also felt the tug of the pulpit; he gave his first sermon in Runcorn in 1856 while still at *Yr Amserau*. As a journalist, he took up liberal causes, opposing slavery and hanging, and campaigning for a secret ballot and the legality of Welsh in courts of law. He also opposed the Crimean War at a time when Russians were vilified and Turks admired. Gwyllt threw his weight behind the peace party. His radicalism probably cost him his candidacy for the Methodist ministry; in politics, the Methodists were strangely passive. In 1858 he moved to Aberdare as editor of *Y Gwladgarwr* (The Patriot) and in 1859, in the politically more tolerant coalfield, he was invited to be minister of a Calvinistic Methodist church in Merthyr. In 1865 he moved again, to Llanberis, where he served as minister of Capel Coch until his retirement in 1869. He died in Llanfaglan, Caernarvonshire, in 1877.

For Gwyllt, as the architect/designer of congregational singing in Wales, the pivotal event was the publication in 1859 of *Llyfr Tonau Cynulleidfaol*, a collection of congregational hymn tunes selected and arranged by him. The collection included several of his own hymns, among them the now celebrated 'Moab', and several from England, Germany and France. In what is regarded as a masterly and unequivocal preface, he declared that his aim was to raise the standard of Welsh hymn singing by familiarizing the Welsh not just with good tunes, but with the best that could be found. In the case of Welsh tunes, his objective was to standardize congregational singing by taking all the local variants of one tune and imposing upon them a single template based on his own taste and judgement. By eschewing 'all that was tawdry, meretricious [and] superficial', L.J. Roberts would write in an article for the *Western Mail*, May 1922, he 'purified the taste of the nation'.

In contrast to modern collectors of folk tunes, who treasure local interpretations, Gwyllt aimed to produce a book of standardized tunes for practical use.[51] The tunes, in old-notation, not tonic sol-fa, were hailed as models of scholarly musicianship and sound judgement even if, as Rhidian Griffiths has indicated, his harmonies tended to be strict and unadorned. Good singing, Gwyllt insisted, could come only from practice, and from services in which the entire congregation had made an accurate and intelligent reading of the hymns. The book was unapologetically didactic, but it sold (in a population of a million and a quarter) 17,000 copies in three years. Gwyllt had reservations about tonic sol-fa for certain kinds of music, but once convinced of its effectiveness for hymn singing he threw his energy into it. In 1863 he published the even more popular *Llyfr Tonau Cynulleidfaol* in tonic sol-fa notation. Adopted by sol-fa classes, chapel-based singing schools and singing societies, it sold 25,000 copies almost overnight. He followed this by editing for four years (1869–73) the journal *Cerddor y Tonic Sol-fa* (Tonic Sol-fa Musician).

If good, standardized hymns were the base of his choral edifice, the next stage was accomplished singing. Only disciplined practice would guarantee this. In Aberdare and Merthyr he founded congregational singing unions to practice singing a list of prescribed tunes from his newly-published *Llyfr Tonau*. By limiting the number of hymns, and introducing new ones, Gwyllt hoped to raise the standard of Sunday singing. He stressed that the practices were for congregations, not choirs, and for learning, not entertainment. Out of them came Gwyllt's unique, and in some ways inadvertent, gift to Wales and the Welsh diaspora: the cymanfa ganu.

On an agreed day, usually at Easter, neighbouring congregations came together in the largest of the chapels to sing before Gwyllt himself, or a guest conductor, the hymns and tunes they had learned. As Easter approached there were practice sessions after the Sunday schools, and a rehearsal on Easter Sunday followed by a gala performance on the Monday. For the single-minded Gwyllt, the annual gatherings were meant to be instructive: a means of raising the level of singing and introducing new hymns. But for the assembled congregations they were festivals, sermon-free occasions for unbridled song. It was the return of carnival that the Nonconformists and the Puritans before them had been at such pains to suppress. The women dressed in their Easter outfits, and if there was a children's cymanfa, the children in their brightest and best. On occasion, they formed up in twos and walked in procession to the chapel. At a cymanfa near Bangor in 1967 they walked behind a truck wrapped in crêpe paper. Had Ieuan Gwyllt been there, he might have barred the chapel doors.[52]

The conductors were extrovert, chosen for their showmanship as well as their musicianship. Divided into their respective parts, the congregations responded to the conductor's good-natured scolding by singing, as John Wesley had urged, 'lustily'. Hymns and choruses were repeated, usually several times, to the conductor's jubilant cry '*Unwaith eto*' (once again), the battle cry of the cymanfaoedd canu.

Cymanfaoedd remained popular well into the twentieth century. On a visit to Llanrwst just after the Second World War, John Sutcliffe Smith, an Englishman, attended a cymanfa at Zion Methodist Chapel. As he drew near to the chapel he found the streets crowded with people wending their way toward it. It was a Saturday afternoon and he wondered if a gathering of that kind could be found in England, or in Europe for that matter, on a weekend afternoon. Before the singing began every seat was taken, benches were set along the passages, and even the doorways were crowded. He found himself asking, 'are all these people singers?', a question answered by the appearance of a hymn book in every pair of hands. The singing did not disappoint. 'The bright tones of the women and children – most of whom occupied the body of the chapel – carried the melody and the alto part ... As to the men, ranged in force along the galleries, they gave out such power (tenor and bass) which I think never to have heard equalled in any place of worship.'[53]

*

In west and mid Wales, a variant of the cymanfa ganu that may, in spirit and tone, be regarded as a forerunner of the singing festivals, was the *cymanfa bwnc* or *holi'r pwnc*. The practice of learning biblical texts through a form of high-pitched chanting, canu pwnc, can be traced to at least Tudor times in mid and west Wales. Early in the nineteenth century, Thomas

Charles introduced the *Pwnc Ysgol* or *Ysgol Ateb*, a question-and-answer session to test the memory of prescribed biblical texts in each class in Methodist Sunday schools. At intervals the schools of a given district would gather and a whole day be devoted to the catechizing. The questioner or catechizer, the *holwr*, when calling for rapid cross-fire responses from sections of the assembled Sunday schools, needed to be, as National Library of Wales librarian John Ballinger remarked, as quick-witted as a conductor at the singing festivals that would follow later in the century.[54]

At special festivals held at Whitsun, known as *Holi'r Pwnc* or *Y Gymanfa Bwnc*, or simply *Y Pwnc*, the holwr, usually a minister from outside the locality, quizzed members of both the adult and children's classes of three or four neighbouring chapels on assigned sections of the Bible. They were festive occasions at which the answers were given in chorus in haunting rhythmic cadences and sometimes in harmony. There were morning, afternoon and evening sessions, the latter generally being crowded, at which hymns were also sung. In some Sunday schools the classes 'sang' the verses in a uniquely Welsh style called *llafarganu*, a forceful speaking-singing in which the text was chanted in a high-pitched monotone. Both llafarganu and the unsung recitations were ritual performances unlike anything performed by English Nonconformists. Cymanfaoedd pwnc at which there was also hymn singing were similar enough to cymanfaoedd canu that in the 1870s some churches in the Upper Neath and Rhigos valleys considered abandoning the former for the latter, and may have done so.

The most dramatic form of Y Pwnc was a kind of religious play, performed before packed chapels, by Baptists and Congregationalists in south Wales. The aim was didactic but the roots of the practice, in Ballinger's view, lay in the dramatic instincts of the Welsh. Gradually, the plays became a kind of religious drama in which the characters were played not by individuals but by an entire class of scholars who delivered, in a monotone, the words of characters from the scriptures. Another variant in the Teifi valley and adjoining districts was *Calan Hen*, when as many as a dozen Sunday schools would meet at the parish church of Llandysul to recite portions of the Bible, answer in chorus questions put to them by the attending clergy, and sing anthems. The meeting was designed in the 1830s as a counter-attraction to *cicio pêl ddu* (kicking the black ball), a game of rough, unorganized football that frequently ended in a drunken brawl. In both the adult and children's sessions, the pitch for the recitations would be set by the leader of the group, and at some sessions men and women recited alternately. At all sessions there was a good deal of singing. Y Pwnc is still practised in a few Carmarthen chapels but the musical, ritual element has been dropped.[55]

*

The dominance of the sermon and the hymn in Welsh chapels inevitably affected their design. Those built in the mid and late nineteenth century were, in Anthony Jones's phrase, palaces for the oral arts. To accommodate the larger congregations, the height was doubled and galleries were built around three of the interior walls. In line with English practice, the façade was moved from the side wall to the gable end and the pulpit placed opposite the entrance. The congregation sat in rows opposite the pulpit instead of in the fan-like pattern of the older chapels. The effect was to make an auditorium of the meeting house and an audience, rather than a gathered church, of the congregation. Carving and decoration of the woodwork, especially of the pulpit, contributed to the concert hall effect. Flat ceilings (which were probably serendipitous) made for good acoustics, and separate galleries (a vital contribution to the development of congregational hymn singing) for men and women allowed for the separation of voices. If there were listeners, *y gwrandawyr*, they sat in the lower levels. At Tabernacl, Morriston, tiers of stepped pews accommodated the singers but because there was no choir there was no need, as in the established churches, for separate choir stalls.[56] In the late nineteenth century, large power organs replaced the little harmoniums, and when placed directly behind the pulpit they were perceived by some to be in competition with it. It was a case of music and singing versus the Word. T.E. Clarke commented on the trend as early as 1850: 'The strains of solemn melody are so often to be heard from within the chapel walls ... but the compositions seem to be arranged that they serve the purpose of pleasing the singers more than producing devotion.'[57]

After the publication of his hymn books, and his founding of the cymanfa and good four-part singing, Ieuan Gwyllt might well have rested on well-earned laurels. But his career would take one more unexpected turn. For the last few years of his life he espoused the gospel music and hymns of the American evangelists Dwight Moody and Ira Sankey. Gwyllt was fastidious socially as well as musically and his embrace of Moody's unschooled rhetoric, and Sankey's sentimental gospel hymnody, has confounded biographers and commentators. Moody and Sankey were not simply evangelists, but evangelists during a particularly strident phase of American history: the era of Buffalo Bill's Wild West show and P.T. Barnum's circus. It was even rumoured that they were advance agents in Britain for Barnum and that Sankey had come to sell American organs. A poem in *Punch* referred to their meetings as a 'Revival American Circus' with 'Ira Clown in the Ring'. But the slurs had no effect upon their appeal. At a Dublin pantomime the clown entered the ring and delivered the line 'I feel rather Moody tonight' and the pantaloon, the traditional butt of the clown's jokes, replied, 'And I feel rather Sankey-monious'. The audience hissed at the slur and rose spontaneously to their feet and sang the gospel hymn 'Hold the Fort'.[58] Even though they were committed Christians and authentic evangelists, in Britain Sankey and Moody never escaped the taint of commerce and hucksterism.

As evangelists, and American evangelists in particular, they were outgoing and extrovert. Gwyllt, on the other hand, is said to have been stiff and humourless. He once objected to the offer of a baked loaf as a prize at an eisteddfod, and on another occasion he brought a cymanfa to a halt while an embarassed mother with a whooping or coughing baby left the chapel. At his formal practices and services, Gwyllt would have no whispering or laughing and he had no toleration for remarks out of keeping with the solemnity of the occasion. When reading out a hymn he demanded absolute silence. The whimper of a child, the whisper of a chorister, or a rustle at the door, would be cause for rebuke. For lively or mischievous congregations he seems to have been irresistible bait. When asked to demonstrate the musical poverty of a particular hymn, a Merthyr congregation sang it with gusto, and repeated the chorus.[59] Gwyllt was furious. In hymnody, dignity was everything and he has been accused of ruining perfectly good folk tunes by corsetting them with strict, unadorned harmonies. Yet for all his stiffness and eccentricity David Morgans, the author of a history of music in Merthyr, regarded him as a 'prophet sent by God' to safeguard religious singing in Wales.[60]

Dwight Moody and his singing partner Ira Sankey came to Britain in 1873. Like Gwyllt, Moody – the preacher of the duo – had backed into the ministry. He had been a shoe salesman in Chicago, with only a primary school education, and had no theological training. Like Gwyllt, he was also a man for causes. He had been an ardent abolitionist and in the post-Civil War Reconstructionist South he challenged the treatment of the emancipated slaves. He also founded schools for the indigent in Chicago and he berated employers for running sweatshops and paying starvation wages. He met Sankey in 1870 and, as a double act and with little preparation, they embarked on a tour of Britain in June 1873. Sankey had been active in the American YMCA movement as a singer, song leader and songwriter. Their ministry began on a street corner in Indianapolis, Sankey singing to draw a crowd, Moody preaching to it, and Sankey singing again as the sinners came forth.[61] The two Englishmen who had agreed to help coordinate their tour of northern England and Scotland – a London vicar and a Newcastle merchant – died before their ship landed in Liverpool. Their early meetings in York, where they began their campaign, attracted only a few handfuls of people. Ignored by the local press, and shunned by the Established Church, only Sankey's singing aroused any curiosity.[62]

From York they went to Sunderland, a town known to be hostile to the use of music in worship, but where Moody had been invited to speak. The invitation came from the minister of Sunderland's Bethesda Chapel, Carmarthen-born Arthur Augustus Rees, one of the few to hear Moody speak at York.[63] After a five-year career in the Royal Navy, Rees attended St David's College, Lampeter, where he joined 'the Lampeter Brethren', a group of earnest, evangelical Christians. He was ordained by the Bishop of Durham in 1843 and appointed to a curacy in Sunderland where his evangelism and his popular, extempore sermons offended both his vicar and the bishop. Rees would later describe himself as a born dissenter. After nine months he was asked to leave Sunderland in spite of a petition with more than 1,000 signatures supporting his retention. His final service attracted an audience of 3,000. He retreated to Bath, where he again offended the bishop, and in 1845 he returned to Sunderland to build, with the aid of an inheritance, the Bethesda Free Chapel. Rees was a musician with a fine singing voice and a 'speaking-trumpet' of a speaking voice. At Bethesda he preached regularly to congregations of 1,400.

Rees's endorsement may have saved Moody and Sankey's British campaign. After a slow start at Bethesda the momentum, against the resistance of local Anglican clergy, quickened, and before the end of their Sunderland campaign the Americans were forced to move to a larger hall. To Arthur Rees they owed not only a crucial endorsement but the engaging phrase 'singing the gospel'. After Sunderland, they appeared in Newcastle, Edinburgh, and Glasgow, attracting large audiences. In Edinburgh they rotated each evening between churches and the city's Music Hall, a carriage taking them from one venue to the next. As their audiences grew, their venues became more secular and when no hall or theatre was large enough to hold the thousands bent on hearing them they used their own portable building, similar to a circus 'big top'. There were also daytime meetings. The churches and halls were invariably packed, with hundreds unable to gain entry. Posters, handbills, sandwich boards – the advertising techniques of a travelling circus – and a massive weeks-long advertising campaign in local and regional newspapers, trumpeting their triumphs in cities they had just left, heralded their arrival. They arrived amid feverish excitement and anticipation.

Yet, among the newspapers there were demurrers. The *Glasgow Herald* berated the city's clergy for falling for 'Yankee tomfooleries'. It deplored Moody's 'theatricality' and the new 'star system' in evangelism. It also criticized the music, finding Sankey's repertoire redolent of the music hall, with unlikely combinations of 'circus quickstep, a negro sentimental ballad, a college chorus and a hymn'.[64] The *Herald* even questioned the disposal of the money the pair were making from the sale of hymnals. In London, where they packed the 20,000-seat Agricultural Hall every night to crowds totalling one and a half million, they were attacked by the *London Daily News* for their 'bumptious conceit' and a 'rural ignorance and roughness' that rendered them 'totally unfit for cultivated society'. The attacks had no effect on their popularity. They left for home to the singing, by a vast crowd at the Liverpool dockside, of 'Hold the Fort', a gospel hymn and a Sankey favourite based upon a heroic Union defence during the American Civil War.

The rallies themselves were part sermon and part song. Typically, Sankey would begin with a round of gospel solos: he was a large man with a fine baritone voice and his singing of 'Hold the Fort' invariably brought down the house. He was also a skilled raconteur who could relax and warm up an audience in readiness for the appearance of Dwight Moody. To lead the audience in song, he recruited 200 choristers from local churches, rehearsed them quickly, and at the rallies lined them up on a platform in front of Moody's pulpit. For Sankey, singing was every bit as important as Moody's preaching. As the crowds filed into the hall, the choir, led by Sankey, sang a few hymns, and when the hall was half-filled he invited the audience to join the choir. The meetings always ended with a hymn sung by the choir and the whole congregation. The gospel hymns, sung at intervals throughout the meetings, were tuneful and melodic and the familiar format of verse-chorus-verse-chorus made them easy to learn and remember.[65] In neither sermon nor song were there any references to Calvin's stern patriarchal god; in American journalist H.L. Mencken's phrase, '[they] put the soft pedal on hell', an observation endorsed by a contributor to the *Cambrian*: 'The mistake of supposing that grim and dismal hymns and sermons are the proper methods for creating reverence ... is one that should be exploded ... and we shall be very much indebted to Messrs. Moody and Sankey if they will help us to get rid of it.'[66]

In Edinburgh, the Sankey and Moody itinerary intersected that of the Fisk Jubilee Singers, an accomplished black American choral group whom Sankey enlisted to sing at some of their rallies. The Jubilee Singers (an eleven-strong group) had been formed to raise money for a college named Fisk, near Nashville, founded in 1866 to educate newly freed slaves. Their song book, *Jubilee Songs*, followed the publication of *Slave Songs of the United States*, the first major collection of spirituals. At first, the group performed in nearby towns and cities and then moved on to Boston, Philadelphia and New York where they were encouraged by Mark Twain and Henry Ward Beecher, the brother of *Uncle Tom's Cabin* author Harriet Beecher Stowe, to undertake a fundraising tour of Britain. They arrived in Britain in 1871, two months before Moody and Sankey, and were an overnight sensation. Among their admirers were Queen Victoria and Prime Minister William Gladstone. Although their haunting spirituals, sung in a minor key, were qualitatively different from the alternately muscular and sentimental gospel hymns of Moody and Sankey, British audiences, and Moody and Sankey themselves, perceived them to be complementary.[67] Congregationalist minister and composer Erik Routley described the gospel hymns as 'the folk music of the music hall [whose] words have almost always the same nostalgic yearning for heaven which is to be heard in the negro spirituals'.[68] For British audiences there were also familiar resonances. Most spirituals, as George Pullen Jackson and other ethno-musicologists have indicated, were black adaptations of British songs and hymns influenced heavily by a history of slavery and oppression. Moody's response to the Jubilee Singers was instinctive: 'they stole his heart and led him at once to appreciate the power of music for good.'[69]

African slaves appear to have been drawn to psalms and hymns soon after their arrival in America at the end of the seventeenth century. 'The negroes ... have an ear for Musick, and [take] a kind of extatic Delight in Psalmody; and there are no Books they learn so soon or take so much pleasure in, as those used in that heavenly Part of divine Worship.' So wrote the Presbyterian missionary Samuel Davies, of Welsh lineage, in 1755.[70] Davies also wrote: 'Sundry of them have lodged all night in my kitchen; and sometimes when I have waked about two or three o'clock in the morning, a torrent of sacred harmony poured into my chamber, and carried my mind away to Heaven. In this seraphic exercise, some spend almost the whole night.' Others recorded that in their lodges the slaves sang hymns and psalms in the evening and again in the morning, long before daybreak. At a Baptist meeting house in Savannah, built by black slaves and visited in 1794 by Morgan John Rhees (a Baptist minister and an ardent abolitionist), the singing touched a Welsh chord. Rhees described it as 'far superior to anything I have yet heard on this continent', and when prostrate with fever a week later, and with an aching and heavy head, his one thought was: 'I'll strive to go and hear them sing.'[71]

On tour, the Jubilee Singers' renderings of 'John Brown's Body' and 'Steal Away to Jesus', their most celebrated songs, enthralled their audiences. But there were no theatrics. 'They arranged themselves,' wrote one London critic, 'in front of the platform in a phalanx three deep. They stand with head erect and somewhat thrown back, and looking upwards, or with eyes nearly closed. It is evident the audience is nothing to them, they are going to make music and listen to one another.'[72] In *The Souls of Black Folk*, William E.B. Du Bois wrote that 'Plaintive rhythmic melody, with its touching minor cadences [is] ... the one true expression of a people's sorrow, despair, and hope.' Sankey's hymns, which one commentator described as the refuge of the dispossessed people of industrial America and England, appear to have touched the same, or similar, chords.

In March 1874 the Jubilee Singers performed at Swansea's Cradock Street Music Hall before an audience of 1,500. Expecting a group of Al Jolson-like blackface singers, the *Cambrian* reporter's review registered surprise and pleasure: 'They were "of true Nigger Minstrelsy" and performed "a programme of Strange Weird Slave songs with concert hall authority and refinement, together with a poise and elegance of dress", in contrast to previous "blackface minstrelsy" troupes who performed in burnt cork.' Audiences were just as perplexed. Even Americans thought of black music in terms of black-faced minstrel troupes. When the Jubilee Singers returned to Swansea in 1875, the reporter had prepared. He described them as 'born as slaves … [who had] all their lives been driven like lepers from any contact with white people'. In the audience was a Swansea woman (Mrs Donaldson) who with her husband had run a 'safe house' for seven years on the banks of the Ohio across from Kentucky, a slave-holding state. Swansea people who were unable to afford the two-shilling ticket price were asked to leave whatever they could afford in a bucket at the entrance – a 'silver collection' from the balcony made up the deficit. Wales contributed $20,000 to the Fisk Development Fund and in 1876 Swansea fielded its very own Jubilee Singers who performed at local literary and musical gatherings.

Moody and Sankey also came to Wales.[73] In 1875 they held rallies in Bala, Blaenau Ffestniog and Wrexham before an estimated total of 10,000 people. In 1875 Sankey, whose wife Fanny Edwards was the daughter of a Swansea man, spent three months recuperating in Caswell Bay near Swansea. In 1882 he and Moody, on a return visit to Britain, conducted missions in Swansea, Cardiff and Newport. For their first mission at the Wood Street Congregationalist Church in Cardiff, the largest church building in town, long queues formed early in the morning. There is no record of Gwyllt having attended any of the Welsh rallies. He heard Sankey and Moody first in Edinburgh, and then in Liverpool where he also met them.[74] Earlier he had cancelled a planned six-month visit to America. Gwyllt had been a slow and careful preacher, a pedant by most accounts, but swept away by Moody's addresses and the music of Sankey he began to preach with fire.[75] The 'terrier-like' Moody is said to have spoken quickly and excitedly in tones that were neither measured nor modulated. Grammar and correct pronunciation were also ignored. His appeal lay in the intensity of his delivery, his addresses culminating in a concluding crescendo that was 'like a cavalry charge. You either had to go with it or get out of the way.'[76]

For Gwyllt to embrace the rhythms, cadences and language of gospel music and the negro spiritual was an epiphany. Sankey's hymns and songs were closer to the music hall than the church but their simple language, overt sentimentality, and singable tunes appealed directly to the poor and underprivileged of the industrial towns and cities whom Gwyllt had espoused both in his journalism and his ministry. In 1874, he published under the title *Sŵn y Jiwbili* his first collection of Sankey's hymns, translated into Welsh and arranged and rendered in tonic sol-fa. He published six separate collections that, after a slow beginning, by 1934 had sold half a million copies. Add to these the sales of the collected edition, then his treatment of Sankey's gospel songs easily outsold his own great hymn book.[77] In answer to Gwyllt's request to translate the hymns, Sankey generously replied:

> Dear Brother Roberts,
> I have so many asking permission to publish my Hymns, &, that I hardly know what I should do. I have as yet given no permission. But seeing that my wife is the daughter of a Welshman, who lived at Swansea many years ago, I cannot refuse you permission to translate into the Welsh language any of my hymns which you may desire ... Please send me a copy of your Book when out ... May God bless the ... sweet singers of Wales.
> Yours, in the best of bonds,
> Ira D. Sankey[78]

In 1882 the poet Watcyn Wyn followed Gwyllt's lead, applying his gift for combining verse and melody to produce *Odlau'r Efengyl* (Rhymes of the Gospel). These were mainly adaptations of hymns in Sankey's *Sacred Songs and Solos* and, like the originals, they were couched in simple language that was free of Calvinistic theology. Throughout Wales, congregational singing in the last decades of the century is said to have become musically less rigorous and more emotional.

*

Tonic sol-fa and and four-part harmony revolutionized congregational singing in Wales and set the stage for an assault on some of the great classical choral pieces. By the 1860s the larger congregations, and choral societies recruited from district chapels in south Wales (where there were dense urban populations), were keen to embark on oratorios and choruses from the works of Bach, Handel, Haydn and Mendelssohn. Haydn and Handel became such familiar names that they were added to the roster of commonly used Christian names in Wales. Joseph Parry, the greatest of the nineteenth-century Welsh composers, named one of his three sons Joseph Haydn and another Daniel Mendelssohn.

A more studied and more ambitious approach to singing led to performance, and performance, inevitably, to comparison and, perhaps just as inevitably, to competition. At the end of the eighteenth century, literary clubs in London and Wales, in an effort to save from extinction medieval systems of bardic composition, revived the competitive medieval eisteddfod. In the following century, the addition of music to the list of events opened the door to choirs. Choral singing first graced the eisteddfod stage in 1825, but not until the introduction of tonic sol-fa and the coming of the railways and cheap excursion fares in the second half of the century could it become a standard event. By mid-century, large choirs could travel to almost any major venue in Wales, in the process converting the musical wing of the eisteddfod into a competitive concert.

When Ivander Griffiths's United Temperance Choir, or Temperance Choral Union, competed at the Cwmamman eisteddfod in 1858, there were six other choral entrants: from Ystalyfera, Cwmllynfell, Carmel, Furnace, Dryslwyn and Llandeilo, all towns and villages within a twenty-mile radius of Pontardawe. The United Temperance Choir began as a small choral society that met on Sunday evenings to sing oratorio choruses in the Reading Room, a small local library in Pontardawe. The choir competed for the first time at an eisteddfod in Cwmafan in 1855, the choristers walking the six miles to Neath and completing the journey by 'Tent Wagon'. A near martyr in the temperance cause, Griffiths initiated a series of temperance singing festivals in Pontardawe, holding the first on Gellionnen mountain, a flat interfluve high above the Tawe valley, as a counter attraction to the Neath Fair, held on the same day. With the announcement of a great eisteddfod to be held at Carmarthen in 1862, plans were made to form a single choir, the United Valley Choir, from towns and villages in or near the Tawe valley. Practice sessions for small groups were held at five or six centres, the choristers taking the train or, if they were some distance from the valley railway, walking several miles in each direction. At Carmarthen there were thirteen choirs of the same dimensions (150 to 200 members), all from south Wales. The size of the audience, 3,000, was unprecedented.

After the eisteddfod, the United Valley Choir, eager for more honours and attracting even more members, began rehearsing Handel's *Messiah*. To coach the separate sections of the choir, now 300 to 400 strong, Ivander Griffiths travelled up and down the valley by train. At Panteg Chapel, Ystalyfera, in January 1863, the choir, for the first time in Wales, performed the *Messiah* in its entirety. The soloists came from London and the instrumentalists from Bristol and Swansea. In the absence of an instrument at the rehearsals of the various subdivisions, the choristers had to rely on the ear and voice of Ivander Griffiths. On arrival in Ystalyfera, the Bristol orchestra found the choir's pitch to be entirely sound. At a subsequent Swansea performance, some music critics complained of the choir's lack of finesse, a criticism countered by an Englishman in the audience who was heard to remark that gathering and keeping together that many choristers, 'especially of the working class', was achievement enough, but that they should combine to perform 'such a magnificent work' was truly remarkable.

At the choral competion in the National Eisteddfod at Swansea, 1863, which pitted the Tawe valley choir under Ivander Griffiths against the Aberdare Choral Society under Silas Evans, the music critic Henry F. Chorley, for the *Athenaeum*, was astonished by the standard of singing:

> The singing of the chorus was a great pleasure and astonishment. The power and the pleasure of cooperation have got hold of the men who come up from the mines and ride home from the forge on a grimy wagon along a tramway, in the midst of scoriae or cinders, or work at a trade in town, or at husbandry in the country. The folk of Cornwall and Northumberland, so far as I know are less tuneful; and I do not fancy that the farm labourers of Kent or Warwickshire would trudge so far, or work so heartily, to get to a singing practice. The spirit of melody lies deep in the hearts of the Welsh ... But the noteworthy fact in respect to the choral societies of Wales is, that not only the members of the choir, but the chorus-masters are, without exception ... working men who have received no professional instruction whatever.[79]

On its approach to Swansea along the last few miles of the Tawe valley, Henry Chorley's train from London would have passed through perhaps the most blighted industrial landscape in all of Britain. Toxic smoke and furnace waste from a string of copper smelters along the river had reduced a once verdant valley to a treeless moonscape of cinders and scoriae.

In his lecture to the British Association for the Advancement of Science at Swansea in 1971, T.J. Morgan, a native of Glais and Professor of Welsh at University College, Swansea, remarked that if one considered the number of chapel choirs and choral societies, and their numerous performances in concerts and eisteddfodau, it would be safe to say that 'a greater quantity of melodious decibels ascended to high heaven from the

Swansea area during those forty years [1870–1910] than from any other part of the world and period of history'. Choral and congregational singing offered not just relief from tedious daily tasks and sometimes excessive and destructive drinking, but transcendence – not, T.J. Morgan emphasised, for a cultivated elite, but for ordinary working men and women. He regretted, as an irreparable and serious cultural loss, the suppression of folk song, music and dance – in the service of 'respectability' – but if he had to choose between the music that was lost and the music that took its place, he would not have found the choice difficult. To accentuate the effect of the drive for self-improvement, represented by the cymanfa and the eisteddfod, he chose a phrase from a temperance hymn by Ben Davies of Panteg, 'to lift the peasant class'.[80]

The quarrymen of north Wales, like the miners and iron workers of the south, also took to song. A temperance choir from Bethesda performed at Exeter Hall, London, where John Hullah held his singing classes, in 1851. David Roberts (Alawydd), the accomplished leader of congregational singing at Bethesda Chapel and author of a musical grammar written in Welsh, trained a choir of 80 to 100 members. Led by three directors (one Anglican, one Wesleyan Methodist, and one Calvinistic Methodist) a choir of 500 combined church and chapel singers, accompanied by the Royal Penrhyn Band, sang the *Messiah* on the floor of Penrhyn quarry in August 1856. Handel was a particular favourite in the quarry areas. To listen to them, an audience of between 12,000 to 15,000 from the district assembled on the galleries, *ponciau*, or flat shoulders of the quarry. A year later, 1,000 people gathered in Bethesda Chapel to hear Handel's *Samson*. When 700 quarrymen gathered to listen to a lecture on music, the editor of the *Caernarvon & Denbigh Herald* wondered if English workingmen would have done the same.[81] Drawn by choristers, Ieuan Gwyllt's last ministry, from 1865 to 1869, was at Llanberis in the heart in the slate district.

For the eastern valleys of the coalfield, and for Welsh choral singing in general, the crowning moment – the 'sunspot of the century' in John Graham's phrase – came in 1872 and 1873 at the National Music Competitions at Crystal Palace, London. To contest the prize in the heavyweight choral contest for choirs of 200 to 500 voices, a group of determined ministers from Aberdare decided to harness the choral resources of south Wales. Their intended strategy was to attract singers from all parts of the coalfield, but practical difficulties limited the catchment area to the northern end. Though shrunken, it was still large enough to necessitate a sectioning of the choir by district, the full choir coming together for the final rehearsals. Conductors were assigned to each of the sections but the overall direction lay with Griffith Rhys Jones, a blacksmith/conductor known by his bardic title Caradog.

At the first competition, 1872, the South Wales Choral Union, better known as Y Côr Mawr or simply Caradog's choir, sang unchallenged in the large choral class. But the 1873 event was a contest. Caradog's opponents were a group of 320 London sol-faists, known as the 'Paris Prize Choir', under the baton of Joseph Proudman, a sol-fa devotee. For the Londoners, the competition was one between rival choirs, or rival communities, but for the Welsh it was a contest between nations, a choral international. Before an audience of 12,500 at the Crystal Palace, the two choirs traded choruses from Handel, Bach and Mendelssohn. Whereas the 1872 Côr Mawr had relied chiefly on 'chest power', the 1873 choir, though considerably larger, tempered strength with finesse. It was a winning combination. The triumphant shout that greeted Y Côr Mawr's victory (a trainload of supporters had travelled with the choir) carried to Wales and rang around the Welsh diaspora. At home foghorns sounded, church bells rang, and rifle corps loosed celebratory volleys. Epic poems appeared in Welsh newspapers and Caradog was carried from Ystrad station to his home in Treorchy in a bardic chair. From overseas, letters, tributes, and gifts poured in, among the latter a gold baton from the goldfields of Australia and a wooden-mounted gold baton from Welsh miners at Cherokee flat, Butte Co., California. The glow of victory burned for half a century. In July 1920, at a ceremony attended by 120 surviving choristers and half the town, Aberdare unveiled a bronze statue (that still stands in the town square) not to a general, a politician, or an industrialist, but to a conductor: the mighty Caradog.[82]

If Caradog was the most heroic of the nineteenth-century Welsh conductors, the most combative and successful – in terms of medals and money won – was Dan Davies of Merthyr, known variously as 'Terrible Dan' and the 'Wellington of choral singing'. His feistiness, and the Welsh love of competition, did not escape the English press. 'Next after a football match', commented the *Musical Times* in 1897, 'Welshmen enjoy a choral fight'. Military metaphors clung to Davies throughout his conducting career and he wore the medals won at choral competitions as proudly as any battle-hardened campaigner. His command over his choirs was so complete that his contemporary, Col. D.R. Lewis, felt certain that if providence had directed Davies to the army he would have become one of its greatest captains.[83] Born in 1859, Dan Davies was entirely self-taught. At nine he conducted a group of elementary schoolchildren in a chapel concert, and while still a boy he began accumulating certificates of proficiency in tonic sol-fa. In 1882 he won the Advanced Certificate and that same year he founded the Dowlais Harmonic Society, named 'The Invincibles' after an unprecedented series of regional and national eisteddfod victories. The choir won money prizes and its conductor gold medals. In 1892 Dan Davies moved to Merthyr where he formed the Merthyr Philharmonic which, after only seven weeks' practice, defeated most of the established coalfield choirs at the south Wales semi-nationals. Choristers and supporters carried him around the town, releasing him only after he agreed to address the crowd from an open window, like a successful parliamentary candidate.

At the eisteddfodau, choirs benefited from informed criticism and, in theory at least, from comparison with other groups. But some rivalries were so intense that choirs and their supporters left the eisteddfod halls without listening to their competitors, returning only for the adjudication. At the Carmarthen eisteddfod of 1862, supporters of the competing choirs were so keen for battle to begin that, before an impatient audience of 3,000, the rector of Neath was forced to cut short his welcoming address. Offending adjudicators were sometimes barracked, and after particularly controversial decisions they had to be spirited out of the halls. To avoid any possibility of bias, and restore a measure of civility to the competitions, eisteddfod committees sometimes engaged English adjudicators.

Competition also worked against the liberating effects of the tonic sol-fa. Instead of using the sol-fa to extend their repertoires, some choirs spent months practising the same selections or test pieces in the hope of carrying off the top eisteddfod prizes. With no new choral works to challenge them, many choristers reverted to learning by rote. A questionnaire distributed by conductors at the 1881 National Eisteddfod, one year after the death of John Curwen, disclosed that fewer than a third of the singers could read any form of music.

3

The Welsh in America

INEVITABLY, THE ZEAL for song and prayer in Wales spilled over its borders. All emigrants, as the renowned French geographer Paul Vidal de La Blache commented, carry their shells with them. By this he meant the customs, language and traditions of the homeland. There is, however, no evidence that Welsh emigrants, in general, sang their way across the Atlantic as assiduously as the Moravians but, in a letter home describing a crossing of the Atlantic in 1795, George Roberts, one of the early Ohio settlers, noted that on fine afternoons the Welsh people assembled in a large boat on the deck and prayed and sang.[1] Many, too, left to the sound of a hymn. As an emigrant vessel left Aberaeron harbour in 1839, carrying 175 passengers bound for Ohio and the Midwest, four young men led the hundreds gathered on the quayside in the singing of the haunting farewell hymn: *Bydd melys lanio draw/ 'Rôl bod o don i don/ Ac mi rof ffarwel maes o law/ I'r ddaear hon.'* (Sweet will be the landing over there/ After sailing wave on wave/ And I'll say farewell forever/ To our native land.) Even the most eager and outgoing passengers on that vessel would have felt some apprehension, and would, despite themselves, have already begun storing memories of the homeland.

On arrival in America they would have to reconcile competing incentives: the instinct to perpetuate the old culture on the one hand, and the need to engage with the new on the other. For the earliest Welsh emigrants to America the immediate goal was to build a new version of the world they had left, and in America this was possible. Like all new lands, America was a tabula rasa, a clean slate. With space enough for everyone, new cultures could make their mark without having to elbow aside those already established.

The first arrivals from Wales were dissident Baptists who, in 1663, founded a settlement (named Swansea) on the Plymouth-Rhode Island border. The accession of Charles II, upon the restoration of the Stuart monarchy in 1660, ended Cromwellian tolerance for religious dissent. They were followed, in 1681, by a group of Quakers who purchased a tract of 40,000 acres in Pennsylvania hoping to make it the nucleus of a self-governing, Welsh-speaking colony, a *gwladfa* or 'barony'. William Penn's verbal promise of a single block of land on which they might preserve their own laws and their own language, however, was never realised.[2] Although granted the land, separate privileges disappeared with the division of the 'Welsh Tract', first between two counties, then between two states (Pennsylvania and Delaware). And instead of an exclusively Welsh (even if politically divided) block, Welsh settlers found that they had German and English, as well as Welsh, neighbours.[3] Quaker exclusiveness also suffered with the arrival in the Tract of Welsh Baptists, Anglicans, Methodists and Congregationalists.

Among the Baptists were a group from west Wales who settled at first near Pennepek in Pennsylvania, in 1701. Two years later they moved across the river to the Delaware portion of the Tract where they built what became known as the Welsh Tract Church. In America, 'church' and 'chapel' carried none of the cultural and class connotions they had in Britain, and 'chapel' was soon dropped. In 1716, the members of the Welsh Tract Church signed a confession, published by the Baptist Elias Keach, containing an article 'Of Singing of Psalms &c'. The article enjoined 'the churches of Christ to sing psalms,

Griffith Jones, rector of Llanddowror. Best known for his system of circulating schools, he was also a spellbinding preacher who could fill churches and their adjacent graveyards to capacity.

Daniel Rowland: A Church of England curate at Llangeitho and Nantcwnlle before his conversion to Methodism. Rowland and Howell Harris were the chief instruments of the Great Awakening in Wales.

Courtesy: Lyn Lewis Dafis

William Williams Pantycelyn: After a friendly contest between exhorters and preachers to determine who might be the most gifted hymnwriter, Howell Harris declared that Williams had no equal. That accolade has never been seriously contested. Williams is generally acknowledged as Wales's greatest hymn writer.

Courtesy: National Library of Wales

Howell Harris: Never ordained, Harris described himself as a *cynghorwr*, an exhortationist not a preacher. He measured the success of his sermons by the force or power he was able to generate.

Courtesy: National Library of Wales

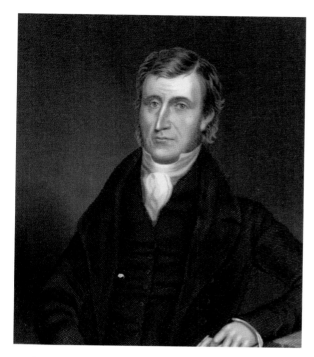

William Williams of Wern: One of the 'big guns' of the denominations accorded the gift, by poet and novelist James Hogg, of encapsulating the thoughts of a philosopher in the language of a child.

Courtesy: National Library of Wales

David Davies of Swansea: Known as the 'silver trumpet of Wales', with a voice so like a silver bell that even the strongest men are said to have been melted by it.

Courtesy: National Library of Wales

Ridley & Holl sc

John Elias: Designated by his admirers as a latter-day Demosthenes for whom sound and rhythm could be as important as meaning. He could preach, said one, 'as if taking down fire from heaven'.

Courtesy: National Library of Wales

Y PARCH. CHRISTMAS EVANS,
Yr hwn a fu farw yn 72 ml. oed.

Christmas Evans. The son of a Llandysul shoemaker, Evans taught himself to read and write in Welsh and English. He was an electrifying preacher and a proponent of singing from the heart, *canu o'r galon*. He lost his eye in a youthful brawl.

Courtesy: National Library of Wales

John Roberts: Known by his bardic name Ieuan Gwyllt, Roberts is generally regarded as the architect of congregational singing in Wales. His *Llyfr Tonau Cynylleidfaol*, in tonic sol-fa notation, sold almost 25,000 copies overnight.

Courtesy: National Library of Wales

Fisk Jubilee Singers, an a cappella group formed to raise funds for Fisk University, a college for newly freed slaves built in 1866. They performed in Swansea in 1874.

Courtesy: Church History Library, The Church of Jesus Christ of Latter-day Saints

Welsh Congregational Church at Poultney, Vermont.

Courtesy: Slate Valley Museum, Granville, NY

Welsh Congregational Church, Granville, Upstate New York.

Courtesy: Slate Valley Museum, Granville, NY

Welsh slate workers, Poultney, Vermont. Standing: Owen Jones; Sitting in back: Lewis Roberts; Sitting in next row: Owen Thomas, Richard W. Parry, Richard G. Jones; Sitting in front: Thomas G. Ellis, Owen W. Owens.

CYMANFA.

Poultney Honored as Place of Annual Meeting of Welsh Presbyterians.

To-day, tomorrow and Sunday will be interesting days at the Welsh church. In it the annual cymanfa of the Welsh Presbyterians of New York and Vermont will be held, and as usual will be attended by great numbers of the denomination. This is the first time in a great many years that Poultney has been selected for this purpose, but we are positive visitors will find that no mistake has been made in the selection.

The first session will be held this evening, when the Rev. John Rowlands of Wales will preach, He is said to be a powerful speaker, and no doubt the opening session will be most interesting. The sessions of Saturday morning and afternoon will be devoted mainly to business, with a preaching service at 6 in the evening. Sunday morning a class meeting will be held at 8.20 and is sure to be largely attended. Preaching will be heard at the 10 o'clock service, and also at 2 in the afternoon and 6 in the evening.

The music will be congregational, led by the large choir under the direction of W. W. Edwards, with Miss Mabel Jones at the organ. Everyone will be welcome at all sessions, excepting, of course, the business sessions.

CERDDOR Y TONIC SOL-FFA.

DAN OLYGIAD

Y PARCH. J. ROBERTS,

(IEUAN GWYLLT).

CYF. III.

WREXHAM:
ARGRAFFEDIG A CHYHOEDDEDIG GAN HUGHES & SON.
1871.

Cerddor y Tonic Sol-ffa.

Cymanfa announcement,
Poultney, 4 October 1907.

UNITED SINGERS OF CITY

They Will Contest at Wilkes-Barre on June 11 and 12.

HISTORY OF PAST EISTEDDFODS

It Shows That Whenever Scranton Singers Have Lost They Have Been Divided Against Themselves—We Have Now One Harmonious Organization.

On June 11 and 12 an eisteddfod will be held at Wilkes-Barre that will be famous in the annals of such musical events in this valley. It is attracting the greatest attention in this state, and ever far outside of the confines of the Keystone commonwealth, because the big choirs of Scranton and Wilkes-Barre will be pitted against one another for the two great prizes, the first of which is $1,000, and the second $300. For the first time in years Scranton will go into the contest with one united choir, which is no little factor in awakening great interest, for if the Electric City could send such wonderful singers as the Cymrodorions and members of the Choral union to the World's Fair and win the big prize when divided against themselves, what ought they not be able to do with one harmonious organization of carefully selected and trained singers to meet the common enemy.

It has, unfortunately, been the fact that rarely have the singers of the city laid factionism aside for the musical advancement of the city as they have at present. The history of the eisteddfod of this region proves this. In 1875 the first big eisteddfod was held in this city in a tent owned by Gilmore, the famous bandmaster, which had a seating capacity of 8,000. It was pitched on the West Side and was the scene of spirited contests.

Three Scranton Choirs.

Three Scranton choirs competed, one under the leadership of Robert J. James, father of Hector James; a second under the leadership of G. M. Williams, now a mine inspector of Luzerne county, while the third was directed by Robert Jones, father of T. Reeves Jones, the eminent pianist. There was one choir from Wilkes-Barre and two from Plymouth, but the big prize was won by Robert J. James' choir, and the second by the singers led by Robert Jones.

In 1880 another eisteddfod was held on the West Side under the auspices of the Welsh Philosophical society. A pavilion, capable of seating 6,000 persons, was erected, and in this the contests took place. Again Scranton entered three choirs for the leading prizes, two from the West Side and one from Providence. A West Side choir, led by William Evans, father of Hadyn Evans, was the victor. It was at this eisteddfod that Bauer's band first entered in a competition, and made itself famous by winning the prize for the best rendition of "The Heavens are Telling."

The Lackawanna rink, on Adams avenue, was the scene of the next big eisteddfod, which was held in 1885. Two Scranton choirs were opposed by a Plymouth choir for the chief prize, and the latter won to the lasting regret of Scranton music lovers, who knew that if but one Scranton choir had entered, culled from the best material in the two, its victory would have been decisive.

Eisteddfod history in Scranton and the intensity of choral competition.

FIRST NATIONAL EISTEDDFOD
SUCCESS BEYOND ANTICIPATION

THIRTEENTH REGIMENT ARMORY.
Where the Big Eisteddfod Was Held.

MR. DAMROSCH'S IMPRESSIONS.

ADJUDICATORS OF MUSIC.

MORNING SESSION.

AFTERNOON SESSION.

EVENING SESSION.

EISTEDDFOD EXECUTIVE COMMITTEE.

ADJUDICATORS OF LITERATURE.

Scranton successes at the first US National Eisteddfod, 1902.

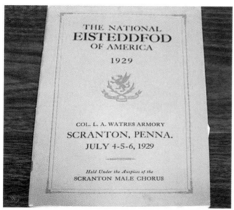

The National Eisteddfod of America, 1929.

Joseph Parry: A pitboy in Merthyr and an ironworker in Danville, Pennsylvania, he became the first Professor of Music at the University of Wales, Aberystwyth. Before his return to Wales he was given the title *Pencerdd America* (Chief Musician of America).

Courtesy: National Library of Wales

Daguerreotype of John Parry, a stonemason from Newmarket, Flintshire, and founding director of the Mormon Tabernacle Choir.

Courtesy: Church History Library, The Church of Jesus Christ of Latter-day Saints

Dan Jones, a former Calvinistic Methodist from Halkyn, Flintshire. Preacher, writer and pamphleteer, Jones led dynamic Mormon missions in industrial south Wales.

Courtesy: Church History Library, The Church of Jesus Christ of Latter-day Saints

Construction of the Salt Lake Tabernacle, completed in 1867, the home of the Mormon Tabernacle Choir.

Courtesy: Church History Library, The Church of Jesus Christ of Latter-day Saints

Quarrying rock for the Salt Lake Temple at the mouth of the Little Rock Canyon.

Building the Latter-day Saints Temple in Salt Lake City.

Cutting the stones and laying the foundation of the Mormon Temple. The Tabernacle is in the background.

Courtesy: Church History Library, The Church of Jesus Christ of Latter-day Saints

Construction workers at the Salt Lake City Temple.

Courtesy: Church History Library, The Church of Jesus Christ of Latter-day Saints

Laying the capstone of the Mormon Temple, 1892. John Parry, founding director of the Tabernacle choir, and his son Caleb, who was also a stonemason, helped build the fifteen-foot wall surrounding Temple Square.

Courtesy: Church History Library, The Church of Jesus Christ of Latter-day Saints

Evan Stephens's choir gathered to perform for Bishop John Sharp c.1888 in front of the bishop's house.

Courtesy: Church History Library, The Church of Jesus Christ of Latter-day Saints

Portrait of Evan Stephens, the tenth child of Pencader farm workers, one of most successful conductors of the Tabernacle Choir.

Courtesy: Church History Library, The Church of Jesus Christ of Latter-day Saints

Evan Roberts: The unassuming twenty-six-year-old theological student, and former colliery doorsman, who in 1904–05 led the Great Revival in Wales.

Courtesy: National Library of Wales

Bible, Mynydd Newydd Chapel.

Courtesy: National Museum Wales

Underground Chapel, Mynydd Newydd, 1899.

Courtesy: National Museum Wales

Colliery prayer meeting, Nantmelyn Colliery, Cwmdare. *Western Mail*, 3 December 1904. One of a number of chapels in the south Wales coalfield at which prayer meetings were held before, during, and after the Great Revival of 1904–05.

RAVENHILL SONS OF REST LECTURE

Under the auspices of Ravenhill Sons of Rest, Mr. Daniel Jones, Bryn-y-Gan, Cockett, an ex-miner and one of the members, spoke on " Cwrdd Gweddi'r Dyfnder," the prayer meetings once held underground at the Mynydd Newydd Colliery.

The speaker said these meetings originated in August, 1845, the year following an explosion at the pit, and were afterwards faithfully held on Monday mornings for a period of 80 years.

'Ravenhill Sons of Rest Lecture' newspaper clipping.

hymns and spiritual songs', and advocated that 'the whole church in their public assemblies, as well as private Christians, ought to ... sing God's praises according to the best light they have received.' In short, singing was to be congregational. Elias Keach, who came to America about 1690, was pastor of the predominantly Welsh Lower Dublin Church in Pennsylvania. Morgan Edwards, who compiled material for a multi-volume history of the American Baptists (he published only two volumes in his lifetime), credited the Welsh Tract Church as the main, if not the sole, vehicle 'for introducing singing ... among the Baptists of the middle States'. The congregation had organized in Wales and moved as a group to Philadelphia in 1701.[4] Edwards, from Monmouthshire, was the pastor of Philadelphia's First Baptist Church, from 1761 to 1771, and a founder of Rhode Island College, later Brown University. Louis Benson, a hymnologist and a more recent historian, endorsed Edwards's opinion, ascribing the initiation of singing in Baptist churches in the colonies to the 'influence of a body of Welsh Baptists settled on the Welsh Tract in Delaware.'[5]

Emigration from Wales slowed toward the end of the seventeenth century, but by the middle of the following century Welsh settlers had moved into south-eastern Pennsylvania, Delaware, and the southern limits of North Carolina where migrants from Delaware founded a new Welsh tract, extending by 1737 over two or three counties. Others, among them Baptists, moved west toward the Appalachians where they joined the migratory stream of Germans and Ulstermen (Scots/Irish) moving south from Pennsylvania into Virginia, North Carolina, and eventually the rest of the Appalachians. Primitive Baptists of the Mountain District Association trace their beginnings in America to the Welsh Tract Church in Delaware.[6] Numerically, the Welsh were among the smallest of the immigrant groups (no more than 8,000 in a colonial population of roughly 250,000), but in matters of hymnody and religious practice their influence was pervasive.

Historians of Appalachia and the South attribute to Welsh Baptists the practice of hymn-lining, or deaconing off, where an elder or deacon chants line by line the verses of a hymn at a quick pace and the congregation (without musical accompaniment) sings the same lines at a much slower, more drawn out pace to a known tune. In seventeenth-century Britain there were two sets of Baptists, the non-singing General Baptists, and the Calvinist singing or Particular Baptists, the set to which most of the Welsh belonged. In America the Particular Baptists were known as Regular and Old Regular Baptists. Significantly, in terms of a supposed Welsh origin for lining out, the Baptists sang in a slow minor tone: 'a sad undertone in all of their singing, which seems to me like the wail of past oppressions.'[7] Mountain Baptists might object to the explanation of a singing style based on history or tradition (as opposed to scriptural authority), but the explanation, as folklorist Beverly Bush Patterson asserts, provides a context.

Lining out is still practised in some mountain churches, but as a matter of revered tradition that has nothing to do with a scarcity of hymnals or an inability to read: 'Today in the Old Regular Baptist services, when the first preacher ... reaches a point of exuberance and some in the congregation have started shouting, an elder will begin lining a hymn which others in the congregation will follow. The preaching, shouting, and hymn-lining continue together apace, with the exhorter increasing his volume and intensity.'[8] According to author Deborah Vansau McCauley and others, a preacher would frequently be 'sung down', or invited to leave his pulpit or platform to join the congregation in the singing that was a constant accompaniment to ministerial exhortations. The singing was determinedly congregational. 'We love to sing with all the people,' noted Elder Cook, 'not with a choir or quartet or duet but ... all of the people joined in together.'[9]

It may also be significant that the theology of the early

Welsh Calvinists and their methods of choosing elders or ministers are preserved practically unchanged in the mountain churches. The ordination of 'called' ministers, the type of person ordained, their relationship to the church, and their preaching styles, according to the Baptist historian Loyal Jones, appear to be similar to those of the early Welsh American churches.[10] Most of the preachers were self-taught, well-informed working farmers and miners who shared the same occupations as members of their congregations. If accepted as candidates for ordination, they served an apprenticeship as itinerant preachers, acquiring, and in turn passing on, accepted preaching styles. Older church buildings, too, may reflect earlier Welsh building styles: common were simple, rectangular buildings with a door for each of the sexes that led to separate seating inside. Interiors were plain and unadorned.

*

In colonial America, Baptist and Methodist preachers employed a melodious style of preaching, known in New England and Appalachia as the 'holy tone' or the 'holy whine', a mode of (sing-song) chanting and intoning that could be hypnotic. Loyal Jones, who is the grandson of Baptist minister Francis Marion Morgan, has proposed that the most likely source of holy tone was the sermons of Welsh Baptist and Methodist preachers. Even today, preachers in some Old Regular Baptist churches employ rhythmic, highly melodic singing tones that, for Loyal Jones, bring to mind Erasmus Jones's 1876 description of hwyl noted earlier.[11] As further evidence of a Welsh connection he points to a liking for poetic turns of phrase, quoting Elder Black of the Indian Bottom Association of Old Regular Baptists who opened his service one morning with: 'We thank thee, Lord, for lengthening out the brittle threads of our lives.'

When working in Appalachia in the 1850s, Hamilton W. Pierson, a Bible distributor and writer, made detailed notes of the 'holy tone' as then practised in mountain churches.

> Scarcely a sentence in the sermon was uttered in the usual method of speech. It was drawled out in a sing-song tone from beginning to end. The preacher ran his voice up, and sustained it at so high a pitch that he could make but little variation of voice upward. The air in his lungs would become exhausted, and at the conclusion of every sentence he would 'catch' his breath with an 'ah' ... This 'holy tone' has charms for [its listeners] not possessed by any possible eloquence. As the preacher 'warms up' and becomes more animated, the more impressible sisters begin to move their heads and bodies, and soon all the devout brethren and sisters sway their bodies back and forth in perfect unison, keeping time in some mysterious manner, to his sing-song tone ... I could not see the slightest evidence ... that he had any idea what he was going to say from one sentence to another ... There was no train of thought or connection of ideas.[12]

It was sound, as John Wesley might have remarked, without sense.[13]

Typical sermons in Old Regular Baptist churches are still extempore. The preacher uses no notes, relying on the inspiration of the moment. As one informant remarked to Howard Dorgan: 'I believe that [Old] Regular Baptist preachers will say that they do not think of what they will say next, and I have heard some say that they have little or no knowledge of what they have said during their preaching.'[14] Some might base their sermons on random selections from the scriptures, a practice equivalent to Daniel Rowland letting his eye fall on whichever page of the Bible happened to be open, while others start slowly, working their way into a theme accompanied by frequent 'Amens' and similar exclamations from deacons and fellow elders sitting close to the stand or pulpit. Frequently, the preacher warms up for exhortation by singing, not talking. On these occasions the speaker moves slowly to the pulpit, thumbs meditatively through his hymn book and begins to sing without musical accompaniment.

After completing the mood-setting hymn, he begins to speak slowly, keeping his voice low and almost inaudible, gradually increasing the volume until he finally hits his stride in impassioned, rhythmical exhorations that will occupy him for the next thirty to sixty minutes. During the delivery, the preacher frequently cups his hand lightly over, or just below, his right ear and rocks forward in time to the beat. At these times the preacher may appear to have closed his eyes and to be rhythmically moving and speaking in a trance-like state. With 'Amens', 'Praise God' and other such exclamations, and with movements that tend to complement those of the preacher, the audience provides a kind of counter-rhythm. 'Given,' writes Dorgan, 'the impromptu nature of these messages, the preacher must maintain his rhythmic form while composing the sermon as he goes. The accomplished mountain preacher is able to sustain his rhythm even when integrating scripture into his sermons or when shifting from one unit of thought to another. In fact, once the speaker reaches a high plateau, everything runs together as if it were one continuous long thought ... Especially noteworthy is the fact that once the rhythm is established, all of the preacher's rhetoric flows in a relatively unbroken stream.'[15]

Howard Dorgan's informed technical observations of the chanted preaching style of contemporary mountain preachers dovetail nicely, according to Vansau McCauley, with both Hamilton Pierson's descriptions of the 'holy tone', and Erasmus Jones's analysis of hwyl, made at roughly the same time.[16] Dorgan's account of the chanting form the sermon takes, once the Holy Spirit has taken possession of the preacher, matches Erasmus Jones's description. The delivery accelerates in pace, volume, and intensity until it reaches a climactic plateau from which the speaker can climb no further or until, as Erasmus Jones phrased it, 'the emotional point is reached'. To affirm the idea of preaching as a dramatic performance, Loyal Jones cites an observation by Elder Ivan Amburgey, a professional musician before he became a preacher. Amburgey liked to use the word 'entertainment' when talking about preaching. 'You got to be an entertainer. That's what preaching is, entertainment.' Preaching should be 'pleasant to hear ... If you go to a concert and listen to songs; you enjoy that. When you go to a church and a fellow gets up to preach and he's boring, that's not much entertainment, is it? ... So, if you sing a good song, it's entertainment, you know. If you preach, if you hear good brethren preaching, to me that's great entertainment.'[17]

In his history of Afro-American Baptists, Walter F. Pitts attributes the intoned, chanted sermon characteristic of Afro-American churches to the merging of two traditions: the evangelical prose sermon of the Protestant (chiefly Welsh) tradition, with the antiphonal or chanting performance style of the African spiritual.[18] The one emphasized the word, both spoken and sung, and the other rhythmic interaction, either in speech or body movements. In the African tradition, music and speech were frequently integrated, running on a continuum from recitative and chant to song. Songs might move into speech and vice versa. The Welsh tradition he describes as a chanted declamatory style, called hwyl, used by poets and preachers to heighten the emotion of their words. He thinks it no accident that the chanted sermon among the whites is strongest in Appalachian pockets where both Revivals and Welsh immigration were prominent features. 'The merging of the African and Welsh oratorical chanting tradition on the American frontier is an example of cultural exchange, in which similar traits reinforce each other. Reinforcement strengthens both practices, with the result that similar practices and ideas are the most likely to survive.' Whatever the exact proportions of the mix, there is general agreement that preaching techniques could be learned and that black Baptist techniques were learned at the hands of whites rather than a deeply felt tribal instinct.

A lone, dissenting critic of the supposed Welsh influence on Appalachian preaching styles is Elder John Sparks, who is both a Baptist preacher and a historian of religion in Appalachia. He contends that the rhythmic, chanted sermon of mountain church services originated not in hwyl but in the vocal techniques of George Whitefield, a trained actor as well as a Methodist evangelist with a voice that Benjamin Franklin likened to a finely tuned organ. Whitefield's cadenced delivery, according to Sparks, was the true source of the holy tone. He suggests that there is no evidence of the use of hwyl in Wales or America before the arrival of Whitefield, and if there is any connection between hwyl and holy tone then it must be mediated through Whitefield. In other words, Howell Harris – the first Welsh evangelist to meet Whitefield – acquired the technique from the Englishman.[19] 'This circumstance by itself is enough for the author to venture the hypothesis that hwyl did not precede the New England Holy Tone historically but that it, like the Tone in America, became a phenomenon of the aftermath of George Whitefield's revivals in Wales, and for the same causes.'

Sparks's assertion, however, is not supported by what is known of Harris, and of his meeting with Whitefield. Harris, who also had a voice that 'thundered greatly', had begun exhorting and evangelizing several years before meeting Whitefield.[20] He was also well aware of his ability, his 'power', to enthrall an audience. Most telling, however, is Whitefield's admission that he learned the 'mad Trick' of field or open-air preaching from Harris when they met in Wales in March 1738, and that his heart 'was knit so closely to him [that he] wanted to catch some of his fire'.[21] On his return to London, after the meeting, he found that parish churches were consistently closed to him and he wrote to Harris to say that he intended repeating his 'mad Trick'. He began field preaching a month after his ordination, in January 1739, 'following,' according to Ted Campbell, 'the pattern that Harris had shown him'.[22]

That pattern, one supposes, embraced his manner of 'persuasive intonation' and the 'godly' or 'holy' tone. In *Revivalism in America*, William Warren Sweet attributed the origin of the rising and falling of the voice in the 'holy whine' to the need for relieving the strain on the voice when preaching outdoors.[23] Until his meeting with Harris, Whitefield's preaching had been confined to Anglican churches, and although his 'irregular' style may have raised official eyebrows, it did not prevent the Bishop of London (who would not have tolerated great fervour in the church) from ordaining him a priest (he had been ordained a deacon in 1736). Whitefield returned to the colonies in the summer of 1739, preaching in both churches and the fields as he moved south.[24] After returning to Britain in 1741 he and Harris embarked on a preaching tour of Scotland and Wales.

Sparks attributes the spread of Whitefield's preaching style in America to Shubal Stearns, a devotee who heard Whitefield preach in the early 1740s and is thought to have mimicked his method of delivery. Originally a Congregationalist from New England, Stearns settled in the Piedmont region of North Carolina and from his base in Sandy Creek he and a cadre of fellow Baptist exhorters converted thousands in North Carolina and Virginia. As described by Tidence Lane, a preacher informant to historian and Baptist pastor Morgan Edwards, Stearns's voice was 'musical and strong' and his delivery so effective that other Baptist ministers copied him 'in tones of voice and actions of the body, and some few exceed[ed] him'. He managed his voice in such a manner as 'to make a soft impression on the heart ... [and] to shake the very nerves and throw the animal system into tumults and perturbations'.[25] Edwards himself never met Stearns or heard him preach. In his own preaching, Edwards, according to Sparks, never employed hwyl and when writing about the preaching mode of Shubal Stearns he made no reference to Welsh antecedents.

Even if Elder John Sparks is right to question a Welsh provenance for Appalachian and Southern singing and preaching styles, Celtic and Gaelic influence may not be denied. Professor Willie Ruff, a black American ethno-musicologist at Yale, who is also an accomplished jazz musician, insists that the roots of rhythmic gospel singing lie in the west of Scotland, not in Africa and the slave past. In churches known to him in Florida the method of lining out, or 'precenting the line', in which the psalms are called out and the congregation sings a response, is virtually identical with Hebridean practice. In Gaelic churches, the psalm singing is without accompaniment; the precentor leads the praise by beginning the tune, which he sings along with the congregation for two lines of a four-line stanza. On the third line, the precentor sings the line solo, which is then repeated by the congregation. This occurs for each line until the end of the item of praise. To support his argument, Ruff cites an advertisement in a North Carolina newspaper, dated about 1740, offering a reward for a runaway slave who would be easy to identify because he spoke only Gaelic. At a church in Alabama, black Americans worshipped in Gaelic as late as 1918. 'We as black Americans,' he concludes, 'have lived under a misconception. Our cultural roots are more Gaelic than Black American. Just look at the Harlem phone book, it's more like the book for North Uist.'[26]

Further evidence of Welsh influence on Southern preaching styles was the enrollment of former students from Howell Harris's college for Methodists at Trefeca, Breconshire, at a similar institution in Georgia opened by George Whitefield just before the Revolutionary War. The objectives of the institution were to maintain orphans, and train missionaries for the 'back settlements' and the Indian territories. One of the missionaries, Lewis Richards, became a Baptist minister successively in South Carolina, Virginia and Maryland, maintaining at the same time a correspondence with his spiritual mentors in Wales with whom he exchanged news of the Welsh Revival and of the evangelization of the backwoodsmen of 'Caintucky'.[27] Under Whitefield's management the centre soon ran out of funds (Morgan John Rhees accused him of using some of the charitable funds to buy a plantation) and was saved by the Countess of Huntingdon, Harris's benefactor at Trefeca.[28]

Supporting the case for Welsh influences upon Appalachian and Southern church practices were the impressions of casual observers. William Davies Evans, a Welsh preacher who travelled in America after the Civil War, attended a Revival meeting of African-Americans in Wilkes-Barre where a man (who 'appeared similar to a warm-hearted, old-fashioned Welshman') began to sing and then speak. The timbre and tone of his voice was so familiar that Evans wondered if the man had Welsh blood in his veins.[29] He, like other travellers in the Appalachians and the South, was also impressed by the prominence of Welsh surnames and place-names. Joneses, Morgans, Bowens and Powells are legion in both white and Afro-American populations. Floyd, a popular Christian name, is a derivation of Llwyd or Lloyd. Welsh place-names are also commonplace. Alabama has counties named Morgan and Montgomery and towns and villages called Prichard, Cardiff, Jones, Rheboth and Morris; Georgia counties named Evans, Montgomery, Jones, Floyd, Morgan, Thomas, Glynn and Jenkins; Louisiana towns and villages called Evans, Jones, Jonesboro, Jonesville, Floyd, Thomas, Powell, and Bowen. Place-names suggest Welsh settlement and surnames Welsh associations. Slaves commonly took their names from places where they had lived and from people who mattered in their lives. Some of these, of course, may have been owners, but the Welsh in general were strongly opposed to slavery.

When travelling in the South immediately after the First World War, the British author and travel writer Stephen Graham was also impressed by similarities between Welsh and Southern pulpits. To be heard or listened to, the Southern preacher, he observed, 'must forget ordinary diction ... and chant in ecstasy and rapture'. When listening to a renowned black woman preacher, a voice next to Graham kept crying out '"Help her, Lord, help her" ... Presently the preacher was lifted out of the ordinary, everyday voice into a barbaric chant, which rose and fell and acclaimed and declaimed in rhythmical grandeur and music. I dared not look at the woman at my side, "She's all right now, Lord; she's all right now", and I thought of the relief of the Welsh when their neighbours get into the strain they call the hwyl.'[30]

Not all Americans, however, look tolerantly upon a Welsh connection with the culture of the Southern states. For the profoundly secular H.L. Mencken, the Welsh Baptist and Methodist infiltration of the South was a catastrophe. In 'Sahara of Bozart,' an essay written in 1920, he delivered a now well-known broadside: 'The religious thought of the South is almost precisely identical with the religious thought of Wales. There is the same naïve belief in an anthropomorphic Creator but little removed, in manner and desire, from an evangelical bishop; there is the same submission to an ignorant and impudent sacerdotal tyranny, and there is the same sharp contrast between doctrinal orthodoxy and private ethics.' He had read Caradoc Evans's collection of short stories, *My People*, and he directed his readers to a preface that would remind them instantly of Georgia and Carolina Methodists. Evans's rural Wales (he was from Rhydlewis, Cardiganshire) was a society riven by greed, jealousy and class conflict, and presided over by repressive Nonconformist ministers. The Welsh historian A.H. Dodd played down Mencken's assault as a *jeu d'esprit*, but Mencken, in his day the dean of American essayists and journalists, was a man for broadsides rather than playful thrusts. While Wales prepared its defences for the publication of Evans's second collection of stories, *Capel Sion*, in 1916, Mencken (in a gesture of support for Evans) offered to buy 100 copies of the book that he would donate to YMCA libraries in America. In Wales, police raided bookshops in an effort to sieze and suppress, on grounds of 'indecency', Evans's book.

Another Methodist, and in some degree Welsh, influence upon Appalachian and Southern culture was the 'camp meeting', the name applied to periodic open-air assemblies or meetings, held in the slack period between planting and harvesting, when Christians of all denominations from forty or fifty miles around came together to celebrate the Lord's Supper. Those who had come from a distance slept overnight in tents and wagons, the women in the wagons and the men on the ground. Populations were rural and scattered and the churches, as in large parts of Wales, were not subject to any central authority and were not large enough to accommodate the numbers who attended. The origin of the American camp meeting has been attributed to Whitefield's field preaching during his first tour of the colonies from 1739 to 1741.[31] But as Whitefield acquired the practice of field preaching from Howell Harris, then Welsh influence may be assumed. The genesis of the great Kentucky Revival at Cane Ridge, near Lexington, in 1801, can be dated to the close of a Presbyterian sacramental service when, after the departure of the ministers, a Methodist itinerant stepped forward and began to exhort those who remained at the meeting house. According to Winthrop Hudson, the excitement he generated swept across the state, reaching a peak at Cane Ridge the following year. Attended by Presbyterians, Methodists and Baptists, the Cane Ridge meeting was a massive Llangeitho, six days of round the clock meetings, sermons and hymn singing attended by an estimated 25,000 frontier people, many of them living on isolated farms and hungry for diversion and sensation.

> The noise was like the noise of Niagara. The vast sea of human beings seemed to be agitated as if by a storm. I counted seven

ministers all preaching at one time, some on stumps, some on wagons. Some of the people were singing, others praying, some crying for mercy shouts that rent the very heavens. Praying, singing and exhorting kept up day and night. In the reports, singing of 'melodious' or 'spiritual' songs stressed, with repetitive refrains set to lively folk tunes. Ministers would preach and then set people to singing. It was requested that there be no singing during sermons but with four or more sermons going on at once, singing continuous. One attendant reported 'there was singing in one part of the camp [or another] without intermission from the time I arrived until the time I left ... a term of seventy-two hours' (James B. Finley).

George Pullen Grant, in his book *White and Negro Spirituals*, presented a similar scene:

As the darkness deepened, the exhortations of the preachers became more fervent and impassioned ... The volume of song burst all bonds of guidance and control, and broke again and again from the throats of the people while over all, at intervals, there rang out the shout of ecstasy, the sob and the groan. Men and women shouted during the sermon, and shook hands all around in what was termed 'the singing ecstasy'.[32]

The emotionalism of the camp meetings horrified novelist Frances Trollope. At a meeting in Kentucky she stood at the edge of the 'pen', a space immediately below the preacher's stand or platform. The mention of the word 'pen' was a signal for the crowd to fall back so that the preachers could begin a ritual descent that signified, as the Pennsylvania historian Ronald Lewis has pointed out, that they were not 'high platform men' separate from the people. This would have been important to Welsh Nonconformists.[33] Fervent hymn singing accompanied the descent and during it the preachers turned to every part of the crowd, beckoning the penitents to come forward. 'Above a hundred' did so, Trollope noted, 'uttering howlings and groans, and on the word being given, "let us pray," they all fell on their knees. But this posture was soon changed for others that permitted greater scope for the convulsive movement of their limbs, and they were soon lying on the ground in an indescribable confusion of heads and legs.'[34]

*

Emigration from Wales slackened again after 1750, but as the century closed Welsh immigrants began to arrive with greater frequency and in greater numbers than previously. In the vanguard were groups of farmers and farm workers seeking inexpensive or affordable land. The standard practice in Wales was for a group from a given district to hire a vessel, or negotiate a group passage, and elect, or acknowledge, a leader. Often, the leader was a Nonconformist minister agitated by high rents, tithes and church taxes imposed indiscriminately on non-Anglicans as well as Anglicans, a callous disregard for tenants, and restricted opportunities, his own included. On arrival, a few emigrants might have struck out on their own, but most, especially if Welsh was their only language, stayed with the group. The monoglot Welsh clung to each other as closely as any other non-English-speaking nationality. By 1830 there were five discernibly Welsh pioneer agricultural settlements in America: one in Cambria County in western Pennsylvania; one in the Mohawk Valley of central New York State – particularly favoured by emigrants from north Wales – and three west of the Allegehenies, in Ohio. Between 1830 and 1860, emigration from west Wales to Ohio's Jackson and Gallia counties was so constant that they were dubbed 'Little Cardiganshire'. Other Welsh settlements in Ohio were near present-day Cincinnatti (Paddy's Run), and in and around the town of Gomer in Allen County. With some 6,000 Welsh settlers by 1860, Jackson/ Gallia rivalled the 7,000 in Oneida and Steuben counties in the Mohawk Valley. As the agricultural frontier moved west, small but cohesive groups of Welsh emigrants settled on the rich soils of Iowa and Wisconsin and, just before the Civil War, Kansas.

Unlike other emigrants from Great Britain who fitted more easily into the majority English culture, communities of Welsh-speaking rural immigrants were tightly knit and geographically distinct, even though Welsh and non-Welsh farms might be interspersed. Intermarriage and recurring waves of migration reinforced the distinction.[35] With little English, and in some cases none at all, and in the case of those affected by Revivals, deeply religious, they assimilated slowly. They were regarded as clannish by some and, in an often rough-and-ready pioneer society, intolerably pious by others. In the Mohawk Valley godlessness, the neglect of Sunday and, most of all, the prevailing drunkenness shocked the Welsh. Whiskey ranked not far below bread and meat in the list of necessities, and in its home-made form open kegs of it with cups attached were available everywhere: in stores, at log rollings, house raisings, and at virtually all social gatherings. In Ohio, the Welsh settlers' insistence on Sundays without work or recreation of any kind earned them the label 'Those God Almighty Welsh'.[36] Because most individuals and families settled on their own land, there were few compact villages or hamlets in the European sense so that the chapels, when built, became community foci, serving as gathering places and a means of identity. Older people living in areas of Welsh settlement in Ohio may still, when asked where they live, name the nearest chapel. In his history of the Welsh in America, the Rev. R.D. Thomas described Jackson/Gallia as a land of the Bible, of preaching, and Sunday schools, much like a more privileged Wales.[37] Paddy's Run, he described thus: 'The village is in the centre of a small plain with hills all around it. The old Welsh congregational chapel is in the centre; a brick building with no gallery, raising seats, about 10 yards by 12 … At the side a large graveyard. Houses all around it and many large holdings to be seen around the plain and on the hillsides. This is the first Welsh settlement in Ohio.'[38]

Until the 1820s, emigrants from Wales were overwhelmingly from the rural counties of mid and west Wales but, with the opening of the coal and ironfields of Pennsylvania and Ohio, the balance shifted to the urban and industrial counties of the south. Mining and manufacturing in the United States gained momentum in the few decades before the Civil War and grew exponentially afterwards. Pittsburgh, Youngstown, Ebensburg, Wilkes-Barre, and Scranton were Pennsylvania boom towns that received thousands of Welsh miners and ironworkers. By 1890 Scranton, which for decades had the largest Welsh immigrant population of any city in America, had been overtaken by Wilkes-Barre, only eighteen miles away, with some 8,600 immigrants and a population of Welsh descent of 21,500. Together, the two cities harboured more than 16,000 immigrants and roughly 40,000 first and second generation Welsh-Americans. After 1850, coal and iron discoveries in Jackson/Gallia also brought Welsh industrial workers to Ohio. Roughly contemporaneous discoveries of slate in south-eastern Pennsylvania and in 'Slate Valley' along the Vermont/ NewYork State border brought quarrymen from north Wales. Among the latter were more than fifty members of the Braichmelyn Choir, Bethesda, who sailed from Liverpool with their conductor William Morris, in 1853, to quarry fine Peach Bottom slate in what is now Bangor, Pennsylvania.

In the towns and cities, as in the country, religion and language were the ties that bound. Industrial workers and their families were more likely to emigrate independently but in the slate quarrying districts of north Wales a plan was aired to collect money in each of the four major quarry districts (Dinorwic, Bethesda, Caernarfon and Llanllyfni) from families who wished to go to America. Collections would continue until there was enough money to charter a vessel. The plan never materialized but its proposal indicated the desire of the quarrymen to stick together.[39] In general, however, industrial workers seem to have left with no conscious intention of preserving a Welsh way of life in America. Yet on arrival in the manufacturing and mining settlements most of these, too, made instinctively for their own kind. In general, however, the Welsh were well received by settled Americans despite – in many cases – the halting nature of their English. Unlike the Québécois and the Irish in the Slate Valley, and Eastern Europeans and Italians elsewhere, they were not Catholic and they were not conspicuously rowdy.

They were also churchgoing, not just religious. For most Welsh migrants, only the provision of shelter and the securing of a livelihood took precedence over the building of a church. 'Where you find the Welsh, you find a church,' a Yankee observer commented. The first step was the formation of a fellowship, or *seiat*, by an experienced elder, that would meet in a home or homes until a church could be built. The waiting period could be several years. Country churches, with few members, were served by part-time resident preachers or by itinerants who moved in a circuit from chapel to chapel. In Jackson/Gallia, the latter were commonly housed in the *tŷ capel*, a building next to the church or attached to it, where the itinerant might rest and eat. Churches were scattered and the clergy often were forced to carry their own provisions. A typical tŷ capel, which might also have been used for Sunday school classes, would have had a kitchen, a parlour, and sometimes a small bedroom.[40]

In the Welsh districts of the mining and manufacturing towns and cities of Pennsylvania and Ohio, where funds were not as scarce, church building could begin quickly. In Scranton, by the late 1850s, the Baptists, Congregationalists and Calvinistic Methodists had built separate churches. By 1870, Scranton had no fewer than seven Welsh churches, some with seating for 800 people, and the state of Pennsylvania about 100. In the Hyde Park district of Scranton, the churches of the three leading denominations dominated the skyline. R.D. Thomas marvelled at them: 'Their spires rise up to

Heaven! They can be seen plainly from Scranton, and for a great distance beyond the city.'[41]

The chapels themselves were American on the outside, but inside they were wholly Welsh. Some of the older country churches had two doors, one for each sex, and the sexes sat separately. Interiors everywhere were plain and unadorned. Crosses and religious scenes were anathema. The Word was the only acceptable representation of God. Worship was a vocal undertaking: the sermon and the hymn, and the hymn singing, as in all the Welsh churches, was determinedly congregational. There was no tolerance for choir lofts and some churches resisted having even a corner set aside for the choir. In pioneer communities, congregational singing was an important symbol of neighbourliness and the four-part harmony in the Welsh churches intensified the feeling of togetherness.

Lincoln Jones Hartford, a musician and Congregational minister of Pennsylvania Welsh extraction, described the 'magical' effect upon his own congregation in Minnesota of the introduction of alto and tenor lines: 'The singing itself has become lively and a new spirit has been evident in the service overall.' Harmony, he asserts, 'is the expression of a Christian tenet: through many, one. So it is then,' he continues, 'that, on any Sunday morning, in almost any church or chapel, people are led to sing together across all sorts of barriers, youth, age, nationality, religious conviction. People sing together, lustily, not knowing who it is they join. The blending of the voices is itself an act of peace-making. Doing one's part, in collaboration, in adjustment with the group, makes for a community of sound.'[42] Few have expressed more feelingly the deep satisfaction of singing communally than Garrison Keillor, the American writer and broadcaster who sang with Lutheran choirs and congregations in his home state of Minnesota: 'To sing like this, in the company of other souls, and to make those consonants slip out so easily and in unison, and to make those chords so rich that they bring tears to your eyes. This is transcendence. This is the power that choral singing has that other music can only dream of.'

*

Preachers were prominent figures in all Welsh-American communities and many were accomplished exponents of hwyl. Robert Williams of Jackson/Gallia spent his youth with a religious family in Anglesey where one-eyed Christmas Evans had lived and preached. The family of Williams's first wife were close friends of John Elias, a prominent Calvinistic Methodist. Like his mentors, Robert Williams was a master of the extemporaneous address. At times, wrote his elegist, 'the power of his eloquence would descend upon the congregation like the falls of Niagara, invincible, sweeping away every obstacle that stood in its path.' A witness to one of Williams's sermons recalled, around 1845: 'Before the end, many could not remain quiet, they gave vent to their feelings until they drowned out the preacher's voice, despite its being so clear and musical.' Nor could they be still after leaving the chapel, but the 'sound of song and praise was heard along the roads as they went home'.[43] Although Williams was from north Wales and spoke with a dialect and an accent different from that of his former Cardiganshire constituents, they would have found the vocabulary and the rhythm of his 'pulpit Welsh' perfectly familiar. Like Daniel Rowland, Williams was a fixed star who seldom travelled outside his home district. In Jackson/Gallia, the chapels were arranged in a ring around Moriah, the central chapel, and the favoured site for all community-wide religious activities.

The siren-like power of Welsh preaching was the subject of reminiscences by the Rev. T. Edwards of Birmingham, Pennsylvania.[44] In 1836, Birmingham's few Welsh families were served by circulating preachers. There was no church so services were held in houses. One warm Sunday afternoon, when not all who came could be accommodated inside the house, the Rev. William Owens preached standing in the yard. The house stood on a hillside on the edge of the town and Owens had a very clear ringing voice. Once the 'Welsh fire' began to burn, he could be heard all over town. People began to run toward the place, attracting others until the pasture below the house was full of people. Although of different nationalities, and ignorant of Welsh, 'they all stood still until Mr Owens had closed'. At one outdoor service there was even a jumper. 'I well remember [Mrs Lewis Jones],' wrote Edwards, 'shouting and jumping in her wooden shoes'. She had attended meetings at Llangeitho and had run fourteen miles with shoes in one hand and hat in the other to hear Daniel Rowland preach.

As on Sundays in Wales, congregational singing ran a close second to the sermon. The chapels reverberated with song. At Poultney, in Vermont's Slate Valley, families in houses next to the Welsh church would come out to their porches to listen to singing that made the church windows rattle.[45] In the 1830s, it was also reported that people living in the anthracite coalfield near Carbondale, upon hearing the strong minor chords of Welsh hymns in the frosty night air for the first time, got out of bed to listen.[46] Fine singing also brought people, who might not have attended otherwise, into church. In the 1860s, the congregation of the Long Street Welsh church in Columbus, Ohio, was too poor to afford a pastor and, possibly, except on Sundays, heat and light for the church. Those who wanted to improve their singing and maintain church attendance on Sundays when no preacher could be there, met in a house at least once a week to practise hymns and anthems, sometimes until midnight. But the more likely explanation for the exclusion of the group is that the church elders would not have wanted to encourage singing separate from the congregation and the creation of what would, in effect, have been a church choir. Whatever the precise dynamics involved, the singing proved attractive enough to hold the congregation.[47]

As in Wales, singing schools were popular, particularly in the 1860s and 1870s. Ieuan Gwyllt's *Llyfr Tonau* had just been published and copies would have been available in America. The schools met in winter – the slack season on the farms and in the quarries – in private houses, schools, barns or the Sunday school. With a minister or leading singer to instruct, people of all ages learned the tonic sol-fa as well as their parts in the more frequently sung hymns. Hymns not sung in their various parts were regarded as flat and unacceptable. In spite of the patent success of tonic sol-fa, and the relative ease with which it could be learned, American choirs and congregations did not adopt it, persisting, in the Southern states especially, with shape note systems that preceded the tonic sol-fa. These substituted shapes or symbols (diamonds, triangles, ovals and squares) for the note heads and they enabled the beginner to recognize pitch through note-head shapes and, as with the tonic sol-fa, dispense with the learning of the names of keys, lines and spaces.[48]

Even if they were disinclined to emulate Welsh four-part harmony, Americans relished the sound of it. Michael Williams, of Welsh Prairie, Wisconsin, wrote to his brother in Plas y Blaenau, 31 May 1849:

> The Americans are delighted with our singing. Two loads of ladies and gentlemen came to Chapel Sunday before last on purpose – to hear the singing. After the services we sung two pieces of Handel's in English and one in Welsh, the last piece of which was the 'Grand Chorus' Worthy is the Lamb that was Slain &c. They were amazed, it was beyond their expectation and declared they had never heard such superb singing, and it had such an effect on one and the young gentleman who had first arrived in Wis. from the Eastern States; that he could not help weeping.[49]

In rural Ohio and Wisconsin, the chapels governed social life with a firm and uncompromising hand. On Sundays, as in Cardiganshire, all secular activity stopped. There were no games, even for children. The contract that granted the Scioto and Hocking Valley Railroad rights-of-way across Welsh-owned farmland in Ohio stipulated that no trains were to run on Sundays.[50] The feeding of animals and people was the only work allowed, and that was kept to a minimum. It was said of one family that they boiled their tea kettle on Saturday so that it would only have to be warmed on Sunday. One summer morning an ineluctable and forgetful David Morgan of Gomer, Ohio, who was a faithful church member, loaded his wagon with hay and, as he drove past the church, he realized to his horror that it was Sunday. It was an experience he never forgot – nor did anyone else.[51] Had he lived in Jackson County, Ohio, he might well have been punished. It was a rule of the county's Horeb Church to 'discipline' members of the seiat who missed three successive meetings. The seiat met for an hours-long session on Friday mornings during seed time and harvest, winter and summer, fair weather and foul. It was the kind of demand – in a farming community – that fuelled 'Those God Almighty Welsh' sentiments.

In contrast to Wales, where the cymanfa ganu had a distinct identity from the outset, in America it began as an adjunct to the cymanfa bregethu, the preaching festival. Unlike the Anglican Synod and the Presbyterian Presbytery, which were primarily business meetings, the periodic assemblies of the Welsh churches were little more than pretexts for serial preaching and congregational singing. Even the elders bypassed many of the business sessions, and the preachers, who often arrived too late for the meetings, seldom missed the preaching and hymn singing. Baptists and Congregationalists from a given district met once a year, and Methodists twice. The Welsh, according to Erasmus Jones, regarded the *cwrdd mawr*, the big meeting, with as much veneration as the Jew did the Passover. Thousands attended, and the festivals usually lasted for days, the singing sometimes lingering deep into the night. Local congregations practised favourite hymns in advance of the meetings and led the singing. As in Wales, choruses were repeated many times. Preachers from the district and the region and – at particularly large gatherings – from Wales, preached in the festival field and in churches around the district. If the churches filled, windows and doors, again as in Wales, were thrown open so that those standing outside could hear.

Moriah, the central, mother church, *Ein Mam Ni Oll*, of Jackson/Gallia, was host to the regional cymanfa every two years. To address the thousands who attended (5,000 to 6,000 in May 1861), the organizers built a raised platform-cum-pulpit in the field adjacent to the church. Local congregations led the hymn singing. At Fairhaven and Middle Granville in the New York/Vermont Slate Valley, a four-day circulating cymanfa bregethu shared by the two communities in 1858 celebrated the opening of a new church. At Fairhaven there were thirteen sermons and at Middle Granville eight. They demonstrated, as Gwilym Roberts noted with what one suspects was deliberate understatement, the capacity of the Welsh for sustained religious observance. But however long-suffering the Welsh, the sermons at the cymanfaoedd seem to have been enjoyed; they were dramatic and, if delivered with hwyl, quasi-musical performances that brought diversion to often humdrum lives. In 1853, some of the mining communities in Pennsylvania requested more cymanfaoedd and even more preaching.[52] The farming Welsh in Wisconsin were just as avid: preaching festivals there were so popular (at one there were no fewer than seventeen preachers) that they led to the general 'neglect of corn and hoe'.[53] But the numbers of sermons delivered at the Wisconsin and Slate Valley cymanfaoedd were nothing like a record. David Harries's official report of a Jackson/Gallia cymanfa, convened around Moriah Church in May 1856, included the startling item: 'There were delivered from the beginning of the cymanfa unto its conclusion [four or five days later] one hundred and one (101) sermons.'[54] As great feasts of preaching and singing the cymanfaoedd, admitted a resigned

Daniel Jenkins Williams, were 'almost an indulgence'.[55] There were no reports of loose behaviour at the American festivals, but in his history of Slate Valley, Gwilym Roberts felt it necessary to note that at the larger and more prolonged preaching festivals in Wales there were charges of drunkenness and immoral behaviour. The Bishop of Caernarfon answered these by studying birth rates and presenting statistics that showed a decline, rather than the alleged increase, in the number of illegitimate births following the meetings. The declines, he noted pointedly, were greatest in places where there had been all-night meetings.

In his history of Calvinistic Methodism in America, Daniel Jenkins Williams described an Ohio cymanfa attended by a multitude that came 'on foot, on horseback, in large lumber wagons and an occasional carriage':

> The cymanfa, when it convened in regular session, was a great gathering in the historic days of Welsh settlements in Ohio. It was the great institution of the Church, and the Church was in control socially as well as religiously in Welsh communities. It was anticipated for weeks beforehand, and the churches held special prayer services for its success ... Many details had to be attended to. Ministers and elders from every church were expected to be present and a great docket was arranged when the outstanding preachers of the cymanfa proclaimed the gospel message. Local choirs and congregations rehearsed special hymns selected for the cymanfa services. These hymns were frequently printed in pamphlet form for distribution at the services ... Enthusiasm ran high. The Welsh hwyl pervaded the assembled worshipers. Great Welsh divines swayed the multitude with their true Welsh eloquence. Congregational singing by the vast throng on these festal occasions was nothing short of a foretaste of things to come, an experience never to be forgotten.[56]

Later in his history, Williams commented on the four-part singing, led by local choirs and congregations: 'The four parts – soprano, alto, tenor and base – could always be heard throughout the vast congregation as well as in the selected choir. When particularly favorite hymns were sung, the refrain was repeated over and over, and each repetition was given with renewed zest and intensified fervour. To hear a great cymanfa audience sing a favorite hymn at the close of a service when a great preacher had carried them to a high plane of religious emotion – all but ecstatic – is an experience which forever lingers in one's memory.'

Although there were practical reasons for itinerancy in rural America, the prevalence of it, combined with the appeal of open-air meetings, pointed to resistance to the idea of a settled ministry. Peter Williams has suggested that the preaching festivals captured the spirit and excitement of the early Revivals in Wales: 'a form of antistructure that may have had deep resonance for those who harbored ancestral memories of the excitement of early revival days.' Citing Émile Durkheim, he likened them to an Aboriginal corroboree in which the excitement and transience of the occasion generated a kind of collective effervescence.[57] Itinerancy also guaranteed fresh, well-honed sermons or performances. Unlike resident ministers, the itinerants, whose audiences were constantly changing, needed only a small repertoire of sermons, each of which improved with the telling. In the course of a season, a sermon would be repeated several times and its cadenced delivery perfected. Preferring newness and change in the pulpit, Welsh Americans, as Daniel Jenkins Williams pointed out, took no pleasure in a settled pastorate, and until the 1850s few rural Calvinistic Methodist churches had a regular, full-time minister.[58]

By the late 1860s there were signs that the cymanfa ganu had begun to break away from the cymanfa bregethu, but it would be years before it would come into its own.[59] In Waukesha County, Wisconsin, John P. Jones founded a choral union very much like Ieuan Gwyllt's. His aim, like Gwyllt's, was to improve standards of congregational singing in Welsh communities.[60] Other communities adopted similar practices, holding rehearsals led by local singing leaders or the appointed conductor. As people entered the church on cymanfa day, ushers asked if they were soprano, alto, tenor or bass and seated them in their respective sections so that they could be cued by the conductor. Smaller communities sometimes dressed the eisteddfod (the most popular cultural event in Welsh communities in the second half of the nineteenth century) in the habit of a cymanfa ganu. At the annual Cattaraugus (Mohawk Valley) eisteddfod, held on New Year's Eve, some 600 to 1,000 people in sleighs and cutters gathered from all over the district. The singing was communal, not competitive; the congregation sang favourite Welsh hymns and songs and, as an expression of loyalty to their adopted land, patriotic American songs. 'One can imagine the old Welsh Baptist Chapel ... filled to capacity. Welsh familes, men, women and children lined the pews. There were so many in attendance that some had to stand. It was the most wonderful event of the year. Light from candles and oil lamps brightened faces and made shadows dance on the walls and ceilings. Heating stoves crackled, popped and hissed as the fires died. The Old Year ended, the New Year began.'

To close eisteddfodau and concerts, a little later in the century, in 1856, Welsh-American audiences sang a plaintive anthem composed in a minor key. Its name: 'Hen Wlad fy Nhadau', Land of my Fathers. It had been written and composed by Evan James, a weaver from Pontypridd, and his son James. According to one account Evan wrote the words in response to his brother's invitation to join him in America. He gave the words to James, a harpist, who set them to music. Another account has James composing the tune while walking along the banks of the Rhondda, then an unspoiled rural valley, and asking Evan to write the words. Whatever the actual sequence, Evan and James named their song 'Glan Rhondda' (Bank of the Rhondda) that, in the early 1860s, was changed to 'Hen Wlad fy Nhadau'. By the end of the century it had become the national anthem, although never officially adopted.

In the larger American towns and cities, in particular, the competitive eisteddfod, whose popularity in Wales (following its late eighteenth-century revival) reached across the Atlantic, tended to overshadow the cymanfa ganu. As a stage for encouraging, and in some cases unveiling local musical and literary talent, the eisteddfod was unequalled. Joseph Parry's musical talents were probably large enough to have surmounted the most unpromising circumstances, but for his rise from pitboy in Merthyr, at age nine, and ironworker in Danville, Pennsylvania, to the founding Chair of music at the University of Wales and composer of the majestic hymn tune 'Aberystwyth', local eisteddfodau in and around Danville could take some of the credit. One of eight children, Parry, with his family, left Merthyr for Danville in 1854 when he was thirteen. He worked as a 'puddler's boy' (eventually becoming head roller) at the Rough and Ready Rolling Mill on Railroad St (named after 'Old Rough and Ready', General Zachary Taylor, and renamed the Glendower Iron Works in 1879), attended the Congregational church, studied harmony in his spare time, and submitted compositions to local eisteddfodau. He learned staff notation, sight singing and the rudiments of harmony from two fellow iron workers, John Abel Jones and John Price, both able musicians. Parry 'held the metal' for Price, that is, he was Price's 'puddler's boy'. It was for a Scranton eisteddfod that he composed 'Ar Don o Flaen Gwyntoedd', now an old favourite. In 1860 he won first prizes for a temperance vocal march at the Danville eisteddfod and for a hymn tune at a Christmas eisteddfod at Fairville in Vermont's Slate Valley. The following year, at the much grander Utica eisteddfod in New York, he won again.[61] By his early twenties he had moved up several divisions; his compositions won prizes at the Welsh National Eisteddfod at Swansea in 1863 and at Llandudno in

1864. At the Aberystwyth National Eisteddfod in 1865, which he attended, the bardic title *Pencerdd America* (Chief American Musician) was conferred on him. He was so precocious a talent that Brinley Richards, an eisteddfod adjudicator, questioned the authenticity of Parry's submissions. In a confessional letter to the *Cambrian*, prompted by an invitation to attend a farewell meeting before Parry's departure for America in 1871, he wrote:

> I shall have very great pleasure in accepting your invitation to attend the meeting at which Mr Parry's friends are to bid him farewell previous to his departure for America. I have a *personal* interest (if I may so speak) in Joseph Parry's career. You doubtless remember the National Eisteddfod at Swansea some few years since, when among more than 100 compositions sent for adjudication, I found one so very well written, and so far above the average of works sent to such meetings, that I doubted its genuiness – as I fancied that the composition was a 'piracy'. I chanced to be at Eastbourne with my friend Sir Sterndale Bennett, and I showed him the manuscript. He, like myself, also questioned the originality of the work, and suggested a search in a volume of Bach's Chorales. The result was in favour of the author of the manuscript. [The author was Joseph Parry.] [62]

After Parry's eisteddfod successes, benefactors in America and Wales raised money to send him to the Royal Academy of Music in London where he sat, successfully, for a Cambridge degree in music. He returned to Danville in 1871 to set up the Danville Music Institute supported by 350 Welsh-American chapels. But Danville could not hold him. Three years later he returned to Wales as the first Professor of Music at the University of Wales in Aberystwyth where he persuaded the college to admit women so that he would have female voices for his choral compositions. When he died, full of honours, in 1903, the obituarist for *Y Geninen* pronounced him without doubt the best-known Welshman in the world. Within Wales he was simply 'the great Doctor'.

In Pennsylvania, Parry's only Welsh rival was William Aubrey Williams (Gwilym Gwent), who was known as the Mozart of the Wyoming Valley. A self-taught Tredegar blacksmith, he emigrated to Wilkes-Barre in his late thirties and worked in the coal mines until his death. In the tradition of miner/composer, he is said to have chalked tunes and notes on pit props and the sides of trams. As well as conducting choirs and brass bands, he wrote more than 100 pieces that included part-songs, anthems and cantatas.

As well as forcing, through competition and adjudication, the talents of local bards and musicians, the eisteddfod enhanced the image of common Welsh culture in the eyes of Americans. Working men and women in America were not in the habit of organizing cultural festivals. But there was, of course, an alter Welsh ego that took its pleasure in the bars and saloons of the iron and coal towns rather than the eisteddfod stage. This alter ego drank and fought and gambled. Big John Thomas and Red Sam Morgan were notorious Hyde Park (Scranton) bruisers in the 1870s. Others were Dic Pedlar (Richard Evans) and Dai Bright (David Jones) who fought eighty-seven rounds in the snow at Wilkes-Barre one Christmas morning. Commenting on a local eisteddfod in 1871, the *Scranton Republican* subtly noted the distinction. Welshmen of every kind were present, 'mostly those with brains, religious and non-religious, rich and poor', but there were also, it added in a sweet note of irreverence, 'a sprinkling of jesters'.[63]

Like the Sol-fa College in London, the eisteddfod made no distinctions of class, gender, or background and, like the College, it became known as the university of the working man. Carbondale, in Pennsylvania, held the first American eisteddfod on Christmas Day 1850, and other Welsh communities in Vermont, New York and Ohio, and eventually across the continent, followed. The great centres of eisteddfodic enthusiasm were the coal and iron districts of Pennsylvania and Ohio's Mahoning Valley. In the early 1870s the Hyde Park Welsh community collected money to help the South Wales Choral Union compete at Crystal Palace against the London sol-faists. The victory of the south Wales choir, in Hyde Park as in Aberdare and Merthyr, occasioned a mass celebration.

In September 1875 Scranton organized the first Welsh National Eisteddfod of America, a measure of the size of its Welsh population and the city's standing as the cultural capital of Welsh America. Held in a large pavilion-like tent with seating for 6,000, for size and scope the two-day Scranton eisteddfod had no equal in the United States. The larger eisteddfodau brought carnival to their host cities. Visitors to Scranton (the tent/pavilion and the flags flying from the six supporting poles could be seen from the centre of the city) thought that Barnum's Circus had come to town. Mines and workshops closed and special passenger trains from the surrounding Lackawanna and Wyoming Valley coalfields funnelled eisteddfod-goers into the city, filling the pavilion to capacity for all six sessions.

The effect of the eisteddfodau was to raise standards of choral singing to heights that non-Welsh adjudicators could only marvel at. The singers were amateurs as, more often than not, were their teachers. There was even tongue-in-cheek speculation that in the coal districts the quality of choral singing might owe something to the solitude of the mine and the background rhythmic beat of hammer on drill. In Pennsylvania, the singing prowess of Welsh miners acquired mythic proportions years before the filming of *The Proud Valley*: 'One of the grandest rehearsals it was ever my good fortune to listen to was the singing of "Coronation" by the miners a mile underground.' A retired Welsh miner who had worked in Pennsylvania mines in the 1870s recalled that, while waiting at the coalface for a tram in which to load the coal they had brought down, 'someone would produce a piece of chalk or pick up a fragment of slate and write a four-part tune on the broad face of the coal still standing. Then those in the room gathered around and soon the deep caverns underground re-echoed with men's voices singing an old Welsh hymn.'[64]

The reverse side of the eisteddfodic coin, however, was competition intense enough, as in Wales, to destroy *communitas*, setting community against community and even factions within communities. The greatest rivalries were in the large choir categories. Competive singing raised standards, but it was the antithesis of congregational singing that rural and small town churches in particular had sought to encourage and preserve. Congregational singing was inclusive and celebratory, not ostentatious or competitive. In rural and small town pioneer communities, where wilderness lay all around, neighbourliness was paramount. Several of Scranton's early choirs were organized specifically to compete in eisteddfodau. At the eisteddfod convened for Philadelphia's 1882 bicentennial celebrations, five 300-voice choirs from the Pennsylvania coal regions battled for honours. That contest ended peaceably, unlike one that spiralled into a free fight outside a Welsh church in Pittston, Pennsylvania, in 1878. The chief choral competition for mixed voices at the World's Fair eisteddfod at Chicago, in 1893, pitted the Scranton Choral Union against its Scranton neighbour, the Cymmrodorion Choral Society, for the largest prize ever awarded ($5,000) at an eisteddfod. Against the odds, the Choral Union took first prize, to resolve at least temporarily a rivalry that had raged for eighteen months and absorbed the attention of the entire city. The two choirs had competed against each other twice during the previous three years and on each occasion the Cymmrodorion Choral Society, under composer and hymnwriter Daniel Protheroe, had won. Protheroe, from Cwmgiedd near Ystradgynlais, emigrated to Scranton when only nineteen. He studied music at the Toronto College of Music, and in 1905 he would receive a doctorate in music from the the Grand Conservatory in New York. He conducted the Cymmrodorion Choir from 1886 to 1894.

In the run-up to the Chicago eisteddfod several top

Cymmrodorion vocalists had been poached by the Choral Union, intensifying the rivalry. To avoid presenting Scranton as a city divided against itself, intrepid mediators suggested that in Chicago the choirs be united, either under Daniel Protheroe or the Choral Union's Haydn Evans, or, failing agreement on either of these, a neutral conductor from New York. Neither choir was prepared to sacrifice its conductor and neither, too, would countenance a conductor from New York. A second option had the two choirs competing in Scranton (using the Chicago eisteddfod test pieces) before going to Chicago. The losing choir would disband before the eisteddfod and its leading singers would strengthen the winner. The Cymmrodorion Choral Society, which expected to win in Chicago, refused the challenge. So divisive was the rivalry that rehearsals were held in camera, ostensibly so that the choristers might concentrate better, but in truth to prevent spying by the other side.

On its return to Scranton, the victorious Choral Union was fêted. A throng gathered at the station and a crowd of more than 20,000 cheered the choristers as they paraded through the streets to a civic feast in the city centre. The defeated Cymmrodorion Choral Society limped into town in the early hours to be consoled by 300 loyal and unbowed supporters. The bad blood between the choirs and their respective supporters is said to have lasted for more than a decade.

Eisteddfod fever also ran high in the Slate Valley of Vermont and in and around Utica in Upstate New York. The choral events in the early eisteddfodau were conducted amicably, a reporter at a Fair Haven eisteddfod in 1870 commenting on 'the uniform good behavior of the audience' and on the intelligence and steady habits of the Welsh that made them ideal citizens. By the 1880s there had been a sea change. Eisteddfodau were larger and the reporting of the main choral events more regular and more detailed. For the May eisteddfod in Middle Granville, in 1883, spectators and contestants, brought by special trains from neighbouring towns, filled the hall for the morning, afternoon and evening sessions. The following year, when all the quarries were closed for the three-day event, the crowds were so large that the Middle Granville hall could not contain them. For the 1887 eisteddfod, a 1,200-seat rink paid for by the valley's 'Slate King', Hugh W. Hughes, proved far too small for the local population and for the supporters who now travelled with the choirs. As in Wales and Scranton, competition bred rancour. When William ap Madoc, a renowned Utica bard and adjudicator, awarded first prize to the Granville Choir at the 1887 eisteddfod, the *Poultney Journal*, whose editor R.J. Humphrey from time to time conducted the Poultney Choir, turned on Ap Madoc: he was either a poor judge of singing or a dishonest one. So undeserving was the Granville Choir that the *Journal* reported a rumour of a Fair Haven man who had offered to lay odds of five-to-one ($500 against $100) if the Granville Choir would sing against Fair Haven in Poultney before a neutral judge. Side betting at eisteddfodau might not have been uncommon. After losing to the Poultney Choir in 1888, the West Pawlet Choir challenged it to a face-off at Rutland before three judges and for a side bet of $500. The Poultney Choir declined the challenge, but at a subsequent concert the people of West Pawlet adopted two resolutions: first, to accept the unanimous verdict in favour of West Pawlet by all the 'musical critics' at the competition; and second, that by awarding the prize to the Poultney Choir the adjudicator had committed an act 'incompatible with justice and contrary to his own adjudication as read at the eisteddfod'. Poultney was not fazed; a 'Yankee' store owner offered a five-cent cigar, labelled 'The Eisteddfod', hoping, one presumes, that it would be smoked defiantly.[65]

The rivalries in the north-east crossed state boundaries. At the Utica, New York, eisteddfod, 1897, the Granville choristers, who had travelled by special train, were so angered when the adjudicator divided the prize for the best male chorus that they refused to participate in the main mixed chorus competition.

In 1899, when J. Hayden Morris, an adjudicator from Mount Vernon, New York, awarded the large chorus prize to Fair Haven rather than Poultney, the Poultney editor accused him of being 'ignorant of music', adding that any friends he might have made on his arrival were friends no longer. A year later, when Morris awarded the large chorus prize to Utica, the Poultney editor cried again: 'A bigger falsehood [Morris judged that the Poultney Choir sang off key] was never uttered by anyone,' and because it was a blatant pretext to award Utica the prize, he 'either lacked ability or integrity'. A Hobson's choice! In 1902 the *Poultney Journal* renewed the attack on Hayden Morris, an adjudicator 'who has before demonstrated his unreliability by rank decisions.' Morris's sin on this occasion was to have awarded a soloist's prize to a man from Pennsylvania after having 'practically admitted' in private that a Poultney man, Bert Race, had won the competition. Morris's performance was 'simply miserable'. The vilified J. Hayden Morris had not only studied with Joseph Parry at the University of Wales, Aberystwyth, but in 1900, 1901 and 1902 he would win major prizes, one of them the coveted Gold Medal for composition at the National Eisteddfod in Wales.

To eliminate discord in the community occasioned by an annual eisteddfod involving two churches at Gomer, Ohio, the organizing committee felt bound to cancel the choral segment of the competition. In a report on the incident for the *Cambrian* magazine, T.D. Thomas, from Gomer, is a reluctant apologist for the choristers: 'Human nature is here as everywhere else, and singers are so exquisitely sensitive (they are trained, so I suppose, in detecting discords) that the least thing grates terribly on their feelings [and they] can hardly bear a defeat without feeling the worse for it … As our object is to make everybody feel *better* after the meeting is over, we discontinued competition in singing between the choirs of the two churches, for the sake of goodwill and maintaining perfect harmony and feeling.' He added that his report should not be 'regarded a general directive, but simply as a statement of how the good people of Gomer do'. Yet he could not resist adding, 'We have no patent on it, should others wish to do the same.'[66]

Rancorous exchanges between competing choirs in the Slate Valley were relieved by interludes when the choirs combined to sing sublimely. After competing at the Poultney eisteddfod in 1891, the Poultney, West Pawlet, Fair Haven and Middle Granville choirs assembled in the Poultney cemetery to sing at the raising of a statue to the late 'Slate King', Hugh W. Hughes. 'It is safe to say,' wrote a Poultney reporter, 'that never was such singing heard in the valley before.' The quid pro quo for unseemly competitiveness was the emergence of many Horatio Algers, rags-to-riches prodigies in the Welsh communities: 'Many a quarry boy,' the American editor of the *Poultney Journal* noted, 'can go from the pit or the slate shanty to the [eisteddfod] stage and [challenge] those trained in our higher institutions.' The common people of other nationalities, he also noted, had no institution like it.

The penultimate eisteddfod in the Slate Valley, which was hailed as the most remarkable ever held there, also ended amicably. For the Granville eisteddfod of 1907, a native son who had prospered in New York put up a large prize for the winning chorus of 75 to 100 voices. The choral pieces were Handel's 'Worthy is the Lamb', and 'Sylvia' by Daniel Protheroe, who had travelled from Milwaukee to adjudicate. For the event the organizers rented, from New York, a tent seating 3,000 and requested that homes be opened to house the overflow from the hotels. At the major choral event, when 5,000 crowded into the tent, a chorus from Utica took first prize. Protheroe softened the blow for the two losing choirs by saying that all three would have graced the stage at the National Eisteddfod in Wales.

More so than the cymanfa, the eisteddfod was vulnerable to the inevitable decline of Welsh as the language of daily exchange. Although Welsh was commonly spoken in some of the Ohio settlements as late as 1890, seventy-five years after the early settlements, the language suffered elsewhere. Second and third generation Welsh-Americans adopted English, and after the First World War the numbers of Welsh immigrants declined dramatically. A Welsh-language press which had flourished for more than a century also dwindled. At the eisteddfodau, literary competitions attracted fewer and fewer entrants and, by the end of the nineteenth century, as competitive recitation, orations and declamations usurped original verse, and sermons in print replaced inventive prose, the literary arm hung by a thread. Music and song, which were less dependent on language, held out for longer but they, too, did not escape. Performance replaced composition, and sentimental and popular songs and choruses' dignified hymns and oratorio pieces. By the first decade of the twentieth century, much of the cultural significance of the eisteddfod had been lost. In August 1908, the *Druid* announced, regarding an eisteddfod organized for the Welsh Day at Scranton, that if it were possible 'the committee would eliminate all the contests as it is plainly evident that everyone without dissent wants the Big Cymanfa and nothing else. They want to hear the two big choirs and they want to join in singing the glorious old hymns of Wales and the patriotic songs of our beloved adopted country. We promise that the contests will be disposed of as rapidly as possible and that the vast throng will be given every opportunity to sing to its heart's desire at the biggest musical festival of its kind to be held in America.' After the event, the same newspaper could declare: 'The Welsh people of Lackawanna and Luzerne Counties have demonstrated to the world that Welsh singers were not prompted to sing for cash prizes only ... They sing because they love to sing.' It was a victory for *communitas*.

Over the years the nature of the cymanfa changed, evolving into a celebration of Welsh culture rather than a dedicated singing festival. By the 1920s, Welsh communities held an area cymanfa ganu in addition to the smaller community gatherings. The larger festivals were non-denominational, and they led to a movement for a national annual cymanfa devoted to the singing of Welsh hymns in both Welsh and English. Led by officers of the St David's Society of Youngstown, 3,000 Welsh and Canadian Americans assembled on Goat Island in the middle of the Niagara River in September 1929. It was the the beginning of what became the National Gymanfa Ganu Association of the United States and Canada. The movement culminated in the formation of the Welsh National Gymanfa Ganu Association at Salt Lake City in September 1971. Each year it organizes a three-day festival over a weekend in September, generally featuring a *noson lawen* (a party with music), a Welsh male voice choir, a banquet and, at its Sunday close, a cymanfa ganu.

4

The Singing Saints

WALLACE STEGNER, THE distinguished novelist and historian of the American West, who as a youth lived in Salt Lake City, labelled the Mormons a singing people. As such, they had fulfilled a prophesy. Within six months of the translation of the *Book of Mormon* into English, and the founding of the Church of the Latter-day Saints, Joseph Smith, to whom the restored gospel had been revealed, prophesied that the Saints would come singing to Zion: 'the righteous shall be gathered from among all nations, and shall come to Zion, singing with songs of everlasting joy.' Brigham Young, Smith's successor as leader of the Church, believed just as strongly that song would ease the path to the promised land. In his proclamation to the Saints at Winter Quarters, Nebraska, in January 1847, he urged them to cultivate lightness of heart during their forthcoming trek into the wilderness: 'If thou art merry, praise the Lord with singing, with music, with dancing, and a prayer of Thanksgiving.' At the second conference of the restored church, at Nauvoo in 1830, Joseph Smith had decreed that the Saints should (like the Israelites) gather in one place because only then could they be assured of escaping the divine wrath that, he prophesied, would be visited upon the unregenerate. After 1847, the gathering place, Zion, was the Salt Lake Basin in Utah.

Because the 25,000 members of the Church in the United States and Canada were too few to build the Kingdom on their own, Smith's decree committed his followers to a programme of planned immigration. Most of the converts would have to come from overseas. Early missionary efforts focused on Great Britain where Brigham Young had been president of the British Mission in 1840–1 and the first emigration agent for Europe. He had seen, as clearly as John Wesley, that the most receptive ground for a faith that promised not only salvation but a promised land (albeit one in a wilderness) lay amongst the mills and factories of the manfacturing and mining towns. In his General Epistle to the Saints, 1848, he repeated the need for a society separate from the Gentiles (non Mormons), exhorting converts to:

> Gather yourselves speedily near this place on the east side of the Missouri River, and, if possible, be ready to start from hence … as soon as the grass is sufficiently grown, and go to the Great Salt Lake City … To all the Saints in the United States and Canada, gather to the same place … To the Saints in England, Scotland, Ireland, Wales and adjacent islands and countries, we say, emigrate as speedily as possible to this vicinity [Salt Lake City].[1]

The first Mormon missionary to Wales, William Henshaw, made directly for Merthyr Tydfil, in 1840 the largest industrial town in the principality. Henshaw did not speak Welsh, and Merthyr then was still largely Welsh speaking. In spite of the promise of the dark Satanic setting as a missionary field, it was a year before he baptized his first converts but, by the end of his mission in 1845, he had established several branches of the Church in Monmouthshire and Glamorgan, with a membership of almost 500.[2] His successor, in 1845, was the legendary Captain Dan Jones. Born in Halkyn, Flintshire, in 1810, Jones went to sea at seventeen and by 1840–1 he was part-owner of a Mississippi steamboat, the *Maid of Iowa* (later purchased by Joseph Smith), that conveyed Mormon immigrants from New Orleans to the Mormon settlement of Nauvoo, Illinois. Disturbed by the vilification of the Saints in the American press, he sought out missionaries, received instruction in the faith, and became a convert himself, in May 1843. He had been a Calvinistic Methodist. Energetic and irrepressible, he quickly worked his way upward in the sect and attended meetings of the ruling Quorum of Twelve Apostles that included both Joseph Smith and the second Mormon leader, Brigham Young. At a meeting of the Quorum, Jones learned that he had been selected to head a mission – that would be delayed by the assassination of Joseph Smith in June 1844 – to Wales. At a two-day celebration of Welsh pioneer heritage in Utah, in 1993, Gordon B. Hinckley, president of the Church, described Jones as 'a stocky little Welshman' who had 'looked into the eyes of those who killed the Prophet and Hyrum'. Dan Jones shared a cell at Carthage with Joseph and Hyrum Smith hours before the assassination of the brothers.

Dan Jones conducted two missions in Wales, from 1845 to 1849, and 1852 to 1856. After a slow start, he was a phenomenal success. North Wales was barren ground that yielded only two or three baptisms in the course of a year. But in the more radical south, which was better disposed to his fiery rhetoric and less sceptical of unorthodox doctrine, he and his fellow missionaries brought some 3,500 converts into the Church. Jones at first relied exclusively on the power of his preaching, but to counter the relentless attacks from pulpits and from a press that denied him the right of reply, he quickly realised the need for pamphlets, magazines and books. In July 1846 he published *Prophwyd y Jubili*, a monthly journal printed at Rhydybont, Carmarthenshire, by his brother John Jones. He followed this, in 1849, with *Udgorn Seion* (Zion's Trumpet). *Prophwyd* was the first Mormon magazine to be published in a language other than

English. During his first mission, Jones published a 104-page history of the Church, a 64-page hymnal, a 288-page defence of Mormon doctrine and thirty issues of *Prophwyd*. At the Rhydybont press worked a twenty-three-year-old printer and typesetter, John Davis, who, in the long hours spent setting the type for Dan Jones's publications, and reading the proofs, became captive to the teachings of the Church and requested baptism.[3] Five years later, in 1851, he translated the *Book of Mormon* into Welsh. Like *Prophwyd*, Davis's translation was a pioneer work, the first translation, other than Joseph Smith's initial translation into English of the golden plates, of the *Book of Mormon*. Samuel Evans, editor of the anti-Mormon Baptist periodical *Seren Gomer*, said it was a 'pity such a valuable labour in producing so perfect a translation had been bestowed upon so worthless a work as the Book of Mormon'. Unable to resist the call of Zion, John Davis would leave for Utah in 1854.

As well as preaching, and defending the Mormon position in his various publications, Dan Jones also wrote and published hymns. Early Mormon practice, followed by Brigham Young and his associates during Young's presidency in Britain in 1840, was to borrow hymns from mainstream Christianity and amend them to reflect Mormon doctrine and belief, emphasizing Joseph Smith's restoration of the gospel and the building of Zion. Aware of a need for hymns in Welsh that would appeal to Saints, Dan Jones published a collection of 139 hymns compiled especially for a service of the Saints at Merthyr in 1847. In the introduction, he noted that some of the hymns, but by no means all, had been adapted from existing ones. The authors were not named and few of the hymns would be familiar to Mormons today. John Davis also recognized the need for new hymns in Welsh and in 1849 he published a collection of 194 hymns, *Casgliad o Hymnau Newyddion*. In the introduction he pointed out that because of a rapid increase in the number of converts, and a larger number of submissions, only a few of the hymns had to be adapted. Aside from one or two hymns from other denominations that had been submitted inadvertently, nearly all the hymns had been written by Welsh Mormons. As a result, critics of the faith could not claim that they had been borrowed from 'the world'. The new collection was less catholic than the old and, by definition, more Mormon. The only well-known borrowing was the doxology, 'Praise God, from Whom All Blessings Flow'.[4]

Among the notable Mormon converts in Wales was Dewi Elfed (David Bevan Jones), a charismatic Baptist preacher who delivered most of his Gwawr Chapel congregation, in Aberaman near Aberdare, to the faith. Elfed could fill large halls, and if there was an overflow he would preach near an open window so that those standing outside could hear. He preached with great fervour and he is said to have caused 'an agitation among the people'.[5] Elfed also wrote hymns (157 of those in the 1852 hymnal were his) and he contributed regularly to *Udgorn Seion*. He also claimed, as his converts, a majority of the more than 700 Welsh Saints who left for America in May 1860.

In April 1851 he had been baptised in the River Cynon (with four others) before 2,000 spectators, by William Phillips, president of the Saints in Wales. Following the baptism, he was inducted as a priest of the Church of the Latter-day Saints in Gwawr Chapel. It was great theatre and a coup for the Mormons, leaving them with a chapel, a baptised minister, and wide publicity. Of all the Nonconformist denominations, the Baptists were the most implacable in their opposition to the Saints. For his espousal of Mormonism, and proselytizing from a Baptist chapel, the Baptist Association excommunicated him and, presumably for their espousal of Elfed, the entire Gwawr congregation. The Association eventually repossessed Gwawr Chapel (which Elfed had refused to leave) after a successful lawsuit and a demonstration by 2,000 Baptists, but it lost most of Elfed's congregation.

Accused, but not convicted, of 'financial irregularities',

Elfed was stripped of office in the Mormon Church in 1855 but he escaped excommunication and in 1860 he left for Utah with his wife and two of their children. He settled in Logan, about 100 miles north of Salt Lake City, and died there in 1863.

Some of the later Mormon missionaries to Wales borrowed a leaf from the Wesleys' book. Joseph Hyrum Parry and his friend and fellow missionary George Emery, from the same ward of Salt Lake City, would stand on street corners in towns and villages in north and mid Wales every day through the summer of 1878 and begin to sing. 'I had a strong voice to carry the air of our favourite hymns, and George put in a fine bass, so we gathered a crowd pretty promptly when we found a promising location.'[6] Joseph Hyrum Parry was the son of John Parry, the founding conductor of the Mormon Tabernacle Choir.

In the October 1848 issue of *Prophwyd y Jubili*, Dan Jones announced that he had received permission to accompany the first contingent of Welsh Saints on their transatlantic journey. In that same issue there was a siren song, 'Hail to California' (California described the entire territory between the Rockies and the Pacific), to be sung by the Saints as they sailed away. The composer isn't credited but it is assumed to have been Dan Jones.

> When pestilence is harvesting the countries –
> Harvesting man like the grass of the field;
> When its foul breezes blow
> Laying waste the green earth,
>   California,
> Yonder across the distant seas for me ...

To which the Baptists replied, in *Seren Gomer*:

> Oh, come to California,
> Dear Welshmen, dear Welshmen
> Stand here no longer,

Dear Welshmen;
There are heavens for us there,
We shall have land without rent or taxes,
...
Dear Welshmen, dear Welshmen,
Do not tarry except for that,
Dear Welshmen.

We can get corn without sowing or harrowing,
Everyone believe, everyone believe.
And bread without baking it,
Everyone believe ...

Ignoring the barb that California was a chimera or a Land of Cockaigne, by December 1848 more than 300 Welsh Saints had declared themselves to be candidates for the emigrating party. Some were leaving for economic reasons but others, like many of the early dissident emigrants from Wales, were genuinely seeking Zion. The itinerary called for the emigrants to meet in Liverpool on 15 February, north Wales's Saints travelling independently and south Walians assembling in Swansea two days earlier and sailing by steamer to Liverpool. South Wales's denominations, from whose ranks most of the converts had been drawn, were incensed, and Swansea itself, agitated by repeated harangues from the pulpits and the press, was in a fever of expectation. In Merthyr there was violence. Dan Jones's house was attacked every night for weeks before his departure, forcing him to leave secretly. The *Cambrian* issued a detailed report of the exodus:

> Emigration to California. – The Latter Day Saints. On Tuesday last, Swansea was quite enlivened in consequence of the arrival of several wagons loaded with luggage, attended by scores of the 'bold peasantry' of Carmarthen shire, and almost an equal number of the inhabitants of Merthyr and the surrounding districts, together with their families. The formidable party were nearly all 'Latter Day Saints,' and came to this town for the purpose of proceeding to Liverpool in the *Troubador* steamer, where a ship is

in readiness to transport them next week to the glittering regions of California. This goodly company is under the command of a popular Saint, known as Captain Dan Jones, a hardy traveller … He entered the town amidst the gaze of hundreds of spectators, and in the evening he delivered his valedictory address at the Trades Hall … Amongst the group were many substantial farmers from Brechfa and Llanybydder, Carmarthenshire; and although they were well to do, they disposed of their possesions to get to California … where their fanaticism teaches them to believe they will escape from the general destruction and conflagration that is shortly to envelop this earth … Their faith is most extraordinary. On Wednesday morning, after being addressed by their leader, all repaired on board in admirable order, and with extraordinary resignation. Their departure was witnessed by hundreds of spectators, and whilst the steamer gaily passed down the river, the Saints commenced singing a favourite hymn. On entering the piers, however, they abruptly stopped singing, and lustily reponded to the cheering with which they were greeted by the inhabitants.[7]

In a letter to *Udgorn Seion*, G.W. Phillips added: 'When the emigrants were about to leave the town, through permission of the captain, they sang "The Saints' Farewell" very beautifully, attracting unusual attention of the observers. Great respect was shown to the occasion by the crowd in general, and many handkerchiefs were being waved in nearby windows.'

Dan Jones described their departure from Liverpool on the *Buena Vista* nine days later. At Liverpool the group had to be divided, 249 sailing on the *Buena Vista* and 77 on the *Hartley*. 'On Monday, the 26th of February, about two o'clock in the afternoon, we set sail from the port, and all the Saints, accompanied by the harp, sang [not "Hail to California"] "The Saints' Farewell" as we left the dock.'

> Farewell now to everyone;
> We shall sail the great ocean,
> In complete longing for God's Zion,
> For it is better to go the land
> Given to us by our Father;

We have lived captive for too long.
Freedom has come to us in the wake of adversity,
We have been called out of Babel
…
Our God, through His great grace,
Will bring us safely to His seemly Zion.

John Davis

The 'sweet voices' of the singers, Jones continued, 'resounded throughout the city, attracting the attention of, and causing amazement to, thousands of spectators who followed us along the shore as if charmed'.[8] William Phillips, who accompanied the Swansea Saints to Liverpool, added: 'On this occasion [at Liverpool], the harpists and singers had a place on the captain's cabin, to sing the "Saints' Farewell" for the last time, when crowds congregated to listen to their music and to be eyewitnesses of their departure to California. They went,' he concluded, 'singing over the ocean / Without a single fear in their breasts'.[9] For departing Welsh Saints the precedent had been set by a group emigrating on the *Metoka* from Liverpool to New Orleans in 1843. As the ship left the Mersey for the sea lanes, the Welsh Saints on board began to sing, so intensely, according to one report, that it moved to tears the bystanders lining the docks.

At sea, the Welsh Mormons were as committed to hymn singing as the Moravians. 'Notwithstanding the roughness of this wintry passage,' noted a passenger on the *Buena Vista*, 'we continued to be a devotional people. At dusk the bugle called all hands to prayer again, by wards … Our evenings, after meetings until bedtime, were spent in singing the songs of Zion, after which the men [went] on deck, while the females retired.' The routines seem to have been similar on all the Mormon vessels. On the *Samuel Curling*, the 703 Welsh converts rose at five for morning prayers, followed by daily ship-cleaning duties: scraping decks and cleaning berths. At dusk, there were prayers and evening meetings followed by singing. One

Sunday in 1863 a violent storm overtook the *Amazon* when ward meetings were being conducted on a lower deck. Water poured down the hatches before they could be closed and one sail was 'torn to ribbons like paper'. The Saints remained as composed as the Moravians. The second mate was heard to exclaim how astonished he was at the 'nonchalance displayed by the sisters in such a season of apparent peril'. The *Amazon* sailed from London with a complement of English and Welsh Saints and docked at New Orleans seven weeks later. Among the Welsh Saints was the entire membership of a brass band from Cardiff.[10]

Until railways reached the American West, Saints from Wales landed at New Orleans and then travelled by river steamboat up the Mississippi to St Louis where another vessel took them up the Missouri to Council Bluffs. At Council Bluffs the *Buena Vista* party divided into two sections, one group going directly to Utah in twenty-four wagons and the rest remaining at Winter Quarters, Council Bluffs, to assemble equipment and provisions and serve as advisers and translators for the next party of monoglot Welsh. Even those going to Utah that season required about eight weeks to get teams, wagons and supplies ready for the crossing. The several hundred Welsh migrants who were either making preparations for the journey west, or settling in for the winter, needed a church, so they built a tabernacle. It was the first Welsh-language branch of the Mormon Church in America. When Winter Quarters was no longer required, the Saints moved west and in the late 1850s floodwaters washed the building away.

After 1856, Utah-bound converts could land at New York or Boston and entrain (some of the *Samuel Curling*'s passengers did so in cattle cars) to Iowa City, then the western terminus of the Rock Island Line. From Iowa City, they walked and hauled handcarts to Utah. Brigham Young calculated that handcarts reduced the cost of the 1,400-mile trek by one third and, especially in the case of Saints unused to handling oxen and wagons, they speeded the journey. The 300 Welsh Saints who sailed from Liverpool in April 1856 on board the *Samuel Curling* made up the third handcart company.

Led by Edward Bunker, an experienced trekker, the Welsh Saints left Iowa City on 28 June with sixty-four handcarts and a number of ox-drawn supply wagons. Few could speak English, and as former miners, ironworkers and labourers, they had no experience of camping or handling oxen and mules. According to Bunker, some could not identify their own teams in the morning and had to be taught how to handle a whip, how to hook and unhook the animals, how to cajole them when driving over rutted trails, and to how to care for their hooves when they became sore – lessons made more difficult by the general lack of English.[11] Like most of the Mormon emigrants, the Welsh Saints knew almost nothing of the geography and climate of North America. Convinced, according to explorer Sir Richard F. Burton, 'that a gay summer reigns throughout the year in Zion,' many of the Welsh Saints discarded their blankets and warm clothing during the crossing of the plains.[12]

The Welsh, however, learned quickly and, as atonement for whatever clumsiness and inexperience they brought to overland trekking, and whatever frustrations caused by the incomprehensibility of their language, they could sing. Singing became their signature as they gathered around the camp fires at night. 'The Welsh are holding up under the difficulties of this journey, and are learning to drive oxen better than my expectations, and are winning praise from all other camps of the Saints for their organization, their virtue and their skill, and especially for their singing.'[13] In a letter from Kanesville, Iowa, to William Phillips and John Davis in Wales, William Morgan quoted a letter from Dan Jones and others: 'They are happy and content [the Welsh Company] and make the camp resound with their evening song.'[14] Morgan then added a footnote of his own:

I am an eye and ear witness to that. I think, as do the Apostles, that the spirit of music has descended on them from out of the evening before their departure from the territory of the Honuhous. About six o'clock Friday afternoon, Bro. Jones ordered me to call the camp together for the purpose of reading the rules of the journey. [After the rules had been read] word was given out to sing to close the meeting. As we sang the first part of the verse, that is, 'When the Saints shall come, etc.,' we saw the English and the Norwegians and everyone, I would think with their heads out of their wagons. With the second part the wagons were empty in an instant and their inhabitants running toward us as if they were charmed … Some asked me where they had learned and who was their teacher. I said that the hills of Wales were the schoolhouse, and the spirit of God was the teacher. Their response was, 'Well, indeed, it is wonderful; we never heard such good singing before.'[15]

The portal to the valley of the Great Salt Lake was a large canyon, Emigration Canyon, which opened on to a grass and shrub-covered bench that sloped gently down to the valley bottom and the city itself. From the city, spiralling columns of smoke-like dust thrown up by the wheels of the wagons or the handcarts signalled the approach of an emigrant train as it crossed the dry bench-land. In preparation for their grand entry to the city, the men and boys had changed their clothes, washed and shaved, and the girls and women were in their best Sunday dresses. Although weather-beaten and deeply sunburned they arrived, in Sir Richard F. Burton's account, shouting and laughing joyfully and singing hymns. Crowds of well-wishers on foot, horseback, or in traps and buckboards, escorted them into the centre of the city. William Hepworth Dixon, a writer and traveller who also edited the *Athenaeum*, left a similar but somewhat grittier portrait of the arrival of a mixed group of English and Welsh emigrants:

[The emigrant train] had just arrived, with sixty wagons, four hundred bullocks, six hundred men, women, and children, all English and Welsh. The wagons fill the street; some of the cattle are lying down in the hot sun; the men are eager and excited, having finished their long journey across the sea, across the States, across the prairies, across the mountains; the women and little folks are scorched and wan; dirt, fatigue, privation give them a wild, unearthly look; and you would hardly recognize … the sober Monmouth farmer, the clean Woolwich artisan, the smart London smith.[16]

In Utah, Welsh immigrants were prized, and there were many of them; by 1850 the official historian of the Mormon Church estimated their number at 25,000.[17] On both the ocean and land crossings they were generally admired for their sobriety, cleanliness, and willingness to work and, no small asset in the eyes of the Mormon leaders as in those of the wagon masters on the trail, most of them could sing. Moreover, they arrived after many months of near daily hymn singing sessions at sea and around camp fires on the plains. Brigham Young welcomed personally Dan Jones's second party of 700 immigrants, and in an unusual step offered them the hilly north-east section of the city (the foothills of the Wasatch Mountains) which he thought would remind them of home.[18] But the Welsh, presumably tired of hills, chose level land some five to eight blocks west of Temple Square in a section referred to for many years as New Wales. Given that, in the interests of harmony, rapid assimilation in mixed communities rather than the convenience of particular cultural groups was Young's objective, favourable treatment appears to have been a major concession.

Choral and congregational singing had been an important part of Mormon worship from the outset. Joseph Smith had encouraged both at Kirtland and Nauvoo, and 'after some altercation' with members who regarded trained choirs as divisive and the work of the devil, he managed to establish a singing school.[19] Brigham Young, his successor, was no less enthusiastic about music in the Church, and about choral singing in particular. Aside from the need for sacred song at the frequent association meetings and semi-annual conferences, singing was an essential ingredient of Young's recipe for a contented society. According to Young, societal contentment rested on two foundations: health and harmony. Harmony depended on a shared faith reinforced by group activities such as communal dancing and singing. Young sensed that in a diverse society, moving rhythmically together and singing harmoniously in groups were the surest ways of creating community.

Young himself sang, as did his wives and children, and in the Young household they all sang together. Brigham also, as he noted in one of his talks, sang (in company) for Joseph Smith: 'After we returned from Missouri, my brother Joseph Young and myself had been singing after preaching in a meeting; and when the meeting was dismissed, brother Joseph Smith said, "Come down to my house with me." We went and sung to him a long time.'[20] He declared his love of harmony in a speech at the dedication of the Salt Lake Theatre in 1862: 'Sweet harmonious sounds give exquisite joy to human beings capable of appreciating music. I delight in hearing harmonious tones made by the human voice, by musical instruments, and by both combined.' In public choral performances, he preferred the oratorios of Handel, Haydn, and Mendelssohn and the masses of Mozart and Beethoven.

Like many pioneers from the eastern states and Europe, Smith and Young had forebodings about the cultural wasteland facing them in the West. As foils against the fearful levelling effects of the frontier, pioneers of all faiths and persuasions often carried with them musical instruments (even pianos) and classics of literature such as Bunyan's *Pilgrim's Progress* and complete sets of Shakespeare. In Nauvoo, Joseph Smith articulated the general apprehension: 'Coming as we did from a highly cultivated state of society in the east, and standing now upon the confines or western limits of the United States, and looking into the vast wilderness of those that sat in darkness;

how natural it was to observe the degradation, leanness of intellect, ferocity and jealousy of a people that were nearly a century behind the times, and to feel for those who roamed about without the benefit of civilization, refinement, or religion.'[21] In each of their major settlements on their exodus west, the Saints built attractive tabernacles and established singing schools, bands and choirs. The charter authorizing the city of Nauvoo to found a university made provision for a department of music. The same charter also granted permission to organize a militia. To provide martial music, the militia quickly organized a fife and drum core that became the Nauvoo Brass Band.

Critics of Mormonism regard Brigham Young's encouragement of choral and congregational singing, and group activities in general, as a form of conditioning, however well meaning. Elsewhere in America, immigrants exchanged their old lives for new ones of relative freedom, but in Utah they moved into tightly structured communities where the pressures to conform were great. Saints danced in lines and groups, not couples, and they sang together, not singly. For the Mormon leaders, the Salt Lake Tabernacle Choir represented the pinnacle of Mormon cultural achievement.[22]

Young also believed that singing would promote health, his second requirement for a contented society. Throughout his life, he had suffered from bouts of 'lung fever'. His mother and several of his wives, including a bride of his youth, had died from consumption. The most effective antidotes, recommended by all American and European physicians in the absence of a scientific understanding of disease, were fresh air and exercise. To these, the American physician Benjamin Rush (d.1813) added robust singing: 'The exercise of the organs of the breast, by singing, contributes very much to defend them from those diseases to which our climate, and other causes, have of late exposed them.' He also claimed that singing could restore victims of consumption, or tuberculosis, to full vigour. In Utah,

Rush's ideas acquired currency in the 1840s through a Mormon apostle and proselyte, Wilford Woodruff. Tuberculosis, in fact, is transmitted by airborne droplets discharged from the mouth during coughing, sneezing and singing, but without knowledge of the transmission of the disease Rush's antidote remained current until the early years of the twentieth century. In an article in the *British Medical Journal* in June 1911, John Frederick Briscoe, a physician and chorister with the Alton Choral Society, recommended singing as a preventative of consumption and diseases of the lungs in general. Members of his own choral society seemed unusually free of throat and chest infections and he thought this could not be coincidence. As prophylactics, Briscoe recommended sight reading classes in particular: he considered them effective in keeping mouths and air passages clear of disease as well as maintaining mental health and good spirits. 'Is there,' he concluded, 'a nicer way of sterilizing the air passages and maintaining them in health than singing the musical scale in harmonious concord in a well-ventilated room or in the open air?'[23]

Early in his presidency, Brigham Young promoted the virtues of exercise and fresh air, pointing out that 'when people are obliged to breathe confined air, they do not have that free, full flow of the purification and nourishment that is in the fresh air, and they begin to decay, and go into what we call consumption'. Confinement of students to their desks would, he feared, restrict breathing and ruin their health. In Utah, as in other parts of America, vocal training came to be seen as part of a programme for general health. In June 1858, *Deseret News* published an article from *Musical World* ('Vocal Music Corrective to Health') based on Rush's principles. The result was a proliferation of singing classes and schools in a movement led by Scotsman David Calder, secretary to Brigham Young. Calder had been trained in the Hullah system of note reading and later had converted to tonic sol-fa. Troubled by the prevalence of lung afflictions in the West, and their heavy toll on life, he had written to an aunt: 'In my visits to the cemetery I found that almost all the causes of death were the diseases of consumption and the lungs.'[24] Encouraged by Brigham Young, Calder founded a singing school that attracted hundreds of students and became more or less an official arm of the Church. He was as convinced as Briscoe about the benefits of singing to health:

> It is an established fact that singing is conducive to health. Nothing is better calculated to produce the power of free and lengthened respiration; and as one of the best preventives of, and surest remedies for, weakness of the chest, vocal music stands pre-eminent. It imparts vigor to the organs connected with the lungs, and thereby conduces to a healthy state of every part of the body.[25]

Calder's singing association made its first public announcement at a parade in July 1862. To demonstrate the contrast between tonic sol-fa and traditional notation, the singers carried two banners, one depicting the old-notation, the other tonic sol-fa. The inference: that the new singing method represented the triumph of simplicity and finesse over complexity.[26]

Building on practices in Nauvoo, where choirs sang at the general assemblages of the Saints, Brigham Young invited John Parry, a passenger on the *Buena Vista*, to form a choir. Born in Flintshire in 1789, Parry was a stonemason who later became a Baptist preacher before joining the Campbellite or Apostolic Church, a rich source of converts to Mormonism but one, paradoxically, opposed to musical training.[27] On hearing of John Parry's conversion and decision to emigrate, Dan Jones expressed his delight in *Prophwyd*, lauding Parry as an ardent revivalist and a giant in the search for truth. Parry could also sing and play the harp, the piano, and the flute, and on the trek west from Winter Quarters, in 1849, with Campbellite prohibitions behind him, he almost certainly led the hymn singing of the Welsh Saints.[28] In Salt Lake City, after leading 85

Welsh converts in hymn singing at the October conference that same year, Brigham Young asked him if he would do the same at future conferences. Parry's choir, which sang well-known hymns in Welsh as well as new Mormon hymns set to familiar Welsh tunes, was the nucleus of the Mormon Tabernacle Choir.[29]

As a working stonemason, Parry was only a part-time conductor. He built a number of houses in Salt Lake City and he and his son Caleb, hired by Brigham Young, helped build a fifteen-foot wall around Temple Square. John Parry was present at the laying of the cornerstone of the Temple in 1853 that Caleb would later (1853–55) help to build.[30] Parry's choir might not have satisfied the purists but a visitor to a Church conference in 1852 wrote of its power to 'exhilarate all present by singing one of their [Welsh] hymns, to one of their charming, wild, romantic airs'.[31] At times of heightened expectation, Mormon choral and congregational singing could be transcendental. 'Singing with the spirit,' according to some accounts, 'brought down angels' and during the singing at the Manti Temple dedication in 1888 people reported, as in Wales during the Revivals, hearing an unseen heavenly choir.[32]

Parry's choir first performed in the Bowery, a temporary outdoor auditorium with heavy timber posts and a brush and earth roof, in the temple block reserved for religious and civic meetings. Burton described it as a 'kind of "hangar", about a hundred feet long by the same breadth, with a roofing of bushes and boughs supported by rough posts, and open for ventilation on the sides; it can contain about 3,000 souls. The congregation is accommodated upon long rows of benches, opposite the dais, rostrum, platform or tribune ... Between the people and the platform was a place not unlike a Methodist "pen" at a camp meeting.'[33] The Bowery's replacement, the 'Old Tabernacle', from which Parry's choir, strengthened by members from the former choir at Nauvoo, took its name, was a large, squat adobe structure, partially underground, with a sloped wooden floor that flooded after heavy rains.

The New Tabernacle, completed in 1867, was even larger, with a domed wooden roof in the shape of an overturned boat or ark, supported by external sandstone piers that enclosed a large elliptical hall with a pulpit, wooden pews, choir seats and a huge organ. Chapel-like, and with excellent acoustics, it was a true theatre for the vocal arts. The domed structure and the elliptical design focused sound and carried it effortlessly to the far end of the building. Adelina Patti, the first celebrity to sing in the Tabernacle, in April 1884, declared it 'as easy to sing in as any parlor'. Billed as 'the greatest singer in the world', she attracted an audience of 7,000. Six years earlier she had bought Craig-y-Nos, a large Victorian house on the Tawe near Abercraf.

So determined was Brigham Young to have choirs and bands in all Mormon settlements that he seeded each new colonizing group with musically gifted members, his 'musical missionaries' who would lead choirs and form bands. Occupation, however, governed the general disposition. Former miners went to the coal districts and farmers to the agricultural communities. 'We will set the Welsh boys to get the ore in the mountains,' ran one directive, 'and then set the Sheffield boys to work in fixing it up into tools'.[34] To encourage community, farmers lived in compact villages, not on isolated farms as elsewhere in America. Mormon communities, no matter how small, usually had a band and a choir, the desire for controlled, harmonious singing outweighing the Methodist fear of cleaving the congregation. But at virtually every Mormon meeting the congregation sang hymns.

Wherever the Welsh settled, bands and choirs inevitably followed, or existing ones flourished. Within a year of his arrival at Ogden, in 1863, William Pugh, who was an accomplished musician, found himself conducting the Ogden Tabernacle Choir as well as the Ogden Brass Band. Pugh had been first cornetist in the Cardiff Brass Band that, induced by Bishop West, emigrated as a group on the *Amazon*. He brought with him manuscripts of well-known oratorios and masses, and to improve singing standards, so that they might be performed, he introduced tonic sol-fa classes. These were held at first in an adobe school building but they grew so large that he moved them to a bigger hall with seating for 200. His Choral Union, formed in 1874, was soon singing 'The Heavens are Telling' from Haydn's *Creation*, the 'Hallelujah Chorus' and the 'Union Battle March' from Faust. None of these had ever been performed in Ogden and no choruses of any kind had been sung with such power. Practising choristers could be heard from several blocks away. Pugh's choir at the Ogden Tabernacle was good enough to alternate with the Salt Lake Tabernacle Choir at general church conferences. At Brigham Young's funeral, Pugh played a cornet solo.[35]

Another of Brigham Young's musical missionaries was the blind harpist Thomas Giles, a member of *Samuel Curling*'s Welsh handcart company. Giles, a former coal miner in south Wales, had been blinded by a head injury from a roof fall in 1848. Sometime after his accident the Mormons gave him a harp. He served the Saints as a conference president in Merthyr, sailing for Zion in 1856 with his wife and three children. En route his wife and a baby died, and although Giles was able to walk and help pull a guided handcart, the journey from Iowa exhausted him. He became so ill that he was left for near dead, with two men assigned to bury him, at Fort Bridger, 115 miles from Salt Lake City.[36]

The handcart company moved on, expecting that Giles would die within hours. They had not reckoned, however, on the ministrations of Parley Pratt, a former missionary to Britain who happened to be returning on the same trail with a group of eastbound missionaries from Salt Lake City. When Pratt came upon Giles he blessed him. Giles recovered, caught up with the company with the help of his burial detail, and reached Salt

Lake Valley in October 1856. He moved to Ogden, 230 miles north of Salt Lake City, where he played the harp and led the community singing of hymns and popular songs. In the absence of hymnals, Mormon communities often resorted to lining out, 'old way singing', that was eventually replaced by 'regular' or 'continuous singing'. Someone who knew the melody started to sing and the congregation, once they recognized the tune, joined in. With a letter of introduction from Brigham Young, Thomas Giles travelled around the state, giving concerts and playing for dances. His sons travelled with him. Hyrum played the violin and Henry the piano and organ. All three sang beautifully. In 1869 Thomas Giles led the Salt Lake Tabernacle Choir at the Weber Stake Conference. His harp is now in the Daughters of Utah Pioneers Museum in Salt Lake City.

John Parry led the Salt Lake choir until 1854 but it was not until after his death, in 1868, that it became a formally organized choir. Early leaders of the Tabernacle Choir were musical men rather than musicians, and performances seem rarely to have risen above the level of good congregational singing. Tensions created by the uncritical needs of the congregation and the more demanding requirements of trained musicians and Church leaders first surfaced in Nauvoo. Congregational singing may have helped to unify the Saints but it did not satisfy the desire for excellence in performance. The Church leaders held that only trained voices could properly glorify God and render Mormon society fit for the second coming of Christ. Leading the chorus of complainants was a former bank clerk from Savannah, Lowell Mason, who was virtually instrumental in changing the direction of Mormon music. He dismissed congregational singing as an indulgence for which 'everything that belongs in taste to music must be given up'.[37] Church leaders took heed and, although congregations continued to sing at religious and civic gatherings, choirs and formality eventually triumphed. To develop a hymn style of their own, the Church invited promising composers to submit new tunes to fit new and old lyrics. Old tunes were discarded and the new tunes, many of them very high pitched, were difficult even for choirs let alone congregations.

*

If John Parry could claim to have been the founder of the Salt Lake Tabernacle Choir, yet another Welshman could take credit for giving it professional shape. Born in Pencader, Carmarthenshire, Evan Stephens was the tenth child of Jane and David Stephens. David Stephens was a farm labourer. Persuaded by the preaching of Dan Jones, the family left for Utah in 1866 on board the *Arkwright*, and alongside 450 other Saints sang 'O Babylon! O Babylon! We bid thee farewell' as two tugs towed the vessel down the Mersey into Liverpool Bay.[38] Evan was then twelve, Welsh speaking but able to read the Bible in English. As a strong, healthy youth he found the trek by oxcart across the plains invigorating: 'The journey across the plains was such an experience of pleasure to me that I found it difficult to sympathize with pioneers who thought it a hardship. I was too elated to walk so I would run ahead, and then I would stop and wait for the crowd.' It was probably the last year when ox trains crossed the entire extent of the plains, from the River Missouri to Utah.[39] The descent from Emigrant Canyon to the Salt Lake Valley he descibed as 'the climax of the most wonderful experience of my life, Salt Lake looking like an absolute paradise'.

The Stephens family settled in Willard, Box Elder County, where Evan for the next eight years herded sheep and cattle and sang as a boy alto with the Willard Choir. Willard and Box Elder County had been popular destinations for Welsh Mormons, among them members of the Cardiff Brass Band. Evan had no musical training but he noted in his memoirs that even in Pencader singing the melody in unison held no interest for him. The choir leaders at Willard, Daniel Tovey,

David Jones, and Edward Woozley, all Welshmen, undertook Stephens's musical education. Painfully, as he put it, he acquired the language of quavers, sharps and flats and went on to work for Shadrach Jones, a Welsh stonemason and housebuilder, and a bass singer with the Willard Choir. Jones, from Llanelli, had sailed from Liverpool to New Orleans in 1849 and had settled first in Logan where he built houses from local granite and worked on the temple.[40]

While working for Shadrach Jones, Stephens began to compose on his brother Thomas's four-octave cabinet organ, and shortly before his nineteenth birthday he was asked to direct the Willard Choir following the departure of Edward Woozley. Brigham Young had sent Woozley to Malad, a preponderantly Welsh Mormon settlement in Idaho that needed a music and school teacher. For Stephens, the novice choir director, it was a baptism of fire. An invitation to sing with the Tabernacle Choir in Salt Lake City required the Willard Choir to learn twenty-four hymns and anthems in two months. Two missionaries, who preached one afternoon at the Willard meeting house, were intrigued by a beardless youth of eighteen leading the choir from his organ stool, playing with his hands and feet, and directing the singers with his head.[41]

In 1880, at the age of twenty-five, when working by day as a railway section hand and a blacksmith's striker, the town of Logan invited him to be their full-time music teacher. For two years he taught and composed and, with the money saved, left to study the organ with the Tabernacle organist in Salt Lake City. Once settled, he approached the Sunday School Board for permission to teach singing-by-note at no charge to children from Sunday school classes in the city. To impress members of the Board at his meeting with them, he offered to sing, and after two songs they applauded enthusiastically. Stephens had found his métier. Children loved him. 'Evan Stephens's pupils not only stick to him, but they accumulate. The number already exceeds 800 and still they choose to join his singing classes. He says he will not take more than one thousand till some of his present pupils are able to assist him in teaching.'[42] For Brigham Young, who died in 1877, the numbers would have been the fulfillment of a dream: hundreds of children sight-reading and singing in the dry, health-giving Utah air. To close their concerts, Stephens led them in singing 'Hen Wlad fy Nhadau', the Welsh national anthem.

While the Salt Lake children's choir blossomed, the Tabernacle Choir wilted, losing members and failing to achieve the professionalism that the Church leaders coveted. Older members had retired, and by 1890 many of the younger male members were in gaol or exile as a result of the federal government's outlawing of polygamy in 1882. As a lifelong bachelor, Stephens was not affected. To halt the decline, in October 1890 the Church elders invited him to direct the Tabernacle Choir. Within six months of his appointment, membership increased from 100 to 300. To accommodate the increase, the west end of the Tabernacle had to be re-modelled. Seats were added and in the process slight improvements were made to the acoustics. Under Stephens the new choir flourished. In 1891, the singing at Tabernacle services overwhelmed W.L. Page, a visiting Presbyterian minister from Rochester, New York: 'Let me do the Mormon music full justice. The second hymn sung by this most wonderful trained choir, a single choral tune of fine harmony, surpassed anything in the way of sacred music that I ever heard in my life. It paid me my journey across the continent and will linger in my memory till the hour I hope to go up to hear higher music and song.'[43]

To confirm his status as director of the Tabernacle Choir, in 1892 the Church elders invited Stephens to compose a hymn (that he named 'Hosannah') for the dedication of the Temple the following year. As the author of a hundred hymns, he would be the most productive of all the Mormon composers. National recognition of the choir occurred at the same time as the confirmation of his own position. Chicago had undertaken to host, in 1893, the World's Columbian Exposition marking the 400th anniversary of the discovery of America. The exhibition, popularly known as the World's Fair, would also celebrate American enterprise and art. Even before the public announcement of the fair, prominent Welsh-American businessmen began to plan an event that would showcase Welsh cultural achievements in both America and Wales. The obvious vehicle, given its popularity in both countries, was the eisteddfod, and one, because of the dying interest in Welsh literary competitions in America, that would highlight choral singing. The event would be organized by the Cymmrodorion Society of Chicago under the general direction of Maesteg-born William ap Madoc, a musician, publisher and poet. Chicago at the time had about 3,000 Welsh residents. 'Nothing,' Ap Madoc declared, 'will tend more to elevate the Welsh name than to hold a four-day international Eisteddfod on such an occasion'. In response to a suggestion that the event should include 'games', he retorted: 'Our "games" are intellectual ones. All racing, ball-playing, quoit-throwing, etc., during the Eisteddfod days at least, we shall leave entirely in the possession of our Keltic cousins.'[44]

To involve Wales in its plans, the Chicago committee invited the National Eisteddfod of Wales to hold the 1893 eisteddfod in Chicago. As the general secretary of the Cymmrodorion Society's organizing committee and the chief instigator and architect of the event, Ap Madoc assured the National Eisteddfod committee that the Chicago eisteddfod would be big enough 'to include the Welsh of both continents'. In his written invitation to the eisteddfod organizers in Wales, he could take flattery no further: 'No other nation can bring to the Columbian Exposition an institution so musical, literary, ancient and of such character as the National Eisteddfod.' The newspaper *Y Drych* was just as forceful: 'What Welshman would wish his unique national institution to appear weak in the middle of the boundless wonders and achievements of the Exposition. We must have an Eisteddfod which will be more than a thread in the quilt of the World's Fair; we must have one which will add to our brilliance as a nation.'[45] To move the National Eisteddfod from Wales would not have been unprecedented as both London and Liverpool had been recent eisteddfod venues. But the Welsh organizers of the National were unmoved, and in the vote of the governing body before the Swansea eisteddfod that year, Chicago lost to Pontypridd.[46]

As an international eisteddfod, competition in Chicago could not be restricted to Welsh choirs, but because the intention was to celebrate Welsh culture, Welsh and Welsh-American choirs would be the preferred contestants. There is no record of the Chicago committee's deliberations, but Evan Stephens's Welsh origins, the prominent role of the Welsh in Mormon music, and strong Welsh representation in the Tabernacle Choir, must have weighed heavily in the decision to issue an invitation. Though flattered, Stephens himself had misgivings about accepting it, convinced that the Tabernacle Choir would have no chance against more thoroughly trained Welsh and Welsh-American choirs. Apostles of the Church, however, must have thought otherwise. They authorized his entry and Stephens, tentatively, began rehearsals. In reaching the decision to go to Chicago, the assessment of a Welsh visitor to a Tabernacle service in 1891 may have been pivotal. He declared the performance of 'Worthy is the Lamb' from the *Messiah* to be as accomplished as anything he had heard in competition in Wales and urged the choir to look to Chicago.[47] Yet Stephens still prevaricated, all the while preparing the choir for competition.

His misgivings about an official entry multiplied when, within a few months of the Fair, the fiercely competitive Scranton choirs, who were declared contestants and clear favourites, succeeded in changing the set pieces. Stephens prepared to withdraw and yielded only after the visit of a persuasive three-man deputation from Chicago, who attended a Sunday Temple service. In the main mixed-voice competition the choir's rivals would be three Welsh-American choirs: two from Scranton, the Scranton Choral Union and the Cymmrodorion Choral Society, and one from Ohio, the Western Reserve Choir from Cleveland conducted by J. Powell Jones. In the subsidiary male voice competion there would be two choirs from Wales: the Penrhyn and Dinorwic Male Choir of quarrymen from Bethesda and the coal miners of the Rhondda Glee Society, and four Welsh-American choirs: the Wilkes-Barre Male Choir, the Iowa Male Choir, the Gwent Glee Society, from Edwardsdale, Pennsylvania, and the Salt Lake Male Choir. The latter would also be led by Evan Stephens.

As a choir director, Stephens was engagingly informal. In appearance he was more peasant than poet: gangly, with the large hands of a labourer or miner, and a powerful, prognathous jaw. His conducting style, too, was unpolished, better suited to a cymanfa than a concert hall. At a concert in St Louis, one of several stops on the way to Chicago, a reporter for the *Globe-Democrat* gave this appraisal:

> There was a lack of conventionality in the concert that both surprised and pleased the hearers. The leader read the program in an old-fashioned style that both interested and amused the people; he pulled the conductor's stand from the platform with an energy that showed that he was accustomed to wait on himself; he forgot to bow on entering and leaving, and generally exhibited unfamiliarity with the tricks of a professional conductor.[48]

The *Globe-Democrat* reporter also noted that the choir sang with a 'magnificent note of religious frenzy' that distinguished it from all other choruses, 'there is fire in their eyes, and thunder in their throats'.

For the main choral contests at Chicago, roughly 7,000 people packed the circular, amphitheatre-like Eisteddfod Hall. There was seating for 5,700 spectators, arranged in rings of seats around a sloping bowl, as well as standing room for several hundred interested contestants in the singers' gallery above the choir. Forty thousand Welsh people from the United States, Canada and Wales itself are thought to have attended the Fair. Stephens's mixed choir was placed second, between the two Scranton choirs. Both of these had been reinforced by polished singers imported from Wales. Unaware of the intensity of choral competition in Wales, H.G. Whitney, the Mormon tour manager, raised the question of imports with the chairman and secretary of the eisteddfod committee only to be told that the practice was 'perfectly allowable', given that it was 'a world contest, and that we could have enlisted Madame Patti had we liked'. Unlike today's footballers, choral singers were not 'cup-tied'. To avoid an accusation of sour grapes, a nonplussed and no doubt speechless Whitney took the matter no further.[49]

Reactions to Stephens's and the Tabernacle Choir's performance were generally favourable. The Rev. J.A. Thomas from New Haven, Michigan, wrote: 'The matchless renditions of 'Worthy is the Lamb', 'Hallelujah Chorus' and 'Lord God of Israel' are still ringing sweetly in my ears ... and had I rendered to my Celtic feelings I would have rushed forward and kissed the talented conductor for that musical feast.'[50] William ap Madoc was equally generous: 'Had the Mormon choir sung as well at the great contest as they did on the Saturday at the Grand Central Music Hall they should have easily defeated all competitors. Their work there was a masterly and magnificent effort.' More critical was the correspondent for the Chicago journal *Music*. He thought Stephens showed disdain for stage protocol, and that he conducted awkwardly, but praised his ability even though the choir went flat from time to time and seemed to lack energy.

For the eisteddfod committee, however, feeling mattered more than protocol and it invited Stephens to conduct the combined choirs in singing the 'Hallelujah Chorus' at the end of the competition.

Caradog, the conductor of the combined valleys' choir that vanquished the London tonic sol-faers, and an honoured guest at the eisteddfod, had no reservations about the quality of the Salt Lake choir. 'You have,' he told Stephens, 'a magnificent choir'. Caradog's appearance in the pavilion was the climactic moment of the eisteddfod. At the end of one chorus, wrote the reporter for the *Chicago Herald*, the applause 'was like checking the tide. Every second added to the wildness of [it].' When the furore had died a little, a young man who had come from Wales with a male choir pointed and shouted 'Dacw Caradog'. Then what had been merely applause grew into 'deafening disorder'. Twenty years after his triumph at the Crystal Palace, Caradog was brought reluctantly from the rear of the pavilion to the stage and, as he faced the audience, was cheered again and again. Then the choir on the stage, the congregation, and the choristers watching from the gallery, all 'vibrating with excitement', burst forth with the anthem 'Hen Wlad fy Nhadau'.

In a reception after a concert at the Omaha Opera House on the way home to Utah, Evan Stephens, in honour of his Welsh connections and the success of both his choirs, was presented with a life-size floral harp, sent by admirers in Salt Lake City. The city revelled in the success of the two choirs but Stephens himself seems to have remained cool and analytic. In a *Deseret News* interview, he admitted that in places the large mixed choir had gone flat a shade and, tired from pre-eisteddfod performances, had sung without sufficient energy in others, but he thought its performance good enough to have taken the first prize (it lost by half a point), 'though I say it who should not'. He seems to have been more interested in the male voice competition in which the Salt Lake choir had taken third place, behind choirs from the Rhondda and Bethesda, the latter led by Dr Edward Broome.

Welsh critics, jealous of the Rhondda choir's victory, pointed out that, thanks to a haulier's strike that paralysed the Rhondda coalfield, the Rhondda choir had been able to practice twice daily, at 2.30 and 7.30. Stephens ignored the barbs. He considered the placing an honour, given the quality of the opposition: 'The greatest compliment paid us – not excepting awarding us the second prize in the main contest – was to declare us third next to these glorious choruses.' He thought 'the contest between male choruses was magnificent, the winners from Wales singing as I never before heard mortals sing. Tone so pure, shading so perfect and full of deep meaning, enunciation so broad and yet distinct. It made me more delighted to lose the prize than I could have been to win at our present stage of progress.' The Welsh, he added 'sing with all their hearts, mind and (too often) lungs, in rehearsal and performance the same'.[51] One of the adjudicators, John Thomas, told Stephens that his choir was 'third in the male voice competition and first on this side of the ocean'.

Stephens was less complimentary about the Pennsylvania mixed choirs. He granted that they were 'magnificent bodies of singers' but under leaders who have 'a dozen times at least led them to victory or defeat at previous contests, on these and similar choruses, they should perhaps have done better'. He considered their shading to have been forced and mechanical and their enunciation 'marred by over accentuation'. He was particularly critical of the 'wild speed with which they rattled off the last part of "Worthy is the Lamb", and the first part of "Now the Impetuous Torrents Rise" ... One might mistake the first [for] a musical representation of the famous race in *Ben-Hur* and the latter [for] a hilarious "Tickling Chorus".' While praising the 'fair and intelligent' adjudication in the male voice contest, he found the adjudication of the main mixed choral event wanting in detail. His choir had been relegated to second place with no adequate explanation from the adjudicators. H.G. Whitney thought them lacking in 'mental girth', while the Mormon Church President Wilford Woodruff, who accompanied the singers to Chicago, insinuated that the contest was fixed by the Welsh organizers. Woodruff's associate, Joseph F. Smith (namesake and nephew of the Church's founder), asserted in a letter to his wife that the Tabernacle Choir deserved the first prize 'fairly and honestly' but that this was 'too much honor to confer on Utah and Mormons'.

In a letter to the *Deseret Weekly*, in late September 1893, Stephens distanced himself from the insinuations of Welsh and anti-Mormon bias, and in post-eisteddfod interviews he made no reference to the Scranton choirs' imports from Wales. But after a visit to Wales in 1900 he spoke freely and witheringly of the damaging effects of competition:

> No one can admire the many fine traits of character I find prevalent in my countrymen in Wales, more than I. Hospitable, warm-hearted, devotional, poetic, and musical – they would be ideal if they would leave beer and competition (with all its strife and haggling) alone. They are critical and truly artistic in feeling, but the long practice in the arena of the Eisteddfod, has warped their art out of shape, into undue effort at effects ... The excitable atmosphere of the occasions has gradually dulled their sense of proper demeanor at such gatherings, until today a musical contest is a pandemonium of disorder such as I have never witnessed elsewhere, instead of the magnificent stately ceremonials one's poetic fancy would paint such a noble meeting of 'bards and minstrels' to be.[52]

For Welsh culture, and for Welsh choirs in particular, the eisteddfod was a huge success. Praise was general and none more fulsome than that in the Welsh-American press. *Y Drych* and the *Cambrian* thought that the eisteddfod had not only confirmed Wales's image as a Land of Song (*Gwlad y Gân*), and the Welsh themselves as a race of singers, but that the Welsh choirs had raised choral singing to a level that no other country could match. For W.D. Davies, in his book, *America, A Gweledigaethau Bywyd*, Welsh music and traditional forms of Welsh literature had graced the stage of the grandest eisteddfod the world had ever seen. Other countries had been able to parade their talents in a single day, but it had taken Wales four.[53]

The Tabernacle Choir under Evan Stephens continued to perform at public concerts and eisteddfodau. After the Denver eisteddfod, 1897, William ap Madoc wrote to *Y Drych*: 'Again, once more comes upon us the spell of music, just as it came when this great choir stood on the platform of the World's Fair eisteddfod ... What is it that creates that spell. There is but one answer. This choir is a unit. There is a oneness and a singleness of purpose that creates its power and influence ... See how the eye watches the face and baton of Professor Stephens! See how every face ... reflects the very soul of the music ... hymn tune or oratorio chorus. To have a chorus of this kind ... to edify and entertain the multitude is a worthy innovation of the modern American eisteddfod.' At the World's Fair, Ap Madoc had written that 'the feeling that took possession of him when the choir began to sing, he should never forget'.[54] A year later, 1898, the choir performed for Joseph Parry who was an adjudicator at the Salt Lake City eisteddfod.

In 1910 the Tabernacle Choir, still under Evan Stephens, hoped to combine a concert tour of the East Coast cities with a visit to Wales to compete at the 1911 National Eisteddfod. The composer and band leader John Philip Sousa had told them that they would be a 'sensation' in New York. The choir sang in New York and in more than twenty eastern cities, including Washington and at the White House, where they had lunch and sang for President Taft. In New York they were fêted at banquets in the Waldorf Astoria and the Hotel Astor. But the excursion to Wales, due to lack of funds, had to be cancelled. The choir also recorded twelve choruses for Columbia Records marred, according to historian Michael Hicks, by Stephens's preference for the minor mode ('ponderous tempi') and an enthusiasm that sometimes masked precision. Preferring passion and feeling to precision, celebrities lined up to perform with the choir, among them a mischievous Dame Nellie Melba who asked Stephens how many wives he had. 'Not so many,' he replied with quick Welsh wit, 'but what I could take, one more'. Melba melted.[55]

After Stephens's retirement in 1916, and his death in 1930, Welsh influence on singing in Utah inevitably declined. Even so, roughly one third of the current Tabernacle Choir can point to Welsh roots, as can twenty per cent of the population of Utah, by far the highest proportion of any of the states. Welsh festivals are still held periodically in Ogden, Spanish Fork and Malad, places where the Welsh settled in numbers, and in 1993 a two-day festival in Provo, the home of Brigham Young University, celebrated the Welsh contribution to Utah culture. The highlights of the occasion were the unveiling at the Mormon Missionary Centre of a painting of Captain Dan Jones preaching in a Welsh village, commissioned by the Sons of Utah Pioneers, and a concert at Brigham Young University featuring Welsh airs and hymns sung by the Tabernacle Choir.

5

The 1904–05 Revival

HAD THE MORMON Tabernacle Choir visited Wales in 1910 they might just have detected the last faint aftershocks of the last of the great Revivals in Wales. The 1904–05 Revival was an eruption of Vesuvian proportions that shook the foundations of the country and reverberated throughout the Christian world. Lloyd George, campaigning in Wales in 1905, commented that the Revival was 'rocking Welsh life like a great earthquake'. Earlier Revivals, however powerful, were preludes: they relieved the mounting pressure but they did not blow the mountain apart. Qualitative differences also distinguished the 1904–05 Revival from its predecessors. In earlier Revivals, singing shared the stage with preaching; in 1904–05 singing was paramount. W.T. Stead, one of the Revival's most reliable chroniclers, recorded the change: 'The Revival has not strayed beyond the track of the singing people. It has followed the line of song, not of preaching. It has sung its way from one end of South Wales to the other. But, then, the Welsh are a nation of singing birds.' By November 1904 the line of song extended from Gorseinon and Treorchy in south Wales to Rhosllannerchrugog and Llangefni in the north. In the same report, Stead repeated his mantra: 'the gospel has been sung rather than preached. Whole congregations singing as if they were making melody in their hearts to God.'[1]

That this was so would not have surprised Joseph Parry. At a cymanfa in Neath that he conducted a decade before his death in 1903, the singing was so fervent that he predicted that the next Revival would be a singing Revival. 'I may not live to see it, but some of you who are here today will see it and you will recall my words.' The Revival was singular in other ways. So explosive or dramatic an event inevitably attracted attention from all parts of the Christian world. At a gathering in Nantymoel in February 1905, covered by the *Western Mail*, there were, apart from dozens of clergymen and laymen from England and Scotland, 'three ladies from Germany who did not understand even English, six French gentlemen, a lady sent from Paris by the Church ... and two missionaries on a visit to this country from China'. A similar gathering in Neath unveiled 'a lady from Silesia, a gentleman from Berlin, another from Hamburg, a lady from Germany, a visitor from Italy, several gentlemen from Scotland, a lady missionary from China and a Russian gentleman'.[2] In addition to the merely curious or interested witnesses, there were professional observers: journalists and writers from the United Kingdom, continental Europe and the United States. By reporting on the Revival from the outset, Welsh dailies, notably the *Western Mail* and the *South Wales Daily News*, were its de facto promoters, broadcasting news of gatherings throughout the country. The *Western Mail* led the way, sending reporters to the main meetings and, each month, combining their articles into a booklet. At Bangor, scores, even hundreds of readers, eagerly tracking the course of the Revival, queued to await the arrival of the *South Wales Daily News*. Among the reporters, two stood out: T.R. Davies, 'Awstin' (Welsh for Augustine), of the *Western Mail*, and W.T. (William Thomas) Stead, former editor of the *Pall Mall Gazette*. Awstin was a Baptist minister's son from Pontypridd and the former owner of a local newspaper. He was an eisteddfod enthusiast and, later in his career, a mining correspondent. Stead was English and a well-known journalist. He was also a social reformer who campaigned against child prostitution and championed women's rights. In 1912 he would die on the *Titanic*.

The two outstanding foreign commentators were Henri Bois and J. Rogues de Fursac, both French scholars. Henri Bois taught theology at a French Reformed (i.e. Presbyterian) theological college in Montauban and, although a professed Christian, he emphasized in the introduction to his book on the Revival that his approach had been that of a student of the psychology of religion, not a theologian.[3] J. Rogues de Fursac was a physician and a specialist in nervous disorders, and the author of standard works on psychiatry and nervous diseases. It is assumed that he was raised a Roman Catholic but his writing is free of religious bias. Wales, and the Welsh people, he clearly liked. 'I passed many weeks in Glamorgan, a district of mining valleys, the cradle and promised land of the Revival. I have entered into contact with this unique people who speak a language older than our dead languages; who have endured centuries of oppression without losing their distinctive and national character.' Bois was also pro-Welsh, noting English criticisms of the Revival in order, in the main, to dispute or dismiss them. An Aberaman minister described Bois as an open, honest man who had not come from France out of curiosity simply to criticize or condemn the Revival.[4]

De Fursac's book on the Revival appeared in a distinguished series containing works by Émile Durkheim, Max Nordau and Herbert Spencer.[5] In 1906 the French Home Office commissioned him to write a report on the recent Revival in Wales as an adjunct to a study by the French Public Health Department on the effect of religious excitement upon people suffering from nervous instability. At the time, anti-clericalism was so rife in France that to contain it the Government, in 1906, severed the State's relations with the Church. Fursac's charge from the Public Health Department was to examine the effects, in Wales, of mysticism upon mental maladies.

While writing their books, neither de Fursac nor Bois seems to have been aware of the existence of the other. Both wrote fine, objective accounts; Bois – who travelled in both north and south Wales and Welsh-speaking Merseyside – a large volume of 613 pages; and de Fursac a more modest book of fewer than 200 pages. They are the most comprehensive and perceptive general accounts of the Revival. De Fursac's book appeared late in 1907, about a year after the book by Henri Bois (December 1905/January 1906). De Fursac travelled from Cardiff up the Taff valley to Pontypridd and Merthyr, then to Neath, Swansea and Bridgend, and finally to the Rhondda valley and Treorchy.

The 1904–05 Revival was also singular in its attitudes to women. Through the chapel-based temperance movement women were beginning to find a voice at a time when most platforms were closed to them. Wives and mothers were of course the chief victims of habitual and excessive male drinking. Sarah Matthews founded the North Wales Temperance Union in 1892 and Sarah Jane Rees, 'Cranogwen', its south Wales equivalent, in 1901.[6] A sister organization, the Salvation Army, which was active in Wales at the time, had made equality of the sexes a cornerstone of its operations, both of its founders, Catherine and William Booth, insisting that women could serve as effectively as men.

As soon as the Revival started, women moved quickly from its wings to centre stage, first as singers and prayer leaders, then as exhorters and organizers. Working alongside men in 'teams', they challenged the notion of separate spheres for men and women, prompting Karen Lowe, a modern feminist writer, to remark that the roots of the women's rights' movement may be found in the Christian Revivals of the late nineteenth and early twentieth centuries. W.T. Stead would have agreed. He described the adjustment of roles as 'the toppling of the hateful and unChristian ascendancy of the male. The old objection of the Welsh Churches to the equal ministry of women has gone by the board. The Singing Sisters who surround Mr Evan Roberts are as indispensable as Mr. Sankey was to Mr. Moody. Women pray, sing, testify and speak as freely as men – no one daring to make them afraid. The Salvation Army has not laboured in vain.'[7]

Aptly, the Revival appears to have been triggered by a woman. In October 1904, Florrie Evans, a young woman from New Quay, interrupted a sermon at her chapel to make an impassioned declaration of faith. The congregation, in what was an already charged religious atmosphere, followed her lead and within weeks a fever of religion had overtaken Welsh-speaking southern Cardiganshire. The Revival came to the attention of Evan Roberts, a retiring but engaging twenty-six-year-old theological student, who became its unlikely leader. The ninth of fourteen children, Roberts from the age of twelve worked as a doorboy in the Broadoak Colliery, Loughor, opening and closing ventilation doors each time trams that carried coal to the pithead needed to pass. At sixteen, despite his slight stature, he had moved up to the coalface as a coal cutter or collier. At twenty-four, in search of a trade that might take him to America, he switched to blacksmithing, but a year later he opted for the ministry and enrolled at a Bible college in Newcastle Emlyn.

He began evangelizing from his home church, Moriah, Loughor, in early November 1904, and after a few sessions so many people came to look and listen that they lined the street on which the chapel stood. Those inside the chapel remained to pray and sing until the early hours, night after night. Shopkeepers closed early to get a seat in the chapel, and tin and steelworkers came directly from their shifts, still in their working clothes. Roberts was a phenomenon whose appeal confounded the well-to-do as well as the ne'er-do-wells in the bars and taprooms. He spoke quietly and confidently, sometimes for an hour or more, but only for as long, he insisted, as the Holy Spirit moved him. He made no attempt at rhetoric, declining even to announce and read aloud the hymns, a practice that experienced preachers infused with dramatic intensity. Yet for all his diffidence and seeming indifference, or perhaps because of them, he was curiously charismatic, holding audiences as much with his penetrating gaze, that ranged methodically over the rows of upturned faces, as his voice.[8] He was quickly dubbed the Wesley of Wales, and despite his disavowal of the role of leader, the Revival came to be identified with him. He held, or appeared at, some 200 meetings but many hundreds of others were led by preachers across the country.

Roberts had no preconceived role for women at his meetings, but one evening in Gorseinon, in late October or early November 1904, he was presented with a Hobson's choice. Five young women from the district came forward to offer their talents as singers: a dressmaker, a Post Office clerk, a stonemason's daughter, the daughter of a phrenologist, and a schoolteacher who left her post without giving notice. Their offer aroused ill-natured gossip, but when evangelizing in the industrial towns and villages all the women were careful to lodge separately from Roberts in respectable homes, often those of chapel deacons and ministers. At various stages on the Revival trail they were joined by women soloists, chief among them Annie Davies from Maesteg, known as the 'Nightingale of the Revival'. Her songs, so it was said, dovetailed so nicely into the prayers and praises of the congregations that she might have been playing a touching accompaniment. Her father, Richard Davies, was a miner and the singing leader at Zoar Congregational Chapel, which Annie attended. She had also trained professionally with Madame Clara Novello of Cardiff and Harry Evans of Dowlais. Her signature hymn, 'Dyma gariad fel y moroedd' (Here is love as vast as the ocean) became the theme song, Henri Bois's 'chant d'amour', of the Revival. Annie was often accompanied, in person and in song, by her sister Maggie Davies, also of Maesteg.[9]

Working men, in general, were not as free or as willing as unmarried women to join the Revival, but a number of male soloists gave up jobs and interrupted careers to travel with Evan Roberts. Among them were Emlyn and Arthur Davies of Cefn, near Ruabon. Emlyn was a promising student at the Royal College of Music in London, with expectations of becoming an opera and concert singer, but, drawn to the Revival, he exchanged opera and oratorio for hymns and gospel songs. His brother Arthur also had a fine voice and eventually became a minister in south Wales. Another singing recruit, Sam Jenkins, a twenty-five-year-old tinplate worker and gospel singer from Llanelli, was soon dubbed the 'Sankey of Wales'. His most popular songs came from Sankey's *Sacred Songs and Solos*.[10] Evan Roberts also had a good singing voice, and he had learned to play the piano and organ. He occasionally sang a solo, but he did not lead the singing, preferring to sit in the *sêt fawr* clapping his hands and urging the congregation to sing on.[11]

From Loughor the Revival moved first to Trecynon, near Aberdare, and then on to the Garw and Llynfi valleys, Mountain Ash and the Rhondda. Meanwhile, there were simultaneous outbreaks in Merionethshire which had no ostensible connection with the southern Revival. The five female singers travelled with Roberts and, to begin the Trecynon meeting, two of them stood beside the young, handsome evangelist at the front of the chapel. Even more troubling was the introduction to the meeting. Instead of the minister announcing a hymn, as was the custom, one of the women began to sing quietly and impassionedly, tears coursing down her cheeks. The approach worked. According to Karen Lowe, a strange stillness is said to have filled the church 'like the presaging of an electric storm'.[12] Trecynon established a pattern of unorthodoxy that would mark Revival meetings. At a typical meeting the congregation gathered early, and for an hour or more sang hymns before the arrival of the principals. The chapels were packed, all seats taken, all aisles filled, and all stairs occupied, even those leading to the pulpit. In one chapel, crowded feet crushed the gas pipes, putting out the lights and ending the meeting. People who couldn't get into the chapels stood outside open windows, joining in the hymns and sometimes starting their own. After the arrival of the principals there might have been a short address and/or the reading of a chapter or a psalm. Then, as W.T. Stead reported, it was usually go as you please for two hours or more. Never was a religious movement so little indebted to leaders. There was no order of service and no set hymns, yet the meetings did not descend into chaos and confusion. Three-fourths of the meetings consisted of singing led, in Stead's phrase, by invisible hands. 'As a student of psychology,' he wrote, 'I have seen nothing like it. You feel that the thousand or fifteen hundred persons before you have become merged into one myriad-headed but single-souled personality.'[13] Awstin reacted in much the same way to a meeting at Tonna, near Neath: 'There was a Babel of voices – a beautiful harmonious Babel, though – breaking forth simultaneously in prayer and song. Often, indeed the prayer would imperceptibly glide into the singing of a stanza or two ... But such singing – singing in which there was a soul full of prayer.'

Evan Roberts himself prepared nothing in advance of his meetings, and at some meetings he did not speak at all, moving down from pulpit or platform to – if there was room – walk up and down the aisles, offering encouragement. When he did speak he made no attempt to inflame his audience with, as one observer remarked, 'the torch of rhetoric'. His addresses were simple, his language colloquial, and his thoughts, for the most part, commonplace. As a speaker, Awstin remarked, he was 'without the remotest claim to the title of orator'. He was also ungainly, walking with a springing step and arms he could not keep still. No watch kept by him, so it was said, would keep time, adding to his aura of otherworldliness.

At the meetings, hymns might be suggested by one of

the Singing Sisters, by the soloists, or by members of the congregation, in each case the protagonist singing the opening few bars. Individuals also offered prayers and confessions but if they threatened to last too long they might, as in the southern Appalachians, be 'sung down' by the congregation. 'If anyone,' Stead reported, 'carried away by his feelings prays too long, or if anyone when speaking fails to touch the right note, someone – it may be anybody – commences to sing. For a moment, there is hesitation as if the meeting were in doubt as to its decision … If it decides to listen and pray, the singing dies away. If, on the other hand, as usually happens, the people decide to sing, the chorus swells in volume until it drowns all other sound.' The most remarkable instances of abandoning the meeting to what Stead called the spontaneous Quaker impulse were those occasions when a hymn begun by the crowd outside the chapel was taken up by the people within. On one of these occasions Evan Roberts happened to be speaking and, on hearing the singing outside, he at once gave way and the singing became general. He required no convincing of the the power of song and the Revival's dependence upon it. When a Londoner asked him if he thought the Revival would reach the capital, he smiled and asked, 'Can you sing?' And in an interview with Awstin he remarked that there were two stages to a Revival, singing first, preaching and prayer second.

The singing itself was often transcendental, reporters having to strain for superlatives to convey a sense of it. W.T. Stead resorted to 'billowing waves of sacred song', the 'sacred psalmody of their native hills', and, in a longer passage, a 'marvellous musical liturgy – a liturgy unwritten but heartfelt, a mighty chorus rising like the thunder of the surge on a rockbound shore, ever and anon broken by the flute-like note of the Singing Sisters, whose melody was as sweet and spontaneous as the music of the throstle in the grove or the lark in the sky'. Once heard, he concluded, 'these hymns remain forever in the mind and the heart, just as the shell retains the sound of the ocean'.[14] Overwhelmed by one hymn singing session, R.B. Jones, in effect, downed his pen: 'The fact is, unless heard it is unimaginable, and, when heard, indescribable.' He pointed out that the whole congregation '*is*' the choir and that it was without a leader. He and others, however, did describe the process: 'Once started [a hymn], as if moved by a simultaneous impulse ... was caught up by the whole congregation almost as if what was about to be sung had been announced, and all were responding to the baton of a visible human leader.' Others commented on the uncanny bonding of the congregation: 'Conventional hymns were sung, but with a supernatural unity. Unannounced, an appropriate hymn would suddenly commence. It was as though the congregation were responding to an invisible baton – as if over one thousand individuals had gelled into one personality.' And this without the benefit of an organ accompaniment: 'No need for an organ. The assembly is its own organ as a thousand sorrowing or rejoicing hearts found expression in the sacred harmony of their native hills.'[15]

Cymanfaoedd canu during the Revival also acquired new energy. The conductor's role at a cymanfa was to complete the preparatory work of the singing classes by controlling the singers and bringing them to some semblance of perfection of form and tone. He was an instructor or singing master, not a preacher. Into this orderly pre-cymanfa world the Revival entered, in Brynmor Jones's phrase, like an 'explosive charge'. He quoted a chorister at a cymanfa in Blaengarw.

> The [afternoon] meeting began in the midst of fire. It flamed in a second. [Of singing], never was heard the note that was heard here this afternoon – volume, strength, tenderness, sweetness, harmony, adoration – and all this inspired. During the meeting, the conductor did try to rein us in a little and put a check on us for the sake of the evening service – lest we should destroy ourselves. It was of no use. They would listen only to the Spirit, and that clear, plain, fiery, audible, in the heart of the people. Girls are

praying sorrowfully: some swooning, some blanching, and paling, and others being transformed as they cried out ... Some were on their feet shouting to heaven; at times, everyone calling out at the same time. We became so unconscious of ourselves that we did not know what happened, what was said, or what was sung.[16]

At the Revival gatherings, hymns, prayers and addresses were in Welsh except in some of the heavily English-speaking urban and mining communities. Sankey's gospel songs were popular but these, thanks to Ieuan Gwyllt's translations, were usually sung in Welsh. Favourites were 'Mae d'eisiau Di bob awr' (I need thee every hour), 'Mi glywaf dyner lais' (I hear thy welcome voice) and 'Taflwch raff bywyd' (Throw out the lifeline). Although there was no order of service and no posted hymns, 'Diolch Iddo' (Thanks be to Him) was sung after each declared conversion. But whatever the hymn, usually it was only necessary for a few bars to be sung before the whole congregation joined in, the voices dropping into their separate parts.

Welsh congregational singing had no greater admirers than Henri Bois and J. Rogues de Fursac, the French scholars. Both were overcome by its quality and exuberance. First, Henri Bois:

The Welsh sing in parts, almost all the time: to listen to them, one would say, that they are a practiced and trained choir. Their singing is measured, spirited, and extraordinarily moving; and this they manage without hymn books. What is just as remarkable is that the truly Welsh hymns are complex and difficult ... But in spite of this everything proceeds powerfully, splendidly without interruption. One scarcely knows which to admire more: the high notes delivered with a crystal-like purity – and the higher the notes the more intense and limpid the delivery – or the majestic rolling bass notes which accompany the melodies ... It is as if the hymns are so much part of their substance that they are able to dispense them with sovereign ease in all manner of combinations.[17]

Bois pointed out that in any hymn book there might be 900 printed hymns and perhaps 300 printed tunes or melodies (in sol-fa) to which to sing them. The imbalance explained why, in its monthly booklets on the Revival, the *Western Mail* printed not only the opening lines of the hymns sung at a particular meeting but also the tune to which they were sung. Thus 'Diolch Iddo' might have been sung to the melody 'Bryn Calfaria' instead of the traditional 'Caersalem'. This Bois regarded as a specifically Welsh practice that he attributed to long acquaintance with the hymns and available melodies from regular attendance at chapels and Sunday schools. In no other country had he witnessed the 'sovereign liberty', the 'supreme ease' with which, without hymn books, and under the inspiration of the moment anyone might start a hymn combining it with a melody of his or her choice.[18] Often it was the women soloists, Annie and Maggie Davies, or one of the five Singing Sisters, whose antennae were finely attuned to the mood of the meetings, who began a hymn appropriate to the circumstances. Invariably the hymn would be taken up by the entire gathering, the Welsh instinct, as Bois affirmed, being to sing *avec* (with).

Bois attributed the choice of an appropriate melody to the Welsh feeling for the tune and not just the words. At a meeting in a Welsh chapel in Birkenhead, a friend who knew no Welsh was gently rebuked by a neighbour, who sat immediately below him on the pulpit stairs, for not participating in the singing. The friend replied that he knew no Welsh and therefore could not sing. His interlocutor countered with the observation that the sentiment or feeling of the hymn lay in the tune as much as in the words, and that if he could not pronounce the words then he should hum the tune. Bois contrasted this Welsh view with that of the American evangelists Torrey and Alexander, then campaigning in England, who advised their audiences to mouth the words if they could not manage the tune, an exercise Bois regarded as empty and mechanical. His book on the Revival is a revealing example of the importance of understanding the tune. No one caught the spirit of the Revival as effectively as he, yet he knew scarcely a word of Welsh.[19]

At the meetings Bois particularly liked the frequent repetition of refrains and final or favourite verses, 'that characteristic expression of Welsh fervour' as Elvet Lewis ('Elfed') wrote. The practice was as popular in 1904 as it had been at earlier revivals. At Nantymoel, in February 1904, Evan Roberts invited people to sing 'Duw mawr y rhyfeddodau maith' (Great God of countless wonders). They rose, Awstin recorded, and sang with 'intense fervour', repeating the last four lines about twenty times. At Maesteg later in the month, the refrain 'Fy nghartref sydd nawr yn y nef' (My home is now in heaven), begun by someone in the congregation, was repeated forty times. Unlike many English visitors to the Revival meetings, who found repeated renderings of the same verse or chorus to be excessive and indulgent, Bois wished that the singing would never end. The English and Anglican landlady of his hotel in Rhos, however, to whom he expressed his enthusiasm for the torrents of song, professed to be 'scandalized' by them as well as by the general disorder of the Revival meetings. For support, Bois turned to a fellow enthusiast, M. Lortscht, who considered ten or even twenty repetitions too few. The repetitions reminded Lortscht of waves crashing majestically on to a seashore, the dying waves reassuringly succeeded by the waves behind. The ocean never lost its strength. So it was with Welsh hymn singing, the singers conveying the same reassuring sense that they could repeat their refrains forever.

Henri Bois was also more tolerant than English visitors of singing in the minor mode, recognizing the suitability of its slower gait and solemn tones to the Welsh temperament. He quoted, with approval, M. Saillens, who found Welsh hymns to be solemn without being heavy and whose indefinable melancholy reminded him of dark Breton landscapes and the sadness evoked by mountains and the sea. Even for the reflective Welsh, however, minor at times could be frustratingly slow. At a cymanfa in Pontypridd, attended by Bois, the conductor brought the singing to an abrupt halt. 'You sing', he interjected, 'as if this were a burial air'. He granted that the tune was in the minor, as it was, after all, *Welsh*. He then reminded them of the jibe that the Welsh were incapable of singing Amen in any key but the minor, the two syllables A-men forming a minor third. But minor, he insisted, was not a synonym for sad. He pointed out that the hymn in question was not at all sad, inferring that they should lighten their singing, but softening his rebuke with the observation that the English did not understand that the Welsh could use the minor to express joy.[20] The conductor then demonstrated how the same minor phrase could express sorrow or joy. While not completely convinced by the demonstration, Bois conceded that the Welsh could infuse a trace of profound and penetrating melancholy into the most joyful hymns. A few years after the publication of Henri Bois's book, J. Vyrnwy Morgan would write that 'to be sad is a necessity of the Welshman's nature. More than that, he is happy in his melancholy.'[21]

Elvet Lewis, too, was in no doubt of the indissolubility of Welsh and the minor: 'The minor tunes of the Welsh sanctuary are as much a part of the people's religion as Snowdon is of the county of Arvon. Strangers have been much impressed with their sweet melancholy – as if they had come down through the funerals of the centuries, and rose heavenward from beneath a yew tree. Why they have been so studiously kept out of English tune-books … is a question worth asking.'[22] To Elvet Lewis the Revival owed the introduction of one of its greatest and most solemn hymns. When visiting Rhos early in 1905 he asked that the old hymn 'Y gŵr wrth ffynnon Jacob' (The man by Jacob's well) be sung to the tune 'Bryniau Cassia' at a Revival meeting. 'The solemn yet triumphant accents of that old Hindu tune have sounded in our ears ever since …

so tender, so solemn, and so overwhelming' wrote a grateful Brynmor Jones.[23]

J. Rogues de Fursac was no less enthusiastic than Henri Bois about Welsh congregational singing, at times finding it so accomplished that he might have been listening to a trained choir. He wrote of being overwhelmed by 'the purity of the melodic phrase, the magnificent simplicity of the harmony and the slow but very rhythmic delivery', all performed to concert standards without direction and often without organ accompaniment.[24] He also liked the sound of Welsh and, like others, thought it a language well suited to song and poetry, pursuits he regarded as intellectual sustenance for the Welsh, not just pastimes.[25] Of the hymns, he was particularly fond of Annie Davies's signature hymn 'Dyma gariad fel y moroedd', sung to the tune 'Tôn-y-Botel' (Tune in a bottle) that he had first heard sung in Pontypridd by 'hundreds of voices with deep feeling'. He described the effect as prodigious. 'I was entranced and penetrated; you sense the religious feeling as transcending this world of space and time.' According to hearsay, the tune was discovered written on a sheet of paper found inside a bottle that had washed up on the coast of Caernarvonshire. Romantically, de Fursac conjured up an image of an emigrant, overcome by emotion at the last sight of the homeland, hurriedly transcribing the melody onto a piece of paper, pushing the paper into a bottle, replacing the stopper, and throwing the bottle overboard.[26] Had de Fursac read Bois's book (published a year earlier than his own) he would have learned that 'Tôn-y-Botel' had been composed around the turn of the century by P.J. Williams of Rhos, near Pontardawe. Its original title, 'Golau yn y glyn' (Light in the valley), had been renamed by a prankster who invented the tune's maritime origin at a private soirée before it became widely known and popular with the public. Once released, the tune's progress was phenomenal. The Welsh, Bois noted, acquire music by ear and a pleasing new refrain would travel quickly. Sung by a congregation on the coast one day it might, the following day, be heard in the interior. Before long children would whistle the tune on the streets and congregations across the country would sing it in four parts. For Bois, 'Tôn-y-Botel' was a measure of the musical talents of the Welsh and the ease with which musical currents crossed the country.[27]

English and Welsh commentators were just as susceptible as foreign visitors to the singing at Revival meetings. For David Matthews, 'it seemed as if an angelic choir had come from heaven to drown the earth's sorrows in a sea of song'.[28] At Pontycymer, in February 1904, Awstin reported singing so dramatic that during the repetitions of refrains and choruses some women had to be carried out of the chapel in a state of collapse. 'The tide rose to its full height when "Marchog Iesu yn Llwyddiannus" was sung to the tune of "Ebenezer", more popularly known as "Tôn-y-Botel". The balance of parts was suggestive of a trained choir, and perfect elocution coupled with the huge volume of song, made the rendering majestic. With the singing came prayers in Welsh and English, singly and simultaneously, so that the service became simply indescribable.' At a Liverpool meeting Gwilym Hughes, a special correspondent for the *South Wales Daily News*, reported that the Rev. Robert Hughes, who had travelled from Rhos, delivered a psalm/prayer in praise of 'a God that sings', a God that saves *'dan ganu'* (through singing). Hughes also referred to a writer in a Liverpool daily who, catching the spirit of a meeting at a Welsh chapel in Birkenhead, acknowledged that the secret of the Revival lay in the power of the Welsh people to sing. At Pontypridd, James L. Brown and his party conceded that 'never before in England, Ireland or Scotland, had [they] heard such beautiful, earnest, hearty congregational singing. It seemed as if the people were all trained to sing, with all the parts going, and all the crowded gatherings were of one heart and voice ... the effect and emotion aroused is indescribable, and, if we are right, cannot be reproduced anywhere else.'[29]

Constance L. Maynard, principal of Westfield College of the University of London, attended meetings at Llansamlet and Llwynbrwydrau, both near Swansea, in January 1904. At Llansamlet she saw Evan Roberts. 'He is a strange offshoot from rough mining districts. I looked at the men around me, mostly of short stature, some with broad shoulders, cropped heads, thick skins, and hard-set, bulldog faces, and among them rises this slender stem, this shoot from another world ... Yet he belongs here ... He is their own, their very own. From this race he springs, in the miner's cottage he was born, and the coal-pit has nurtured him; he is their making, their property.' She found the singing and the meeting itself extraordinary: 'The service began in a wholly informal manner. It was all in Welsh; guttural sounds of fiercely energetic prayer ... and wonderful singing, prompt, tuneful, and exceedingly loud. Again and again came the choruses ... repeated with piercing intensity that swallowed up all else in a storm of vibrating sound. There was too much of it for my taste, breaking in as it did upon the prayers, but now and then it was exquisitely sweet, arising from some corner of the building and gathering volume as it rolled along. The whole meeting went on as if there were no audience at all, but every one was alone with God.'

Her second meeting, at Llwynbrwydrau, was six miles west of Swansea. The chapel had filled by 4.15 for a service not due to begin until 6.30. Among the early arrivals were fourteen miners who had walked the ten miles from Carmarthen and intended to walk home that evening. The singing at Llwynbrwydrau was 'even more extraordinary' than it had been at Llansamlet, 'the bass and tenor voices closing in a flood over the powerful sopranos, and making a thunderous body of sound that thrilled the very walls of the building ... Think of the congregations of our Sussex villages singing like that!' Like other observers she noted the absence of hymn books and the disregard for a set or accepted order of service, such was, she noted, Evan Roberts's determination that the 'Spirit', not he, should control the meeting.[30] As a boy James Griffiths, the Labour politician and cabinet minister, attended with his parents a Revival meeting at Betws, near Ammanford, conducted by Evan Roberts. In his seventies, Griffiths couldn't recall a word of Roberts's address but his memory of the curious spell he cast remained vivid: 'I can still see him standing up in the pulpit, tall, with dark hair falling over his face, and the quiet voice reaching the gallery as if he were singing.'[31]

The laissez-faire character of the Revival meetings, Bois, Fursac and others attributed to the power and importance of the laity in Welsh chapels and Sunday schools. These, as they had once been described, were 'ecclesiastical republics' in which there was no overall direction or leadership. Classes were led by monitors or older members who, to promote discussion, encouraged every member to speak.[32] There was no opening address and no imposition of doctrine. As in the earlier circulating schools, young and old read their Bibles in Welsh, becoming thoroughly familiar with the scriptures. With large adult memberships, the Welsh schools were unusual, and in rural districts they embraced entire communities. As centres of social life, Bois remarked, they served the same function as the café. If the preacher failed to appear at the Sunday school or at a midweek prayer meeting the members simply carried on with their readings and discussions. It may not have been the questing 'new theology' promoted by R.J. Campbell (*New Theology*, 1907), but it was an alternative to dogmatic, authoritarian and institutional Christianity.[33] With no great preachers, no promotion in the Sankey and Moody and Torrey and Alexander mode, and gatherings that ran themselves, 1904 was unique in the history of revivals.

For Bois, de Fursac and Elvet Lewis, only years of preparation in Sunday schools, prayer meetings, singing schools, and cymanfaoedd could explain the sublime singing at the Revival meetings. A decade before the 1904 Revival, Elvet Lewis noted how visitors from England and other countries were startled by the readiness of entire congregations to participate in prayer and song, not realizing that long rehearsals lay behind. 'Those prayers,' he wrote 'those refrains at meetings never to be forgotten by the stranger from near or far, were no sudden shower from the sky either: they were ordinary men and women that prayed and sang, trained in the school of long years.'[34] For Henri Bois, only an advanced state of readiness could explain the 'explosion' of sound that occurred in 1904. In a society conditioned by generations of Bible reading and hymn singing, 'a breath of wind from on high' would be enough to light the spark that kindled a Revival. Everyone in Wales, he noted, was thoroughly familiar with the most popular hymns and he thought it no coincidence that Joseph Parry should have predicted a singing Revival while conducting a cymanfa. Bois added that a minor factor not to be overlooked when examining the fervour of the Revival singing was the vigorous reaction of Welsh Nonconformists to a new school law giving special privileges to the Anglicans. He quoted the inscription on a chapel foundation stone, or tablet, reading: 'Beulah, 1905, the year of the Revival and the struggle for religious liberty.'[35]

While Bois considered the solemnity of Welsh singing to be a kind of prayer, he pointed out that the reverse was also true – that prayer in Wales could be a kind of song. This was the 'famous' Welsh hwyl that he considered the most puzzling phenomenon for all visitors from abroad. In prayers that ended in hwyl he thought there was a telling moment when the voice dropped and became scarcely audible. Little by little it increased in pitch and volume until, suddenly, the sound was continuous. Hwyl had begun. At the same time, there were rhythmic arm movements, slow at first but, at their most vigorous, not unlike the movements of a miner wielding a pick at the coalface. Bois identified several types of hwyl. The *hwyl simple* began as just described. The voice rose and increased in volume until a plateau, a certain musical height, had been reached. Speech then expanded into chanting or singing, but it was only the last word or syllable of each phrase that was truly sung. The voice remained at this level and then subsided. The second type was the *hwyl chromatique*. As in the first, the voice rose following a musical scale but, unlike the first, it continued to rise after moving from speech into chant. At the point when it seemed that the voice could go no higher, the word or phrase was repeated in a manner that reminded Bois of the repetitions of Alleluia in the *Messiah*, and the mounting cries of the martyrs in the fifth act of Meyerbeer's opera *Les Huguenots*. His third category was the *hwyl alternant* when the voice, having arrived at a musical height, remained at that level. The rhythmic phrases, ended by a sung syllable, followed each other on two notes, creating a minor third. This was always in the minor. Sometimes the prayers ended abruptly in full hwyl but more often the voice descended little by little until reaching the original vocal point.[36]

De Fursac was also intrigued by hwyl. His treatment of it, as befitted a psychiatrist, was analytical. He regarded it as an energizing force, or current, sustaining both the preacher and the congregation:

> [The Welsh are] essentially [an] emotive people and for emotion to pass into the congregation, it must appear in the officiating minister ... The first duty of the preacher is to be, or at least appear to be, moved ... Sometimes his voice becomes tearful and for a moment I really believe he is weeping. Then again the emotion grips him and he is strangled ... The tone and the gestures are more important than the words, and even I, who understands no word of Welsh, can say, I am the sermon.
>
> When the exaltation is at its height, the preacher stops and starts to chant. Words are insufficient, music is necessary. This transformation takes place progressively. As the emotion increases, so the tone rises and the inflexions of the voice become more extensive. Gradually, imperceptibly, the discourse is transformed into a kind of plaintive and very impressive chanting. This is the Welsh hwyl, or rather the external expression of hwyl.[37]

During the Revival, hymn singing could occur almost anywhere and at almost any time. One unlikely venue was the smoke-room at University College of North Wales in Bangor. A student in a philosophy class heard the singing, and at the end of the class he and a fellow student were told that the Revival had broken out in the smoke-room when someone had begun to hum 'Aberystwyth':

> Now I understood the explanation of the sound of the singing which I had heard during the lecture in our Professor's room. Away we both went up the stairs and along the corridor to a door at its far end that opened to the smoke-room. We could go no further than the door for the room was full to overflowing. About forty or fifty people were present ... When I arrived they were singing 'O! yr Oen, yr addfwyn Oen' (Oh! the Lamb, the gentle Lamb). No one was leading the meeting. No one was leading the singing. But one hymn followed another ... The meeting went on until about mid-day, if not longer. Then, about two o'clock in the afternoon, without anyone, as far as I know, arranging or announcing, a great number of students ... came to a large lecture room called the 'New Hall' ... [where] almost all the seats were taken, with about 120 to 150 present. Again, there was no one leading, but everything went on exactly as though there was a leader.[38]

In mid February 1905, students at Bala also caught the Revival fire, parading en masse in the streets, filling the spacious schoolroom of Capel Mawr and singing fervently. Several were so overcome that exams had to be deferred until the following term. At Ystradgynlais, one evening after chapel prayer meetings, a group of young men gathered in the square about 10p.m. and began to sing hymns. A crowd assembled and, instead of protesting at the noise, many residents of nearby houses left their beds and went to join the meeting, by this time in a ferment of feeling. No one worried about the early morning shift. A large procession formed, and the people made their way to Sardis vestry, singing their favourite hymns as they went. They reached the vestry about 11 o'clock and within a few minutes the meeting was ablaze, young men and women praying, singing and repeating their favourite hymns with 'indescribable intensity of feeling'.

Sometimes a chapel or prayer meeting spilled on to the streets, the revivalists going into pubs to persuade the habitues to join them in song and prayer. But the results were not always the desired ones. After a prayer meeting at Rhos, a group walked through the village and opposite the pub paused to sing 'Dowch o'r dafarn; dowch o'r dafarn ... yr awr hon' (Come from the tavern ... now this hour). After three verses of the impromptu ditty the landlady came to the door and said: 'There's nobody here. They have all rushed out of the back door.'[39] On Saturday nights in Aberdare and some of the other coalfield towns there were singing processions through the streets. In Neath, Constance L. Maynard counted 500 marching men, ten in a row, arms linked, singing 'All hail the power of Jesu's name' with 'magnificent blended voices'. There were also daytime gatherings in town centres and in market squares. Awstin reported that it was not unusual to see the market square of Caerphilly thronged, while two or three chapels were crowded to overflowing. Farmers and tradesmen came on horseback or in traps, while colliers and other workmen trudged on foot. Hundreds too, who had some distance to travel, came by car or train.[40] At Pontycymer, in November 1904, Awstin also reported that three or four hundred people gathered in front of the largest hotel and sang 'Diolch Iddo' and other familiar hymns.

Evan Jenkins of Blaenau Ffestiniog wrote to his wife after his arrival in Treorchy:

> I have arrived here [Treorchy] safely. I am writing this at midday. There is a great revival here, praying and singing in every chapel, and it is as if nobody is working here at all. Singing and praying all night through, almost, and along the street. The colliers come from their work in the morning and sing all along the road. I went

to chapel at 10 o'clock this morning; I've never seen such a place in my life, praying and singing ... I thought I was in the fair at Llan when I first went into the chapel and heard everyone speaking at once, but I soon saw I was not in a fair, but was hearing everyone sing like angels ... Everyone giving out a hymn and striking up the tune himself.[41]

There were also prayer and hymn-singing sessions between shifts in steelworks and mines. In the former they were conducted against a background of whirring wheels and the heavy lumbering of the rolls and, at night, the red glare of furnace fires. Coal mines had attracted thrill-seeking tourists for more than a century and the added attraction of hearing miners sing and pray in the echoing chambers of a mine added a touch of froideur to the occasion. For the services, colliers on the night shift remained underground until joined by those on the morning shift who came in early. An unnamed correspondent from Maesteg wrote to a London paper:

At the invitation of the management I went down the Coegnant Pit ... at Nantyffyllon. Reaching an open space called the Baltic, I saw a strange sight. Hundreds of colliers were gathered together. Some were seated on the ground, others were kneeling, and still others stood in recesses. Without waiting for a leader, one of the men started to sing 'Diolch Iddo'. This was repeated again and again. Then several prayed and then again the gallery rang with 'Guide me, O Thou great Jehovah'. As an old collier prayed in Welsh, every head was bowed. He was followed by another, who started singing 'There is a fountain filled with blood'. This was taken up with vigour, the horses on their way to the workings seeming puzzled at such strange sounds.

In some collieries the miners, at the end of the service, raised their lamps as an expression of faith. The gesture inspired Elvet Lewis's hymn, 'Lift up the Lamp for Jesus'.

With eight other visitors, Henri Bois dropped early one

morning into 'the entrails of the earth' to be met, after their descent, by the distant singing of familiar hymns 300 metres below the surface. They came to a large gallery where sixty to a hundred miners, sitting, kneeling or crouching on bended knees in a characteristic coal miner's posture, their safety lamps hanging from their belts or from props supporting the roof. After a short address, they sang John Henry Newman's 'beautiful' hymn 'Lead, Kindly Light', a choice so appropriate to the circumstances that Bois reprinted it in full. The words alone, however, could not convey the disarming effect of the miners singing softly and with contained emotion in the darkness and deep silence of the mine. It would, he admitted, have taken someone with far greater control of his emotions than he to prevent his eyes from filling with tears.[42] Readings underground could be equally moving. 'A lad', one visitor recorded, 'recited with exquisite effect the fifteenth chapter of John, in Welsh, and the melody of his uttererance came like a musical ripple on the air … It was an awe-inspiring sight to see the lamps gleaming out of the blackness of the galleries; to hear the echoes of the musical choruses of the Welsh hymns ringing through the pit. Promptly at seven the service ended, and the colliers wended their way down the tunnels into the darkness, singing with gladness.'[43]

In some mines there were underground chapels, dating from earlier revivals, in which there was seating, a lectern, and regular services. The best-known of them were in the Five and Six Foot seams, respectively 350 and 750 feet below the surface, in the Mynydd Newydd pit at Fforestfach near Swansea. These were used again in 1904–05. Management approved because the services did not interfere with the miners' shifts and, at least for a while, they improved the quality of coal. Less muck or dirty coal reached the surface and relations with the sometimes-belligerent miners were easier. The change of heart also improved the lives of the horses underground. They were no longer sworn at or kicked, at least for a while, and the hailer's commands – formerly a string of oaths – had to be re-interpreted by the animals. Beyond the pit there was also much less drinking, even to the forsaking of a dust-settling pint at the end of the shift – at least for a while.

As well as singing underground there were reports, as in earlier revivals, of singing in the air. Henri Bois cited a Miss Jeffreys who woke in the night, on two separate occasions, to a choir of angels singing admirably.[44] He quoted from a brochure by poet Edgar Vine Hall that a family in the neighbourhood of Egryn on the Lleyn peninsula also heard soft and sweet singing in the air. They were returning after midnight from a Revival meeting when suddenly, a few yards from their house, in the calm air they heard singing so unearthly that it made them tremble. A respondent in A.T. Fryer's study of the psychological aspects of the Welsh Revival also reported singing in the air:

A few days before Christmas 1904, I was riding to see some parishioners … They lived about three miles up the hillside. As I was gradually ascending I fancied I heard voices singing. I took little notice for the moment, believing it was pure fancy. Gradually the voices seemed to increase in volume, until at last they became quite overpowering. I was trying to imagine it could be nothing outside myself, as it were, but the wonderful harmony seemed to be borne on me entirely from the outside, and was as real to my senses as anything I have ever heard. I could distinguish the words distinctly. They were the last four lines of the first verse of 'Dyma Gariad fel y Moroedd':

Pwy all beidio â chofio amdano?
  Pwy all beidio â thraethu'i glod?
Dyma gariad nad â'n anghof
  tra bo nefoedd wen yn bod.

The moment the refrain would come to an end it would be restarted, the volume becoming greater and greater. To me it was an exquisite sensation. When about arriving at my destination the voices suddenly ceased. I have had no trace of the recurrence of such a thing, and never had such an experience previously. I am not given to study or dwell upon any such manifestations.[45]

In a reversal of the historical pattern, the Welsh Revival triggered a Revival in America. Every Protestant religious journal in the United States carried reports of the Revival in Wales. Welsh-American communities, such as Wilkes-Barre in Pennsylvania, were among the first to be affected, in December 1904, followed by eastern seaboard towns and cities from Philadelphia to New York during the first months of 1905. Philadelphia claimed the largest number of converts since the campaigns of Moody and Sankey. New Jersey reported overflowing churches, and Atlantic City claimed that out of a population of 60,000 only fifty people remained unconverted. By April all of New England and much of New York State had been affected. At Northfield, Massachusetts, the birthplace of Dwight L. Moody, news of the Welsh Revival prompted a wave of confessions and repentance. Further south, Louisville in Kentucky claimed the largest Revival in the city's history. In Houston, Texas, churches were crowded and gambling dens closed. Michigan reported the greatest Revival in the history of the state. In Denver, on 'Revival Day', in January 1905, the Colorado state legislature adjourned, and stores and schools closed; 12,000 are said to have packed churches and theatres for midday prayer. Except perhaps in some of the Welsh-American communities, it was not, as in Wales, a singing Revival, but the fervour ignited by Florrie Evans in New Quay rolled across the New World from New York to Los Angeles on the Pacific coast where, in a matter of days, 180,000 are said to have attended Revival services.

*

In Wales, 1905, the second and penultimate year of the Revival, ended in a crescendo of song from an unexpected and a profane stage. That winter had seen the emergence of a national rugby team that brought joy to the hearts and song to the lips of everyone in Wales that saw them play. It is a teasing irony that rugby, Wales's national game and as vital a facet of the country's identity as its proclivity for song, should have been the invention of an upper-class English public school.

From Rugby, the school where William Webb Ellis first picked up the round football, the practice of handling and running with the ball instead of just kicking it spread to other public schools and from these, in the 1870s, to St David's College, Lampeter, an Anglican foundation. Other Anglican schools in Wales followed suit, in some cases supporting local teams, but the game's greatest appeal was to the industrial workers of south Wales, the vast majority of whom were Nonconformist. Rough ball games had been a feature of Welsh life for centuries, and although tolerated and even encouraged by Anglicans as manifestations of local culture, Nonconformists in general had afforded them only a grudging tolerance. During the Revival some were undisguisedly hostile. To prevent the formation and entrenchment of a rugby club, a chapel community at the head of the Swansea Valley cut down the posts and deposited them at the local police station.[46] A number of players renounced the game and several clubs were forced to disband as a result – at least for a season. The loudest opponents of the game seem to have been zealous converts; Evan Roberts and his intimates said little, possibly taking to heart the advice of a Canadian visitor who asked what will your young men do if they can't play rugby and cricket.[47]

The national rugby team, however, was beyond censure. For the first time in its history it was successful and nothing could reduce its appeal. In the years leading up to 1905 it had won three Triple Crowns, beating each of its English, Scottish and Irish rivals in the same season. In 1905, Great Britain prepared to receive New Zealand's national team, the All Blacks, as they were dubbed during the tour. Just before leaving home, their prime minister, Robert Seddon, told them that he didn't care if they lost all their other matches as long as they beat Wales. English, Scottish and Irish teams, both at national and club level, put up no opposition, the All Blacks amassing 800 points in twenty-seven games, conceding only three tries, and keeping twenty-two clean sheets. In the seven matches before their arrival in Cardiff they had not conceded a point. Only the Welsh, it was thought, had any chance of restraining them.

Their clash with Wales, scheduled for Saturday, 16 December, was billed the match of the new century. The New Zealanders arrived by train on Thursday to a curious and welcoming crowd that filled the streets outside Cardiff station. The All Blacks were a greater draw than Sankey and Moody or Barnum and Bailey. On Friday work slowed, and on Saturday most offices and works closed so that the men could watch the game. They had been paid on Friday night instead of, as was customary, on Saturday. The atmosphere in Cardiff was said to be, as it is still on international days, electric. On match day dozens of special trains brought 25,000 supporters down from the mining valleys and in from the neighbouring coastal towns. Some 40,000 to 50,000 watched the game itself.

Before play began the New Zealanders performed the 'haka', a Maori war dance designed to strike fear into the hearts of the enemy. In the haka the players, standing in a group, brace their legs, stamp their feet, and make rapid thrusting and chopping motions with their arms, as if they were weapons, all the while showing the whites of their eyes and uttering fearsome cries. The spectators, who were seeing and hearing it for the first time, were enthralled and at its close 'thundered their approval'. A day or so before the match the *Western Mail* reported that Tom Williams, a member of the selection committee, had suggested that the Welsh players respond to the haka, if not with a war dance then with a stirring song of their own. Once the crowd had settled, the Welsh players, led by their captain, began to sing 'Hen Wlad fy Nhadau', then established as the national anthem. Within moments the crowd picked up the refrain 'and from every corner of the ground', reported Christchurch's *Lyttlelton Times*, 'rose the deep, swelling, heart-stirring chorus'. No national anthem had ever been sung in a sports ground, and none anywhere by such an enormous crowd that, thanks to the Revival, was in exceptionally good voice.

The haka and the anthem changed the tone of the proceedings and brought them into sharper focus. What had been perceived as a match between the two best rugby teams in the world was now a test of nations. No game is as territorial and as manifestly physical as rugby; the ultimate objective is to defend not just the space between two posts but, as in American football, the line itself. Cardiff Arms Park was now a darkling plain and the teams' two warring, or at least struggling, armies. Dave Gallaher, the New Zealand captain, articulated the change: the singing of the Welsh anthem, he said later, 'was the most impressive incident' he had ever witnessed on a football field, adding that it gave 'a semi-religious solemnity' to the contest. Long after the details of the game have dimmed, noted one reporter, 'the memory that will linger still vividly will be that vast chorus sounding the death knell of the All Blacks'. An English international player commented later that in Cardiff 'there was a Celtic electricity in the air' that '[threw] an invading fifteen off its balance'.[48]

Even Welsh commentators were nonplussed. 'One felt,' wrote the reporter for the *Cambrian Daily Leader*, 'as if a gigantic battery had been set in motion, for a feeling which cannot quite be described came over us as the minutes flew along. I recall putting my hand on the shoulder of a big strong man sitting in front of me, and also hastily withdrawing. He was trembling to an extent to make one feel alarmed.' And another: 'It became not merely a contest between the thirty men in the arena but between the whole 47,000 persons, from out of whose eyes their very soul seemed to pour ... it is not outside the realms of possibility ... that they can share to some small degree in having directly contributed to the glory of old Gwalia.'

On the field that gave the world what Jan Morris has called the 'mighty anthem', the All Blacks, in their hearts, must have known that they could not, and perhaps should not, win. A nation as small as their own with so much of its esteem invested in rugby and song could not have been more expectant, and defeat would have been unbearable. Mercifully, on that day, the gods of poetry and song were as vigilant as the gods of war. Not that the game wasn't Homeric. Wales won a titanic struggle by the narrowest of margins, an undisputed try to nothing scored by Teddy Morgan, a flying Welsh wing. It was the All Blacks's only defeat in their thirty-five-match tour.

After 1905, the singing of popular hymns and songs, accompanied by a military band, and followed by the national anthem, became a standard feature of pre-game festivities at rugby internationals in Cardiff. For enthusiasts, this alone was worth the price of admission. But as the chapels and Sunday schools emptied, and as day schools dropped hymn singing from their morning assemblies, the practice atrophied. 'Cwm Rhondda' and Max Boyce's 'Hymns and Arias' may still be sung during the game, but the only pre-game offering today is the anthem.

6

A Brotherhood of Song

'The Welsh male choir sound reaches parts of the human condition that other music cannot. The range of notes produced may be limited (far more limited than a mixed choir, a brass band, or an orchestra) but the range of colour and emotion is far greater.'

Dr Alwyn Humphreys MBE,
Conductor Emeritus – Morriston Orpheus Choir

RHIDIAN GRIFFITHS HAS dated the beginning of the decline of chapel culture and congregational singing from 1914. The world war, followed by another twenty-five years later, combined with increases in wealth and mobility, led to a questioning of traditional teachings and a widespread loss of faith. Chapels and churches were no longer indispensable social and cultural foci and membership slumped. Pantycelyn's hymns, which used to be on every lip, were known only to a shrinking minority. The near universal familiarity with sol-fa, inevitably, was also a casualty. The change, according to Professor Geraint Jenkins, was one of the most decisive cultural breaks in the history of Wales. He quotes a lapsed convert: 'The [1904–05] Revival was the swan-song of the old religious tradition in Wales ... the consumptive's flush of death.'[1] Only occasionally today does one hear the uplifting, full-throated sound of Welsh congregational singing. For the American author and Congregationalist minister Lincoln Jones Hartford, a passionate admirer of the Welsh in full voice, the loss is immeasurable. Yet a people whose singing, as he wrote, swells from deep within them as though they were a pipe organ, need to sing.[2] Richard Llewellyn's Huw Morgan, who employed a different metaphor, would have agreed: 'For singing is in my people as sight is in the eye.'[3] But whether the Welsh, failing a Revival of religious belief, will ever again find a medium as tailored to the national temperament as a solemn hymn sung in a minor key is a question no one can, or dare, answer.

The Welsh still sing, however, but today the singing is more often choral, in organized groups and choirs, than spontaneously communal. In a population of just over three million there are more than 200 mixed, male, and female choirs, as well as dozens of others that form, disband and re-form as circumstances require. The best known and most popular of them are the male voice choirs, several of which, after years of intercontinental travel and performance, enjoy near worldwide fame. In the chapel congregations and chapel choirs, women were as prominent and as vocal as men. But as chapel attendance declined and the role of the chapel in the community atrophied, women – who had been prominent in the temperance movement – lost their platform and their social niche. Long, and often solitary days, cooking, cleaning and washing for a houseful of working men and children, also left little time or energy for other activities. Men, on the other hand, gathered and bonded in the mines and works and, after their shifts, in the pubs of the industrial towns and villages of south and north Wales. In the industrial towns there were also more of them. By migrating from farming districts in search of work in the mines, the quarries, the steel and the tinplate works, they frequently upset the natural balance of the sexes. In the Rhondda in 1891 there were roughly 50,000 men to 38,000 women. From these male bases emerged the male voice choirs who practised in schools, halls and the long rooms of pubs, gave concerts and competed in local, regional and, if they were good enough, national eisteddfodau. The conductors invariably were local men: teachers, headmasters, steelworkers and bakers, many of them self-taught, whose social standing would not have separated them from the choristers.

A few of the choirs came out of the chapel tradition. Dunvant Male Choir, named after the mining village west of Swansea, was founded in 1895 by a group of miners and steelworkers, members of the Ebenezer Congregational Chapel. It was known first as the Ebenezer Excelsior Male Voice Party. Its first conductor, Tom Richards, a tinplate worker, the son of a stonemason, and father of the renowned painter Ceri Richards, founded the choir with two friends and remained its conductor for the next twenty-five years. The choristers were brickworkers, colliers, railwaymen, steelworkers and foundry hands. Tom Richards often conducted his evening rehearsals dressed for the nightshift at the tinplate works. He was a strong advocate of the tonic sol-fa and is said to have paid for lessons for some of his choristers. His insistence paid off. In 1901 the choir won first prize at the prestigious Neath eisteddfod. It was a remarkable achievement for a young choir and a jubilant, still chapel-going village placed Tom Richards's prize, an oak chair, in Dunvant Chapel.[4]

Typically, however, the roots of the choirs were secular, but the beginnings were equally inauspicious: small groups of working men in a town or village gathering under a local conductor and practising in a schoolroom. The founders of the great Pendyrus Choir were two out-of-work young miners, Ben Jones and Emlyn Drew, from Tylorstown, a village in the Rhondda Fach (the smaller of the two Rhondda valleys) who, in the 1920s, approached a local baker and musician with conducting experience and asked if he would direct a choir. They canvassed friends and former workmates, set up rudimentary voice tests, and within weeks had assembled a group of more than a hundred men. The choir was formally inaugurated on 24 May 1924 at the local miners' federation hut. They called it Pendyrus after the name Alfred Tylor had given to his mine. On the rough, uncultivable land above the mine were two long-abandoned ancient hill farms, the higher called Pendyrus Uchaf and the lower Pendyrus Isaf. The choir practised in Tylorstown Junior School, its home for the next seventy-five years. Its conductor, until 1960, was the dynamic Arthur Duggan, a bakery salesman for the local Cooperative Society; his accompanist was the formerly out-of-work Ben Jones, Pendyrus's co-founder.

The image of the singing Welsh miner received, in the 1930s, the incalculable endorsement of Paul Robeson, the great African-American bass. In 1928, when performing in *Showboat* in London, Robeson, a committed and active socialist, is said to have met a number of unemployed Welsh miners who had walked to London to draw attention to widespread poverty and hardship in south Wales. There is no evidence to corroborate that he did, but Welsh miners were ardent supporters of the Republican cause in Spain. Of the 170 men from Wales who joined the International Brigades, 118 were from the mining valleys and 39 from the adjoining coal ports. To support the miners and encourage anti-Fascist sentiments, Robeson, between 1929 and 1939, gave many concerts in south Wales. After a concert in Neath, the organizing centre for anti-Fascist activity west of Cardiff, he told a reporter that he was studying Welsh airs from gramophone records. He loved 'the depth and richness of the language' and believed that Welsh airs, like most folk songs, were well suited to his voice.[5]

To the Welsh, Robeson became as powerful a symbol of oppression as the Fisk Jubilee Singers who had sung in Swansea fifty years earlier. He was assured of his iconic status in Wales when he accepted, in 1939, the role of David Goliath, an out-of-work African-American sailor, in the film *The Proud Valley*. Without a ship, and looking for work, Goliath walked to the Rhondda from Cardiff. He enters the film when a miners' choir, which he can hear from an open window, is rehearsing

Elijah, but without their bass soloist. At the appropriate moment Robeson, from the street below, sings the solo 'Lord God of Abraham' in his magnificent bass, and in cinemas wherever the film played he brought the house down. Throughout the film he is accompanied in song by miners from the Cwmbach Male Choir, formed in 1921 when, during a strike, the miners were locked out of work.[6]

Robeson's communist sympathies and his activism led to the siezure of his passport, in 1950, after his return to America. Repeated invitations to attend the annual miners' eisteddfod in south Wales failed to mollify the State Department, but in 1957 a transatlantic telephone link allowed him to address, and sing to, the 7,000-strong audience packed into the pavilion at Porthcawl. He sang, in English, 'Ar Hyd y Nos' (All through the night) and, also in English, 'Hen Wlad fy Nhadau'. The Treorchy Male Choir returned the compliment with what was described as a 'magnificent rendering' of 'Y Delyn Aur' (The golden harp). After the return of his passport in 1958, Robeson attended the National Eisteddfod in Ebbw Vale and sang at the miners' eisteddfod in Porthcawl. His final concert in Britain was at the Royal Festival Hall, London, in 1960; at his side, providing choral accompaniment, were the miners of Cwmbach Male Choir. In 2007, just over thirty years after his death, the Rutgers University-Newark Chorus, which now has both black and white members, visited Wales and sang at locations where Robeson had sung. While at Rutgers, from 1915 to 1918, Robeson sang with the Glee Club at local functions but he was never invited to join or attend social functions, nor travel with choir.[7]

The 1950s and '60s, the years of Paul Robeson's celebrity in Wales, were halcyon days for male voice singing. Rivalling Pendyrus, in the eastern valleys of the coalfield, was Treorchy Male Voice Choir. Treorchy's roots (the suffix 'choir' is hardly needed in south Wales) were older, traceable to 1883 when a group of twenty-five young men, after winning two small local eisteddfodau (one for a rendition of Joseph Parry's 'Myfanwy' at the Red Cow Hotel), asked a local conductor, William Thomas, if he would direct them. Thomas, a school attendance inspector, had been a member of Caradog's victorious South Wales Choral Union. The twenty singers soon swelled to eighty and the choir began winning major prizes. Its rival in the Rhondda was the Rhondda Glee Society, who beat Treorchy by a point in what amounted to a play-off, in Pontypridd, to attend the Chicago World's Fair. The Glee Society took first prize in the male voice competition. Its conductor was publican Tom Stephens, who had been the principal boy alto in Caradog's Côr Mawr at the Crystal Palace. The two choirs were bitter rivals and neither one would have described the other, as Evan Stephens had done so generously in defeat by the Glee Society in Chicago, as a 'glorious chorus'. Both were, of course. After a triumphant performance at Windsor Castle, when Treorchy received the designation, Royal Welsh Male Choir, i.e. official singers to the Queen, William Thomas promptly shrank the choir to a select twenty-five. He then embarked on two exhaustive tours, one to North America in 1906–07 and the other, in 1908–09, to the rest of the world: a 50,000-mile tour and 310 engagements.

The modern Treorchy was the child of the late John Haydn Davies, a diminutive, self-taught schoolmaster. The choir re-formed in 1917 but not until the accession of John Haydn (as he was known) in 1946 did it assume its modern shape, or more accurately, sound. John Haydn Davies's mantra was that the choir should sing as if it were one voice. After a performance of Schubert's '23rd Psalm' (Duw yw fy Mugail, The Lord is my Shepherd) at the Aberystwyth National Eisteddfod in 1952, W. Matthews Williams, one of the adjudicators delivered this paean: 'It is only once in a century one hears such marvellous singing which was so moving that tears came in to my eyes and I was not the only one so affected. If there is singing like this in heaven then I am eager to get there quickly. It was so beautiful that the whole panel of adjudicators … put their pencils and notebooks down … and listened.' John Haydn had risked interpreting literally the adagio instruction on the score. The performance lasted five minutes, overwhelming not only the audience but, as Matthews Williams noted, the adjudicators. At an earlier eisteddfod in Llanharan, Alan Bush, Professor of Composition at the Royal Academy of Music in London, was so affected by the choir that he dedicated his composition *Owain Glyndŵr* to them and presented the original manuscript to John Haydn Davies. At a recording session in 1969 under the baton of John Cynan Jones, John Haydn Davies's successor, the internal balance of the choir was so nearly perfect that the chief sound engineer was able to record them on one microphone.

A close Rhondda associate of John Haydn Davies was the mercurial Glynne Jones, conductor of the Pendyrus Choir. Jones had been regarded by many as Davies's natural successor but, instead, he became musical director of the Rhymney Male Silurian Choir – a group of mostly miners and steelworkers – in Rhymney, just over the hill from Dowlais. In 1962 he returned to the Rhondda to conduct Pendyrus, the choir founded by the unemployed miners of Tylorstown in 1924 and led by the baker Arthur Duggan. Glynne Jones, echoing Caradog, the blacksmith conductor, once remarked (to Meic Stephens) that the rich, reverberating texture of their singing had something to do with the strenuous nature of their work in mine and furnace. Caradog attributed his fine ear to the ringing sound of his hammer striking the anvil. Glynne Jones was the son of a Dowlais foundry worker and, mimicking Joseph Parry, described himself as a *'bachgen bach o Dowlais, erioed, erioed'* (a small boy from Dowlais, ever, ever). A bachelor, Glynne Jones lived in his mother's house in Dowlais, and died there in December 2000. Unlike most of the coalfield conductors, he studied music formally – at University College, Cardiff – with the intention of composing but, a natural extrovert, he quickly realised that his talent was for performance. His aim was to encourage music-making among his neighbours and extend the boundaries of what they sang and what audiences might tolerate. Pendyrus's first concert under Jones's direction was a rendering of David Wynne's cantata 'Owain ab Urien' in 1962. Sixteenth-century Italian church music, and compositions by modern Welsh, English and American composers followed. If John Haydn Davies brought a new sound to male voice choral singing in south Wales, Glynne Jones introduced a new choral landscape.

Where Glynne Jones and John Haydn Davies succeeded by persuasion, Ivor Sims, the founding conductor of Morriston Orpheus, one the great choirs of the western half of the south Wales coalfield, could do so only by ultimatum, albeit inadvertently. Except for a hiatus during the First World War, there had been an unbroken sequence of male voice choral singing in Morriston since 1893. Located in the Tawe valley a few miles above Swansea, Morriston in the nineteenth century was a copper smelting and coal mining town; in the twentieth a steelmaking and tinplate one. In 1926 Ivor Sims, who until then had been the accompanist of the Morriston United choir, became its conductor. In 1930s the question arose of whether to continue with the same popular repertoire, and thereby increase revenues, or be ambitious. In a referendum seventy members of the 100-man choir voted for more of the same. Sims resigned, but the following year the disgruntled members of the Morriston United Choir asked him if he would form a new one. The phoenix was the Morriston Orpheus Choir. Under Sims it embarked on a more sophisticated repertoire that, before his untimely death in 1961, included the works of Cherubini, Max Bruch, Brahms and Schubert.

Just before Ivor Sims's death, Ian Thomas, who longed to join the choir, attended a rehearsal at the invitation of one of the committee men: 'I sat on my own at the back of the room whilst it filled up with a huge number of men, many still in working clothes, and many speaking Welsh – it was very noisy. Then, a small elderly man with a shock of silvery hair appeared at the front. He tapped his conductor's baton against the lectern in front of him, said "ready boys", and instantly there was total silence. The very first delicate but rich sound that came from those hundred or so voices turned my knees to jelly and [they] stayed that way for the rest of the evening.' Aware that Ian Thomas hoped to join the choir, Ivor Sims, at the end of the rehearsal, asked him to stay behind to sing a few lines with the accompanist. When he'd finished, Ivor Sims – to Ian Thomas's delight – said: 'Congratulations Mr. Thomas, welcome to the choir as a second tenor, perhaps we will make a top tenor of you later.'

Ivor Sims died not long after that rehearsal. At his graveside the choir, in what had become a ritual for the burial of revered conductors in south Wales, gathered to sing. They had chosen 'Steal Away to Jesus', a spiritual made popular by the Fisk Jubilee Singers and Paul Robeson. It was, wrote Ian Thomas, probably the most moving rendition of that spiritual ever aired.[8]

Ivor Sims's most public performance, and according to a near-anonymous donor to the choir's archives (he signed himself RGM) one his greatest performances, was at the St Helen's rugby ground in December 1951. The occasion was the match between Swansea and the Springboks, the touring South African rugby team. Before the game, 'a loose-limbed grey-haired man walked into the centre of the pitch, and stood on a wooden box which had been placed there for him. He wore a brown sports coat and grey trousers, and looked as unremarkable as a man can look under [those] circumstances except that he carried in his hand a slim white baton. He had come to conduct the singing.' It was, of course, Ivor Sims.

Quite naturally without a word being spoken, the hullabaloo of the crowd [diminished] into a kind of murmuring calm. With a single imperious gesture, the man raised the baton above his head … and abruptly all noise ceased … A small silver band, hitherto unnoticed in the lee of the stands, introduced the opening bars of

'Blaenwern'. The baton descended. The singing of a Welsh rugby crowd in those far-off chapel-bred days was justifiably one of the world's unique cultural experiences. It was a time, now also long past, when every other man seemed able to harmonise at will in 3ds and 5ths ... What followed on that day was a demonstration of mass singing of an excellence never to be heard again on a rugby ground. All around St Helen's and beyond into the streets of the town, people stopped what they were doing to listen as the great chord structures took hold ... In a matter of minutes he had turned Babel into Arcady and us ordinary mortals into messengers of the spirit. It was not just singing, but also a people – rejoicing in awakening kinship, in the oneness of their emotional identity – I had seen my first great choral conductor.[9]

Within a few miles of Morriston, in what was once the western coalfield, there are other accomplished male choirs: Dunvant, Manselton (now the Swansea Male Choir) and Pontarddulais, all based in former mining and manufacturing communities. In his history of Pontarddulais, E. Lewis Evans described it as a community, in the last quarter of the nineteenth century, of *'Cymry oddi cartref yn gwneud cân'*, literally translated, Welsh people away from home making song. They had come to the Bont (its colloquial name) from neighbouring valleys in search of work in the mines and tinplate works and, like most communities in industrial south Wales, they formed choirs. Pontarddulais Male Voice Choir owed its origins, like many of the choirs, to the energy and inspiration of one man. Noel Davies, the son of a coalminer and a mother who sang with the distinguished Pontarddulais Choral Society, was another in the line of distinguished schoolteacher-conductors.[10] He began with mixed youth choirs until asked by a group of young men if he would direct an all-male choir. It was the nucleus of the now renowned Côr Meibion Pontarddulais. Noel Davies was a friend and great admirer, if a frequent rival on the eisteddfod stage, of John Haydn Davies, the legendary Treorchy conductor. Like John Haydn, Noel Davies perennially challenged choir and listeners, and after a visit from the Harvard Glee Club to the Bont he embarked on the works of contemporary American composer Randall Thompson. To acknowledge (one suspects) the Bont's industrial past, Elliot Forbes, the Glee Club's conductor, also introduced Noel Davies and the choir to 'Red Iron Ore', a folk song lauding the men and the boats that carried iron ore down the Great Lakes to the steel mills at Buffalo and Gary, Indiana.

In north Wales, where there are now about forty male voice choirs, the nurseries of the large choirs, as in the south, were industrial towns and villages. The slate quarrying towns of Blaenau Ffestiniog and Bethesda, in Caernarvonshire, are home to three choirs: Penrhyn at Bethesda; and Brythoniaid and Moelwyn Male Voice Choir at Blaenau Ffestiniog. A Penrhyn and Dinorwic Choir, assembled for the event and directed by twenty-three-year-old Edward Broome, took second place in the male voice competition at the Chicago World's Fair in 1893. Brythoniaid's conception, in Blaenau Ffestiniog in 1964, was quintessentially Welsh: a small group of men in a chapel hall, directed by a local musician Meirion Jones, preparing to compete at a local eisteddfod. The original Moelwyn Male Voice Choir at the beginning of the last century visited the USA on two occasions to raise money for sufferers from silicosis and other chest diseases of the slate quarrying districts. Rhos (shortened from Rhosllannerchrugog), the pre-eminent choir of the Denbighshire and Wrexham coalfield in the north-east, has equally long roots. It was founded in 1891 by Richard Mills, the son of Richard Mills of Llanidloes, the well-known composer and musician. He apprenticed as a printer and in Rhos he set up his own press on which he mastered the difficult craft of printing staff notation. He also launched the *Rhos Herald*, composed anthems, and arranged and wrote hymn tunes at the same time as he directed the choir. Today, Rhos, a village (as it describes itself) of nearly 10,000, and the surrounding district, support two accomplished male voice choirs. The second is Rhos Orpheus, founded in 1957.

Two major north Wales choirs, Trelawnyd and Froncysyllte, lie outside the quarrying and mining belts. Trelawnyd, on the road from Holywell to Rhyl, in the middle of the nineteenth century was noted for its religious radicalism; it had a small 'Mormonite' meeting house and villagers left for Utah in some numbers in 1856. Seventy-seven years later, in 1933, thirty-five villagers assembled under the baton of a local schoolmaster, William Humphreys, father of the novelist Emyr Humphreys, to compete in a local eisteddfod. Froncysyllte, a village in the pastoral Vale of Llangollen that once knew heavy work, stands on a high outcrop of limestone below several quarries, and in the nineteenth century was home to limekilns and brickworkers. In 1947 members of five chapels and a church met in a Baptist chapel to discuss the possibility of forming a choir to compete in the male voice competition in the recently founded International Eisteddfod at Llangollen, a few miles down the road. 'Fron' is today a hugely popular choir.

Yet in spite of the acclaim brought by often exquisite performances, countless invitations to sing at home and abroad, and repertoires that embrace sacred, folk, popular and classical music, the choirs have thinned and greyed and most of the community-based ones admit that maintaining numbers is difficult. In 1961 only twenty of Treorchy's 114 choristers were over forty, whereas now more than ninety per cent fall into that category. Most choristers today are in their sixties and recruitment relies heavily on the recently retired. Seventy per cent of the Pontarddulais choir are now retired. The other great change is that quarrymen, miners, steel and tinplate workers have been replaced by teachers, accountants, tradesmen and policemen who typically drive rather than walk to practices. Singing is less of a neighbourhood affair, and becoming less so as specialised, concert-oriented choirs, such as the North Wales Male Chorus, draw members from the entire region. The male bonding that was natural to the mine and the works has gone. So too, and more seriously, has the easy familiarity with tonic sol-fa, the simple code-breaking system that allowed musically untrained singers to tackle even difficult compositions. The decline in chapel attendance, the loss of the school assemblies and their sung hymns or anthems, and the misconceived fear that sol-fa would deny access to music's broad uplands, has left the majority stranded in the foothills, unable to follow sol-fa or the old-notation, and reduced to singing by ear.

The days of the male voice choir in its traditional form may well be numbered. Continued popularity may depend not just on wider repertoires but on more adventurous and more popular arrangements, even choreography. The Welsh, to repeat the mantra of Lincoln Hartford, will always need to sing chorally and Welsh choirs, presumably, will always find ways of engaging their audiences. Toward the end of the last decade, the BBC launched a competition, *Last Choir Standing*, to determine Britain's favourite amateur choir. Applications on tape came from 1,000 choirs, sixty of which were invited to audition live. Twenty-seven were asked to return, and from these fifteen were eventually chosen to perform in three rounds of studio heats. Elimination was by viewer votes. The winners were two choirs from Wales: the young Cardiff-based male choir Only Men Aloud and, the runners-up, Ysgol Glanaethwy, a mixed youth choir from north Wales. For a nation that produced the cymanfa and the eisteddfod it was, as triumphant Welsh rugby spectators might say, a no contest.

Endnotes

Foreword

[1]   Wyn Griffith, *The Welsh* (1950), 158.

Chapter 1: Breaking the Silence

[1]   Howell Elvet Lewis, *Sweet Singers of Wales* (Aberystwth, 1889), 16–17.

[2]   Geraint H. Jenkins, *Literature and and Society in Wales* (Cardiff, 1978), 148.

[3]   Quoted in Anthony Jones, *Welsh Chapels* (Cardiff, 1996), 3.

[4]   Quoted in David Ian Allsobrook, *Music for Wales* (Cardiff, 1992), 14.

[5]   Ellis Wynne, *Visions of the Sleeping Bard* (London, 1703).

[6]   David Ceri Jones, '*A Glorious Work in the World*', *Welsh Methodism and the International Evangelical Revival, 1735–1750* (Cardiff, 2004), 39–40.

[7]   Eifion Evans, *Daniel Rowland and the Great Evangelical Awakening in Wales* (Edinburgh, 1985), 33.

[8]   Geoffrey F. Nuttall, *Howel Harris, 1714–1773, The Last Enthusiast* (Cardiff, 1965), 15.

[9]   W.E.H. Lecky, *A History of England in the Eighteenth Century*, Vol. 2 (London, 1913).

[10] Eifion Evans, trans.

[11] Nuttall, 16.

[12] Ibid., 54.

[13] E.P. Thompson, *The Making of the English Working Class* (London, 1963), 13.

[14] Howell Elvet Lewis, *Howell Harris and the Welsh Revivalists* (London, 1911), 111–12.

15 Cited by D. Ben Rees, *The Saga of a Revival: Early Welsh Pentecostal Methodism* (Lerpwl, 2010), 59–60.

16 Derec Llwyd Morgan, *The Great Awakening in Wales* (Peterborough, 1988), 17.

17 Eifion Evans, 353.

18 Ibid., 41.

19 Ibid., 165.

20 Ibid., 172.

21 Ibid., 74.

22 Ibid., 75.

23 John Wesley, *Journal*, 31 March 1731.

24 Edwin Sidney, *The Life of the Reverend Rowland Hill* (1834), 61.

25 John Gillies, *Historical Collections* (1754), quoted in Eifion Evans, 159.

26 Erik Routley, *Hymns and Human Life* (New York, 1952), 63.

27 David Stowe, *How Sweet the Sound* (Cambridge, Mass., 2004), 17.

28 T. Crichton Mitchell, *The Man with the Dancing Heart* (Kansas City, 1994), 249.

29 Carlton R. Young, *Music of the Heart* (Carol Stream, Illinois, 1995), 92.

30 Quoted in Young, 97.

31 Young, 63.

32 Lightwood, 138–9.

33 Mark A. Noll, *Wonderful Words of Life, Hymns in American Protestant History and Theology* (Grand Rapids, 2004), 5.

34 Arnold A. Dallimore, *George Whitefield: the Life and Times of the Great Evangelist*, Vol. 1 (Edinburgh, 1970), 33.

35 Harry S. Stout, *The Divine Dramatist* (Grand Rapids, 1991), 95.

36 Geraint Jenkins, 213.

37 Ceri Jones, 23.

38 Alan Luff, *Welsh Hymns and their Tunes* (London, 1990), Chapter 4.

[39] Glyn Tegai Hughes, *Williams Pantycelyn* (Cardiff, 1983), 46.

[40] Theron Brown and Hezekiah Butterworth, *The Story of Hymns and Tun*es (New York, 1906), Chapter 11.

[41] John Davies, *A History of Wales* (Cardiff, 1990), 309.

[42] Tegai Hughes, 85.

[43] R.D. Griffith, *Hanes Canu Cynulleidfaol Cymru* (Cardiff, 1948), 32.

[44] Sidney G. Dimond, *The Psychology of the Methodist Revival* (London, 1926), 123.

[45] Ibid., 117.

[46] James Bissett Pratt, *The Religious Consciousness* (New York, 1949), 173–76.

[47] Sidney J. Dimond, 123.

[48] Eifion Evans, 216.

[49] Ibid., 264–5.

[50] Eifion Evans, 315–6.

[51] Eryn White, 'The World, the Flesh and the Devil: Early Methodism in South-West Wales', *Transactions of the Honourable Society of Cymmrodorion*, 3 (1996), 53.

[52] Derec Llwyd Morgan, 25.

[53] John Wesley, *Journal*, 27 August 1763; see also R.A. Knox, *Enthusiasm, a Chapter in the History of Religion* (Oxford, 1950), 533.

[54] T.M. Bassett, *The Welsh Baptists* (Swansea, 1977), 118–19.

[55] Ibid.

[56] W.E.H. Lecky, *A History of England in the Nineteenth Century*, Vol. 3 (Cambridge, 1878–90), 77–8.

[57] Eifion Evans, 145.

[58] Geoffrey Nuttall, 51.

[59] Eifion Evans, 320.

[60] Derec Llwyd Morgan, 29.

[61] Barbara Ehrenreich, *Dancing in the Streets* (New York, 2007).

[62] Victor W. Turner, *The Ritual Process: Structure and anti-Structure* (New York, 1969), 128.

63 Barbara Ehrenreich, *Dancing in the Streets* (New York, 2006), 2–5.
64 Ioan M. Lewis, *Ecstatic Religion* (London, 1971), 29–30.
65 Yi-Fu-Tuan, *Segmented Worlds and the Self* (Minneapolis, 1982), 139.
66 Laurinda S. Dixon, *Perilous Chastity: Women and Illnesses in Pre-Enlightenemnt Art and Medicine* (New York, 1995), 178.
67 Nicholas Murray, *Aldous Huxley: A Biography*, 41.
68 Aldous Huxley, *The Devils of Loudon* (New York, 1953), epilogue. On boundary loss, see also William H. McNeill, *Keeping Together in Time* (Cambridge, 1995), 8–9.

Chapter 2: Controlling the Voices

1 Anne Kelly Knowles, *Calvinists Incorporated: Welsh Immigrants on Ohio's Industrial Frontier* (Chicago, 1997), 112.
2 Cass Meurig, 'The Fiddler in Eighteenth-Century Wales', *Welsh Music History*, 7 (2007), 22–40.
3 Richard Suggett, 'Festivals and Social Structure in Early Modern Wales', *Past and Present*, 79 (1996), 79–111.
4 D. Roy Saer, 'Traditional Dance in Wales during the Eighteenth Century', Lecture, September 1984.
5 James Hogg, 'The Welsh Pulpit', *Titan*, XXVI (1858), 345–49.
6 Kenneth O. Morgan, *Rebirth of a Nation* (Oxford, 1982), 16.
7 R. Tudur Jones, *Congregationalism in Wales* (Cardiff, 2004), 119.
8 Sioned Davies, 'Performing from the Pulpit: An Introduction to Preaching in Nineteenth-Century Wales', *Identifying the 'Celtic': CSANA Yearbook*, 2 (Cardiff, 2000), 127.
9 Bruce A. Rosenberg, *Can These Bones Live?: The Art of the American Folk Preacher* (Urbana, 1988), 65.
10 Abel Stevens & James Floy, 'The Welsh Pulpit', *The National Magazine*, 12 (1858), 451.

11 Edwin Paxton Hood, *Christmas Evans, the Preacher of Wild Wales* (London, 1881), 59.

12 'Lives of the Illustrious', *Biographical Magazine* (1855), 173.

13 Paxton Hood, 213.

14 Ibid., 171.

15 Ibid., 14. Andrew Wilson-Dickson, a contemporary musician, would agree with Lord Lyttleton. He writes in *The Story of Christian Music* (2003): 'Like Italian, the Welsh language is a wonderful vehicle for song; its strong stresses and lilting quality are already halfway to music. The exceptional hymnody of Wales has benefited from it as much as the folksong.'

16 Sioned Davies, 136.

17 T.M. Bassett, 187.

18 Ibid., 126.

19 George W. Henry, *Shouting Genuine and Spurious* (1859), 296.

20 Quoted in Eiluned and Peter Lewis, *The Land of Wales* (1937), 91–2.

21 Erasmus W. Jones, 'The Welsh in America', *Atlantic Monthly*, 37 (March 1876), 305–13.

22 Paxton Hood, *Christmas Evans: the Preacher of Wild Wales* (London, 1881), 17.

23 Tudur Jones, 120.

24 Sioned Davies, 115–37.

25 Sally Harper, 'Dafydd ap Gwilym, Poet and Musician' (April 2007).

26 Ackerman cites his recording of 'And Death shall have no Dominion'.

27 Howell Elvet Lewis, *With Christ among the Miners* (London, 1906), Chapter 2.

28 *Y Traethodydd* (1882), 849.

29 Owain T. Edwards, 'Music in Wales' in R. Brinley Jones, *Anatomy of Wales* (Peterston, 1972), 208–30.

30 R.D. Griffith, *Hanes Canu Cynulleidfaol Cymru* (Cardiff, 1948) 55.

[31] James T. Lightwood, 66.

[32] T.J. Morgan, 'Peasant Culture of the Swansea Valley', *Glamorgan Historian*, 9, 105–22.

[33] T.M. Bassett, 185.

[34] R.D. Griffith, 133.

[35] Ibid., 55.

[36] Lincoln Jones Hartford, 'A Good Tune: A Dissertation on the Phenomenon of Welsh Hymn Singing as it Demonstrates the Inherent Relationship of Worship and the Arts' (Chicago Theological Seminary, Th.D. thesis, 1987), 43.

[37] Owain T. Edwards, op. cit.

[38] R.D. Griffith, 65.

[39] David Morgans, *Music and Musicians of Merthyr and District* (Merthyr Tydfil, 1922), 22.

[40] Ibid., 39.

[41] W.A.C. Stewart & W.P. McCann, *The Educational Innovators 1750–1880* (London, 1967), 184.

[42] D. Leinster-Mackay, 'John Hullah, John Curwen, and Sarah Glover: a Classic Case of "Whiggery" in the History of Musical Education', *British Journal of Educational Studies* 24, 2 June 1981, 164–7.

[43] Jones's printing press is now in the Rhondda Heritage Museum.

[44] Lincoln Hartford, 69.

[45] T.J. Morgan, 115.

[46] *Musical Times*, 61 (1920), 94–6.

[47] Gareth Williams, *Valleys of Song* (Cardiff, 1998), 32.

[48] Eifion Evans, *Two Welsh Revivalists* (Bridgend, 1985), 19.

[49] Lightwood, 376.

[50] Anthony Jones, 104.

[51] Rhidian Griffiths, 'The Best Composer: Ieuan Gwyllt and the Welsh Melody', in Sally Harper & Wyn Thomas, *Bearers of Song* (Cardiff, 2007), 106–16.

[52] Patricia Schultz, 'A Comparison of the Traditional Welsh Cymanfa Ganu with Contemporary Local American Practices', (University of Missouri Ph.D. thesis, 1984), 79.

53 John Sutcliffe Smith, *Impressions of Music in Wales* (London, 1948), 28–9.

54 John Ballinger, 'Further Gleanings from a Printer's File', *West Wales Historical Records*, 11 (1926), 219–25.

55 'Holi'r Pwnc', *West Wales Historical Records*, 12 (1927), 225–31.

56 Anthony Jones, 106.

57 Ibid., 111.

58 Janice Holmes, *Religious Revivals in Britain and Ireland, 1859–1905* (Dublin), 62.

59 Gareth Williams, 16.

60 David Morgans, 17.

61 Don Cusic, 58.

62 Bruce J. Evensen, *God's Man for the Gilded Age* (Oxford, 2003), 19.

63 Timothy C.F. Stunt, 'The Early Development of Arthur Augustus Rees and his Relations with the Brethren', unpublished ms., 20pp.

64 David W. Stowe, *How Sweet the Sound* (Cambridge, Mass., 2004), 98.

65 Don Cusic, *The Sound of Light: A History of Gospel Music* (Bowling Green, 1990), 58–9.

66 'Public Opinion and Messrs. Moody and Sankey', *Cambrian*, 12 March 1875.

67 Stowe, 92.

68 Routley, 238.

69 Stowe, 108.

70 Stowe, 34.

71 Gwyn A. Williams, *The Search for Beulah Land* (London, 1980), 87.

72 Ibid., 109.

73 W.J. Phillips, 'Diwygiad Sankey a Moody a Chymru', *Y Traethodydd* (1962), 8–15.

74 John Owen, *Traethawd ar fywyd ac athrylith y Parchedig John Roberts* (Pwllheli, 1879), 41.

75 Alan Luff, 202

76 Timothy George, *Mr Moody and the Evangelical Tradition* (London, 2005), 4.

77 Alan Luff, 202–3.

78 Reprinted in John Roberts, *Sŵn y Jiwbili* (Wrexham, 1876), Nodiad. See also T.J. Davies, *Ieuan Gwyllt* (Llandysul, 1977), 96.

79 Henry Richard, *Letters and Essays on Wales* (London, 1889), 50–1.

80 T.J. Morgan, Ibid., 118.

81 Gwilym R. Roberts, 62–3.

82 Gwilym P. Ambrose, 'The Aberdare Background to the South Wales Choral Union', *Glamorgan Historian*, Vol. 9, 191–201.

83 David Morgans, 155. See also Gareth Williams, 91.

Chapter 3: The Welsh in America

1 NLW, The Wales–Ohio Project, J. Luther Thomas Archives.

2 Edward George Hartmann, *Americans from Wales* (New York, 1978), 44–5.

3 A.H. Dodd, *The Character of Early Welsh Emigration to the United States* (Cardiff, 1957), 15.

4 Beverly Bush Patterson, *The Sound of the Dove: Singing in Appalachian Primitive Baptist Churches* (Urbana, 2001) 27.

5 Louis F. Benson, *The English Hymn: its development and use in worship* (Michigan, 1962), 99.

6 Bush Patterson, 27.

7 A nineteenth-century witness, quoted in Deborah Vansau McCauley, *Appalachian Mountain Religion, a History* (Urbana, 1995), 106.

8 Vansau McCauley, 107.

9 Bush Patterson, 41.

10 Loyal Jones, 'A Preliminary Look at the Welsh Component of Celtic Influence in Appalachia' in *The Appalachian Experience: Proceedings of the Sixth Appalachian Studies Conference* (1983), 26–33.

[11] Loyal Jones, *Faith and Meaning in the Southern Uplands* (Urbana, 1999), 122.

[12] Hamilton W. Pierson, *In the Brush: or Old-Time Social, Political, and Religious Life in the Southwest* (1893). Quoted in Vansau McCauley, 383.

[13] For a discussion of the effectiveness of rhythm vis-à-vis meaning, see Bruce A. Rosenberg, *Can These Bones Live?: The Art of the American Folk Preacher* (Urbana, 1988).

[14] Howard Dorgan, *Giving Glory to God in Appalachia* (Knoxville, 1987), 56.

[15] Ibid., 64.

[16] Vansau McCauley, 215.

[17] Loyal Jones, *Faith and Meaning in the Southern Uplands*, 124.

[18] Walter F. Pitts, *The Old Ship of Zion: the Afro-Baptist Ritual in the African Diaspora* (Oxford, 1993), 89.

[19] Elder John Sparks, *The Roots of Appalachian Christianity* (Lexington, 2001), 68.

[20] Ted A. Campbell, *The Religion of the Heart: A Study of European Religious Life in the Seventeenth and Eighteenth Centuries* (Columbia, 1991), 109.

[21] Nuttall, 23.

[22] Ted Campbell, 109.

[23] William Warren Sweet, *Revivalism in America* (New York, 1944), 95.

[24] Ibid., 109.

[25] Elder John Sparks, 65.

[26] Willie Ruff, International Conference on Line-Singing, Yale, 2007.

[27] A.H. Dodd, 19.

[28] Gwyn A. Williams, *The Search for Beulah Land: the Welsh and the Atlantic Revolution* (London, 1980), 86.

[29] Margaret Morgan Jones, *Travels of a Welsh Preacher in the USA* (Llanrwst, 2008), 16.

[30] Stephen Graham, *The Soul of John Brown* (London, 1920), 90–1.

31 Catherine M. Bell (ed.), *Teaching Ritual* (Oxford, 2007), 127.

32 Quoted in Don Cusic, 48.

33 Ronald Lewis, *Welsh Americans: A History of Assimilation in the Coalfields* (Chapel Hill, 2008), 144.

34 Frances Trollope, *Domestic Manners of the Americans* (London, 1832), 132–3.

35 Cherilyn A. Whalley, 'The Old Man's Creek Welsh Community of Johnson County, Iowa', *North American Journal of Welsh Studies*, Vol. 2, 1 (2002), 36–49.

36 William E. Van Vugt, *British Buckeyes: The English, Scots and Welsh in Ohio 1700–1900* (Kent, Ohio, 2006), 79.

37 R.D. Thomas, *A History of the Welsh in America* (Utica, 1872), 133.

38 Clare Taylor, 'Paddy's Run: a Welsh Community in Ohio', *Welsh History Review*, 11 (1983), 302–16.

39 Gwilym R. Roberts, *New Lives in the Valley: Slate Quarries and Quarry Villages in North Wales, New York and Vermont, 1850–1920* (New Hampshire, 1998), 16–17.

40 Michael T. Strubble and Hubert G.H. Wilhelm, 'The Welsh in Ohio', in Allen G. Noble (ed.), *To Build a New Land: Ethnic Landscapes in North America* (Baltimore, 1992), 79–92.

41 Quoted in William D. Jones, *Wales in America: Scranton and the Welsh 1860–1920* (Cardiff, 1993), 91–2.

42 Lincoln Hartford, 44.

43 Anne Kelly Knowles, 143.

44 'Reminisences of the Welsh Congregational Church, Birmingham, Pa', *The Cambrian*, Vol. 3, 3, 131.

45 John S. Ellis, *A Centennial History of the Welsh Presbyterian Church of Poultney, Vermont 1901–2001* (n.d.), 7.

46 Ronald Lewis, 151.

47 NLW, The Wales–Ohio Project, 'Some facts with reference to the Welsh of Columbus Ohio, from its earliest times up to 1800'.

48 Don Cusic, 94.

49 Patricia Bowers Schultz, 'A Comparison of the Traditional Welsh Cymanfa Ganu with Contemporary Local American Practices' (Ph.D. thesis University of Missouri, Kansas City), 22.

50 Van Vugt, 79.

51 NLW, The Wales–Ohio Project, 'Gomer's First 150 Years' (Vol. 1), 40.

52 Jenkins Williams, 115.

53 *Harvard Encyclopedia of American Ethnic Groups* (1980), 1,014.

54 Daniel Jenkins Williams, *One Hundred Years of Welsh Calvinistic Methodism in America* (Philadelphia, 1937), 141.

55 Ibid., 115.

56 Ibid., 117–18.

57 Peter Williams, 'Seeing beyond the Word: Visual Arts and the Calvinist Tradition' in Paul Corby Finney, *Metamorphoses of the Meeting House: Three Case Studies* (Grand Rapids, 1999), 479–505.

58 Jenkins Williams, 14–20.

59 Gwilym Roberts, 61.

60 Patricia Bowers Schultz, 26.

61 Dulais Rhys & Frank Bott, *To Philadelphia and Back: The life and music of Joseph Parry* (Llanrwst, 2010), 26–8.

62 *Cambrian*, 21 July 1871.

63 Ronald Lewis, 151.

64 Ibid., 154.

65 Gwilym Roberts, 285–92.

66 *The Cambrian*, Vol. 2, 3, 21.

Chapter 4: The Singing Saints

1 Milton R. Hunter, *Brigham Young the Colonizer* (Independence, 1945), 73.

2 Ronald D. Dennis, *The Call of Zion* (Provo, 1987), 1.

3 Ronald D. Dennis (ed.), *Zion's Trumpet: 1849 Welsh Mormon Periodical* (Salt Lake City, 2001), 73.

4 T.H. Lewis, *Y Mormoniad yng Nghymru* (Cardiff, 1956), 97–8.

5 D.L. Davies, 'From a Seion of Lands to the Land of Zion' in Jensen & Thorp (eds), *Mormons in Early Victorian Britain* (Salt Lake City, 1989), 152.

6 Joseph Hyrum Parry, *Memoir*, Vol. 2.

7 *Cambrian*, 16 February 1849.

8 Dennis, *The Call of Zion*, 14.

9 Ibid., 145.

10 'Voyage of the Amazon', *Ensign*, 16 March 1980.

11 Wallace Stegner, *The Gathering of Zion* (New York, 1964), 237–8.

12 Richard F. Burton, *The City of the Saints and across the Rocky Mountains to California* (New York, 1842), 229.

13 *Udgorn Seion* (April 1850), 108.

14 Dennis, *The Call of Zion*, 183.

15 Ibid., 207.

16 William Hepwoth Dixon, *New America* (Philadelphia, 1867), 140.

17 Edward G. Hartmann, 75.

18 Memoir of Joseph Hyrum Parry, 1855.

19 Michael Hicks, 'What Hymns Early Mormons Sang and How they Sang Them', *Brigham Young University Studies*, Vol. 47, 1 (2008) 95–118.

20 David L. Bollinger, 'An Historical Investigation of the Recreational Philosophy, Views, Practices and Activities of Brigham Young' (Brigham Young University M.A. thesis, 2009), 41–2.

21 Terryl Givens, *People of Paradox* (New York, 2007), 127.

22 Stephan Thornston, *Harvard Encyclopaedia of Ethnic Groups*, 273.

23 John Frederick Briscoe, 'Choral Singing as a Preventive of Tuberculosis', *British Medical Journal*, 3 June 1911.

24 Michael Hicks, *Mormonism and Music* (Urbana, 1989), 47.

25 *Deseret News*, 19 December 1860.

26 Hicks, 48.

27 Givens, 128.

28 Geraint Bowen, *Ar Drywydd y Mormoniaid* (Llandysul, 1999), 46.

29 Dennis, *The Call of Zion*, 60.

30 Bowen, 47.

31 Hicks, 44.

32 Hicks, 40.

33 Burton, 258.

34 Pam Taylor, 'Religion and Planning in the far West: the first generation of Mormons in Utah', *The Economic History Review* (1958), 76.

35 Merlin Ray Sorensen, 'The Ogden Tabernacle Choir: its History and Contribution to the Cultural History of Utah' (Brigham Young University M.A. thesis, 1961), 15–19.

36 LeRoy R. Hafen & Ann W. Hafen, *Handcarts to Zion* (Glendale, 1960), 87–8. A handcart company travelled, on average, 8.5 miles daily.

37 Hicks, 43.

38 Bergman, 32.

39 Dale A. Johnson, 'The Life and Contributions of Evan Stephens' (Brigham Young University M.A. thesis, 1951), 110.

40 Bowen, 105.

41 Bergman, 71.

42 Johnson, 12.

43 *Deseret Weekly*, 4 June 1892.

44 Hywel Teifi Edwards, *Eisteddfod Ffair y Byd Chicago, 1893* (Llandysul, 1990), 90.

45 *Y Drych*, 2 July 1891.

46 William Jones, 159.

47 L. Ray Bergman, *The Children Sang: The Life and Music of Evan Stephens* (Salt Lake City, 1992), 112.

48 Bergman,121.

49 'The Choir Returns', *Deseret Evening News*, 13 September 1893.

50   Ibid., 32.
51   *Deseret News*, 13 September 1893.
52   Ibid., 48.
53   William Jones, 172–3.
54   *Deseret News*, 24 July 1897.
55   Hicks, 154.

Chapter 5: The 1904–05 Revival

1   W.T. Stead, *The Revival in the West* (London, 1905), 24.
2   Noel Gibbard, *Fire on the Altar* (Bridgend, 2005), 82.
3   Henri Bois, *Le Reveil au Pays de Galles* (Toulouse, 1906).
4   Basil Hall, 'Two French Contributions to the History of the Revival in Sidney Evans and Gomer Roberts', *Cyfrol Goffa Diwigiad 1905–1906* (Caernarfon, 1954), 75.
5   J. Rogues de Fursac, *Un Mouvement Mystique Contemporain* (Paris, 1907).
6   Sarah Jane Rees was the first woman to be awarded the coveted bardic chair. She was also an ardent supporter of tonic sol-fa and a local examiner for the Tonic Sol-fa College.
7   Stead, 32.
8   A.T. Fryer, 'Psychological Aspects of the Welsh Revival', *Proceedings of the Society for Psychical Research*, XIX (December 1905), 113.
9   Karen Lowe, *Carriers of the Fire; the Women of the Welsh Revival* (Llanelli, 2004), 59–60.
10   Brynmor Jones, *Voices from the Welsh Revival* (Bridgend, 1995), 54–8.
11   Noel Gibbard, 'Songs of Praises: Hymns and Tunes of the Welsh Revival, 1904–05', *Merthyr Historian*, 17 (2004), 67–73.
12   Lowe, 52.
13   W.T. Stead, 'Evan Roberts and the Welsh Revival', *Daily Chronicle*, 13 December 1904.
14   Ibid.

[15] R.B. Jones, *Rent Heavens: The Revival of 1904* (Porth, 1931), 49–50.

[16] Brynmor Jones, 85.

[17] Henri Bois, 245–6. All translations from the French are my own.

[18] Bois, 247.

[19] Bois, 249–50.

[20] Bois, 47.

[21] J. Vyrnwy Morgan, *The Welsh Religious Revival 1904–5* (London, 1909), 63.

[22] Elvet Lewis, *Sweet Singers of Wales*, 13.

[23] Brynmor Jones, 172–3.

[24] Fursac, 55.

[25] Ibid., 58.

[26] Ibid., 61.

[27] Bois, 259.

[28] David Matthews, *I Saw the Welsh Revival*.

[29] James L. Brown, 'On the Track of the Welsh Revival', *Bright Words*, Part 3, 16 January 1905.

[30] Constance L. Maynard, *Between College Terms* (London, 1910).

[31] James Griffiths, 'Glo Carreg: Memories of the Anthracite Coalfield', *Carmarthenshire Historian*, 12 (1968), 7–16.

[32] Prys Morgan & Rhys Davies, *Wales: the Shaping of a Nation* (Newton Abbot, 1984), 155.

[33] Basil Hall, 'The Welsh Revival of 1904–5: A Critique', in G.J. Cuming (ed.), *Popular Belief and Practice* (Cambridge, 1972), 295.

[34] Elvet Jones, *Sweet Singers of Wales*, 22.

[35] Bois, 45–7.

[36] Bois, 271–5.

[37] Quoted in William Linnard, 'A French View of Merthyr Tydfil and the Evan Roberts Revival', *Merthyr Historian*, 17, 57–63.

[38] Brynmor Jones, 98.

[39] Ibid., 121.

[40] Awstin, *Western Mail*, 5 December 1904.

[41] Brynmor Jones, 125.

[42] Bois, 598–9.

[43] Brynmor Jones, 149.

[44] Bois, 383.

[45] Fryer, 136.

[46] Gareth Williams, *1905 and All That* (Llandysul, 1991), 76.

[47] Gareth Morgan, 'Rugby and Revivalism in Sport', *International Journal of the History of Sport*, Vol. 22, 3 (May 2005), 434–56.

[48] Ibid., 152.

Chapter 6: A Brotherhood of Song

[1] Geraint H. Jenkins, *A Concise History of Wales* (Cambridge, 2007), 171.

[2] Lincoln Hartford, 1.

[3] Richard Llewellyn, *How Green Was My Valley*.

[4] R.G. Mainwaring, D.G. Richards, J.C. Evans, *Dunvant and its Male Choir 1895–1995* (Swansea, 1995), 19–20.

[5] Mark A. Exton, 'Paul Robeson and South Wales', University of Exeter M.A. thesis, 1984, 32–9.

[6] Ibid., 59.

[7] Sheila Tulley Boyle and Andrew Bunie, *Paul Robeson: The Years of promise and Achievement* (Massachusetts, 2005), 54.

[8] Archives of Morriston Orpheus Choir, 1961.

[9] 'The Miracle of St Helen's', typescript 1953, signed RGM, Archives of Morriston Orpheus Choir.

[10] Eric Jones, *Maestro: Cofiant Noel Davies* (Llandysul, 2007).

Bibliography

Allsobrook, David Ian, *Music for Wales* (Cardiff, University of Wales Press, 1992).

Ambrose, Gwilym P., 'The Aberdare Background to the South Wales Choral Union,' *Glamorgan Historian*, 9, 191–201.

Ballinger, John, 'Further Gleanings from a Printer's File', *West Wales Historical Records* (1926) 219–25.

Bassett, T.M., *The Welsh Baptists* (Swansea, Liston House, 1977).

Bell, Catherine M. (ed.), *Teaching Ritual* (Oxford University Press, 2007).

Benson, Louis F., *The English Hymn: its development and use in worship* (Whitefish, Montana, Kessinger, 1962).

Bergman, L. Ray, *The Children Sang: the Life and Music of Evan Stephens* (Salt Lake City, Northwest, 1962).

Bois, Henri, *Le Reveil au Pays de Galles* (Toulouse, 1906).

Bowen, Geraint, *Ar Drywydd y Mormoniad* (Llandysul, Gomer, 1999).

Boyle, Sheila Tulley & Bunie, Andrew, *Paul Robeson: The Years of Promise and Achievement* (University of Massachusetts Press, 2005).

Brown, Theron & Butterworth, Hezekiah, *The Story of Hymns and their Tunes* (New York, Biblio Life, 1906).

Burton, Richard F., *The City of the Saints and across the Rocky Mountains to California* (New York, Longmans, 1842).

Campbell, Ted A., *The Religion of the Heart: a Study of European Religious Life in the Seventeenth and Eighteenth Centuries* (University of South Carolina, 1991).

Cusic, Don, *The Sound of Light: a History of Gospel Music* (University of Wisconsin, 1990).

Dallimore, Arnold A., *George Whitefield: the Life and Times of the Great Evangelist* (Edinburgh, Banner of Truth, 1970).

Davies, John, *A History of Wales* (Cardiff, University of Wales Press, 1990).

de Fursac, J. Rogues, *Un Mouvement Mystique Contemporain* (Paris, 1907).

Dennis, Ronald D. (ed.), *Zion's Trumpet: 1849 Welsh Mormon Periodical* (Provo, Brigham Young University, 1987).

Dennis, Ronald D., *The Call of Zion* (Provo, Brigham Young University, 1987).

Dimond, Sidney G., *The Psychology of the Methodist Reviva.* (Oxford University Press, 1926).

Dixon, Linda S., *Perilous Chastity: Women and Illnesses in Pre-Enlightment Art and Medicine* (Cornell University Press, 1995).

Dodd, A.H., *The Character of Early Welsh Emigration to the United States* (Cardiff, University of Wales, 1957).

Dorgan, Howard, *Giving Glory to God in Appalachia* (Knoxville, University of Tennessee, 1987).

Edwards, Hywel Teifi, *Eisteddfod Ffair y Byd Chicago, 1893* (Llandysul, Gomer, 1990).

Edwards, Owain T., 'Music in Wales' in *Anatomy of Wales*, R. Brinley Jones (Peterston, Gwerin, 1972).

Ehrenreich, Barbara, *Dancing in the Streets* (New York, Metropolitan, 2007).

Evans, Eifion, *Daniel Rowland and the Great Evangelical Awakening in Wales* (Edinburgh, Banner of Truth, 1985).

Evans, Eifion, *Two Welsh Revivalists* (Cardiff, Evangelical Library of Wales, 1985).

Evensen, Bruce, *God's Man for the Gilded Age* (Oxford University Press, 2003).

Exton, Mark A., 'Paul Robeson and South Wales' (Exeter University M.A. thesis, 1984).

Fryer, A.T., 'Psychological Aspects of the Revival', *Proceedings Society for Psychological Research*, 1905, 113–15.

George, Timothy, *Mr Moody and the Evangelical Tradition* (London, Continuum, 1905).

Gibbard, Noel, *Fire on the Altar* (Bridgend, Bryntirion, 2005).

Gibbard, Noel, 'Songs of Praises: Hymns and Tunes of the Welsh Revival 1904–5', *Merthyr Historian*, 2004, 67–73.

Givens, Terryl, *People of Paradox* (Oxford University Press, 2007).

Graham, Stephen, *The Soul of John Brown* (London, Wentworth, 1920).

Griffith, R.D., *Canu Cynulleidfaol Cymru* (Cardiff, 1848).

Griffiths, James, 'Glo Carreg: Memories of the Anthracite Coalfield', *Carmarthenshire Historian*, 1968, 7–16.

Griffiths, Rhidian, 'The Best Composer: Ieuan Gwyllt and the Welsh Melody' in Sally Harper & Wyn Thomas, *Bearers of Song* (Cardiff, University of Wales Press, 2007).

Hall, Basil, 'The Welsh Revival of 1904–5: A Critique' in G.J. Cumming (ed.), *Popular Belief and Practice* (Cambridge University Press, 1972).

Hall, Basil, 'Two French Contributions to the History of Revival' in Sydney Evans & Gower Roberts, *Cyfrol Goffa Diwigiad 1905* (Caernarfon, 1954).

Hartford, Lincoln Jones, 'A Good Tune: A Dissertation on the Phenomenon of Welsh Hymn Singing' (Chicago Theological Seminary, Th.D. thesis, 1987).

Hartmann, Edward George, *Americans from Wales* (New York, Octagon, 1978).

Henty, Richard, *Letters and Essays on Wales* (London, James Clark, 1889).

Hicks, Michael, *Mormonism and Music* (Urbana, University of Illinois Press, 1989).

Hicks, Michael, *What Hymns Early Mormons Sang and How They Sang Them* (Provo, Brigham Young University Studies, 2008).

Hogg, James, 'The Welsh Pulpit', *Titan*, XXVI, 1858, 345–9.

Holmes, Janice, *Religious Revivals in Britain and Ireland 1859–1905* (Dublin, Irish Academic Press, 2001).

Hood, Edwin Paxton, *Christmas Evans, the Preacher of Wild Wales* (London, Hodder & Stoughton, 1881).

Hughes, Glyn Tegai, *Williams Pantycelyn* (Cardiff, University of Wales, 1983).

Hunter, Milton R., 'Brighmam Young the Colonizer', *Pacific Historical Review*, 6, 4, 1937.

Huxley, Aldous, *The Devils of Loudon* (New York, Chatto & Windus, 1953).

Jenkins, Geraint H., *Literature and Society in Wales* (Cardiff, University of Wales Press, 1978).

Johnson, Dale A., 'The Life and Contributions of Evan Stephens' (Provo, Brigham Young University M.A. thesis, 1951).

Jones, Anthony, *Welsh Chapels* (Cardiff, National Museum of Wales, 1966).

Jones, Brynmor, *Voices from the Welsh Revival* (Bridgend, Bryntirion, 1995).

Jones, David Ceri, *A Glorious Work in the World; Welsh Methodism and the International Evangelical Revival, 1735–1750* (Cardiff, University of Wales Press, 2004).

Jones, Erasmus W., 'The Welsh in America', *Atlantic Monthly*, March 1876, 305–313.

Jones, Loyal, 'A Preliminary Look at the Welsh Component of Cetic Influence in Appalachia', *Proceedings of the Sixth Appalachian Studies Conference*, The American Experience, 1983.

Jones, Loyal, *Faith and Meaning in the Southern Uplands* (Urbana, University of Illinois, 1999).

Jones, Margaret Morgan, *Travels of a Welsh Preacher in the USA* (Pwllheli, Llygad Gwalch Cyf., 2008).

Jones, R.B., *Rent Heavens, the Revival of 1904* (Porth, Revival Library Reprints, 1931).

Jones, R. Tudur, *Congregationalism in Wales* (Cardiff, University of Wales, 2004).

Jones, William D., *Wales in America: Scranton and the Welsh 1860–1920* (University of Scranton, 1993).

Knowles, Anne Kelly, *Calvinists Incorporated: Welsh Immigrants on Ohio's Industrial Frontier* (University of Chicago Press, 1997).

Knox, R.A., *Enthusiasm, a Chapter in the Hstory of Religion* (New York, Wagner, 1951).

Leinster-Mackay, D., 'John Hullah, John Curwen, Sarah Glover: a Classic Case of "Whiggery" in the History of Musical Education,' *British Journal of Educational Studies*, June 1981, 164–7.

Lewis, Howell Elvet, *Howell Harris and the Welsh Revivalists* (London, Religious Tract Society, 1911).

Lewis, Howell Elvet, *With Christ among the Miners* (Revival Library, 1906).

Lewis, Howell Elvet, *Sweet Singers of Wales* (Aberystwyth, 1889).

Lewis, Ioan M., *Ecstatic Religion* (London, Routledge, 1971).

Lewis, Ronald, *Welsh Americans: a History of Assimilation in the Coalfields* (Chapel Hill, University of North Carolina, 2008).

Lewis T.H., *Y Mormoniad yng Nghymru* (Cardiff, University of Wales, 1956).

Lowe, Karen, *Carriers of the Fire: the Women of the Welsh Revival* (Llanelli, Shedhead, 2004).

Luff, Alan, *Welsh Hymns and their Tunes* (London, Hope, 1990).

Maynard, Constance L., *Between College Terms* (University of Michigan, 1910).

McCauley, Deborah Vansau, *Appalachian Mountain Religion, a History* (Urbana, University of Illinois, 1995).

McNeill, William H., *Keeping Together in Time* (Cambridge, Harvard, 1995).

Meurig, Cass, 'The Fiddler in Eighteenth-Century Wales', *Welsh Music History*, 2007, 7, 22–40.

Mitchell, T. Crichton, *Charles Wesley: The Man with the Dancing Heart* (Kansas City, Beacon Hill, 1994).

Morgan, Derec Llwyd, *The Great Awakening in Wales* (Peterborough, Epworth, 1988).

Morgan, Gareth, 'Rugby and Revivalism in Sport', *International Journal of the History of Sport*, 2005, 434–56.

Morgan, J. Vyrnwy, *The Welsh Religious Revival 1904–5* (London, Chapman and Hall, 1909).

Morgan, Kenneth O., *Rebirth of a Nation* (Oxford University Press, 1981).

Morgan, Prys & Davies, Rhys, *Wales: the Shaping of a Nation* (Newton Abbot, David and Charles, 1984).

Morgan, T.J., 'Peasant Culture of the Swansea Valley', *Glamorgan Historian*, 9, 105–22.

Morgans, David, *Music and Musicians of Merthyr and District* (Merthyr Tydfil, 1922).

Murray, Nicholas, *Aldous Huxley: an English Intellectual* (London, Abacus, 2003).

Noll, Mark A., *Wonderful Words of Life: Hymns in American Protestant History and Theology* (Grand Rapids, Eerdmans, 2004).

Nuttall, Geoffrey F., *Howel Harris, 1714–1773, The Last Enthusiast* (Cardiff, University of Wales Press, 1965).

Patterson, Beverly Bush, *The Sound of the Dove: Singing in Appalachian Primitive Baptist Churches* (Urbana, University of Illinois, 2001).

Phillips, W.J., 'Diwygiad Sankey a Moody a Chymru', *Y Traethodydd*, 1962, 8–15.

Pitts, Walter F., *The Old Ship of Zion: the Afro-Baptist Ritual in the African Diaspora* (Oxford University Press, 1993).

Pratt, James Bissett, *The Religious Consciousness* (New York, MacMillan, 1920).

Rosenberg, Bruce A., *Can these Bones Live, the Art of the American Folk Preacher* (Urbana, University of Illinois, 1988).

Routley, Erik, *Hymns and Human Life* (New York, John Murray, 1952).

Schultz, Patricia, 'A Comparison of the Traditional Welsh Cymanfa Ganu with Contemporary Local American Practices' (University of Missouri Ph.D. thesis, 1984).

Sidney, Edwin, *The Life of the Reverend Rowland Hill* (New York, Appleton, 1834).

Sorensen, Merlin R., 'The Mormon Tabernacle Choir: its History and Contribution to the Cultural History of Utah' (Provo, Brigham Young University M.A. thesis, 1961).

Sparks, Elder John, *The Roots of Appalachian Christianity* (Lexington, University of Kentucky, 2001).

Stead, W.T., *Revival in the West* (London, 1905).

Stegner, Wallace, *The Gathering of Zion* (New York, McGraw Hill, 1964).

Stewart, W.A.C. & McCann, W.P., *The Educational Innovators 1750–1880* (London, MacMillan, 1967).

Stout, Harry S., *The Divine Dramatist* (Grand Rapids, Eerdmans, 1991).

Stowe, David, *How Sweet the Sound* (Cambridge, Harvard, 2004).

Strubble, Michael T. and Wilhelm, G.H., 'The Welsh in Ohio' in Allen G. Noble, *To Build a New Land, Ethnic Landscapes in North America* (Baltimore, Johns Hopkins University Press, 1992).

Suggett, Richard, 'Festivals and Social Structure in Early Modern Wales', *Past and Present*, 1996, 79–111.

Sutcliffe, Smith John, *Impressions of Music in Wales* (London, Venture Press, 1948).

Sweet, William Warren, *Revivalism in America* (Nashville, Abingdon, 1944).

Taylor, Clare, 'Paddy's Run, a Welsh Community in Ohio', *Welsh History Review*, 1983, 302–16.

Thomas, R.D., *A history of the Welsh in America* (T.J. Griffiths, 1872).

Thompson, E.P., *The Making of the English Working Class* (London, Gollancz, 1963).

Trollope, Francis, *Domestic Manners of the Americans* (London, 1832).

Tuan, Yi-Fu-, *Segmented Worlds and the Self* (Minneapolis, University of Minnesota, 1982).

Turner, Victor W., *The Ritual Process: Structure and anti-Structure* (New York, Routledge, 1969).

Van Vugt, Willem E., *British Nuckeyes: the English, Scots and Welsh in Ohio 1700–1900* (Kent State University Press, 2006).

Whalley, Cherilyn A., 'The Old Man's Creek Welsh Community of Johnson County, Iowa', *North American Journal of Welsh Studies*, 2002, 36–49.

White, Eryn, 'The World, the Flesh and the Devil: Early Methodism in South-West Wales', *Transactions of the Honourable Society of Cymmrodorion*, 1996, 53–4.

Williams, Daniel Jenkins, *One Hundred Years of Welsh Calvinistic Methodism in America* (Westminster, 1937).

Williams, Gareth, *1905 and All That* (Llandysul, Gomer, 1991).

Williams, Gareth, *Valleys of Song* (Cardiff, University of Wales Press, 1998).

Williams, Gwyn A., *The Search for Beulah Land* (London, Open Library, 1980).

Wynne, Ellis, *Visions of the Sleeping Bard* (London, 1703).

Young, Carlton R., *Music of the Heart* (Hope, 1995).

Index